Consumer Panels
Second Edition

D1530253

Consumer Panels

Second Edition

Seymour Sudman
Walter H. Stellner Professor of Marketing
University of Illinois, Urbana-Champaign

Brian Wansink
Professor of Business Administration
University of Illinois, Urbana-Champaign

AMERICAN
MARKETING
ASSOCIATION

Chicago, Illinois

Library of Congress Cataloging-in-Publication Data

Sudman, Seymour.
   Consumer panels.—2nd ed./Seymour Sudman and Brian Wansink.
     p. cm.
   Includes bibliographical references and index.
   ISBN: 0-87757-297-6 (alk. paper)
   1. Consumer panels. I. Wansink, Brian. II. Title.

HF5415.3 .S8 2001
658.8′34—dc21   2001053522

American Marketing Association
311 S. Wacker Dr., Suite 5800, Chicago, Illinois 60606 USA
Francesca Van Gorp Cooley, Director
Charles Chandler, Editorial Assistant
Mary Loye, Design and Compositor

Cover design by Matt Cheney and Liz Novak

Manufactured in the United States of America

Dedication

This book is dedicated to the memories of Robert Ferber and Seymour Sudman.

Robert Ferber's death in September 1981 ended a brilliant career in research. Ferber was the coauthor of the first edition of this book and, among his many achievements, made major contributions to the development of consumer panel methodology. He has been sorely missed.

Seymour Sudman helped bring me to the University of Illinois. Even at his sudden death at age 71 in the year 2000, his bright-eyed energy, enthusiasm, curiosity, creativity, and wit were a youthful inspiration to people one-third his age. His impact on the profession of panel and survey research, as well as on legions of scholars across disciplines, will be felt directly and indirectly for many, many years. Proceeds from this book contribute to a scholarship fund established in his honor.

Brian Wansink

Author Bios

Seymour Sudman

Seymour Sudman (Ph.D. University of Chicago 1962) was the Walter H. Stellner Distinguished Professor of Marketing at the University of Illinois from 1968 until his death in 2000. Through a lifetime of active research, he contributed immeasurably to the area of survey design, sampling, and methodology. He was actively involved in providing guidance to the U.S. Census Bureau, and he served as Deputy Director and Research Professor of the Survey Research Laboratory at the University of Illinois.

Brian Wansink

Brian Wansink (Ph.D. Stanford University 1990) is Professor of Marketing, Nutritional Science, and Agricultural and Consumer Economics at the University of Illinois, and is Professor of Marketing at Wageningen University in The Netherlands. His research focuses on how marketing-related variables increase the consumption frequency, quantity, and volume of packaged goods. Wansink was a professor at Dartmouth College and at the Wharton School at the University of Pennsylvania before moving to the University of Illinois to found the Food and Brand Lab (www.ConsumerPsychology.net), the Food Psychology Panel, and the Brand Revitalization Panel.

Table of Contents

Acknowledgments

Much of the information about how company-specific panels operate was obtained from the marketing literature and the research departments of major suppliers, but when this information was insufficient, we went directly to individuals in these companies for additional information. We would like to acknowledge the help we received from Andy Korman, Kim Chui, Wally Balen, Julie Stewert, and Adam Patterson. Special thanks to John Caspers at NPD for his insights on continuous tracking, balancing, and projecting.

Several of our colleagues read drafts of this book and made useful suggestions. We acknowledge the help of our University of Illinois colleagues James D. Hess and Madhu Vishwanathan, as well as that of some of the most stimulating, hard-working, thoughtful, and fun coauthors I could hope for—Pierre Chandon, Joost Pennings, Se-Bum Park, and Koert van Ittersum.

Much gratitude goes to four top Illinois MBA alumni who helped with the book in various stages. Justin Anderson helped review international academic research on panels. Jason Baculoski located unpublished, non-proprietary research on privacy issues and regulations. Elizabeth Cooper conducted telephone interviews of panel operators and panel users. Jer-Yuan Chao helped double-check the cost analyses and the numerical illustrations. Also, thanks goes to project leaders in the Food & Brand Lab at the University of Illinois who helped review chapters.

Introduction

Why a New Edition?

The first edition of *Consumer Panels* was published by the American Marketing Association in 1979. It has been out of print for some years, but there continues to be a growing demand by increasingly savvy researchers for information about the uses and operation of consumer panels. Shortly before his untimely passing, Seymour Sudman asked me to help him undertake a major revision of this book. Not only was there a need for such a reference book on consumer panels, but there had also been major changes that occurred both in the uses and users of panels.

Changes in Methodology

As a reminder to readers, in 1979 when the first edition was published, there were no store scanners; indeed, there was no Universal Product Code. The Internet was in its infancy, primarily used for defense communications, and the World Wide Web had not been conceived.

It is clear that technological developments have revolutionized data collection methods, though many of the procedures used in 1979 are still used today and will be used long into the future. It is likely that technological developments will continue at a rapid pace. Yet, though some of the methods described in this book may be superceded in the not-too-distant future, most of the basic procedures, mechanics, and strategies for effectively using panels will remain the same.

Changes in Market Structure and Needs

Since the first edition, there have been various changes that have occurred in the organizational structure of both suppliers and users of consumer panel data. Two stand out. The first is the increased size and diversity of both suppliers and users, caused primarily by mergers and acquisitions. This trend has the potential to make communication between users and suppliers more difficult, but it has been countered in several ways, as we will discuss. More and more, users have direct online access to panel results without waiting for published reports or oral analyses. In addition, large panel operators now locate their data analysts at the offices of major users to facilitate communications.

The second major change that has occurred has been increased globalization, first by users, but quickly followed by suppliers. As users have expanded their products and services into Europe and Asia, panel operators have expanded their panels to provide information for their users. Of course, issues of cross-cultural comparability have become increasingly complex. Although some cross-cultural issues are discussed, most of this book is based on U.S. experience, and generalizations to other countries must be treated cautiously.

Organization and Structure

This book is intended to be both a basic tool and a source of ideas. The first portion of the book provides basic overviews of panels and is intended to stimulate ideas as to the wide range of questions that can best be answered using continuous and discontinuous panels. Instead of being an encyclopedic, definitional overview, Chapter 1 is written to "make someone smart in 10 minutes." The strength of Chapter 2 lies in the power of examples. That is, whereas questions being answered by a household cleaning panel may appear to have little relevance for non-perishable food products, a creative manager might find that the relationships between inventory stockpiling and usage frequency would be valuable for him or her to examine. For this reason, the chapter offers descriptions of panels—including some from academia—that have been making pioneering advances in the areas of consumption clusters, preference affiliation, affinity marketing, and usage frequency antecedents.

Chapters 3–5 focus on different aspects of obtaining the most accurate data desired. The goal of these chapters is to help users obtain the most valuable data for the lowest possible expenditure of time, effort, and money. Because there are trade-offs among precision (accuracy), speed, and cost, these three chapters outline how to estimate and reduce sample biases (Chapter 3), recruit and compensate members (Chapter 4), and improve panel accuracy and reporting (Chapter 5).

One frequently ignored consumer panel topic is conditioning. Not only is it difficult to observe, but it is also expensive to correct. Chapter 6 examines three types of conditioning—recruitment conditioning, short-term conditioning, and long-term conditioning—and shows how these can be estimated and inexpensively corrected.

The details of organizing, processing, maintaining, and operating a panel are the focus of Chapters 7 and 8. Although this is of practical use primarily to researchers, it provides a behind-the-scenes view of the processing and economics of panel research to those who may be interested.

If Chapters 7 and 8 are for researchers, Chapter 9 may initially appear to be targeted more to managers. Titled "Choosing a Consumer Panel Service," it examines 12 common mistakes that can be made with panels and the opportunities for getting as much from panel research as is possible. Although this may appear managerial in nature, the other side of the coin is relevant to researchers. In effect, it offers a checklist that researchers can use to determine how they stack up on a panel service scorecard.

Chapter 10 shows how a successful convenience panel can be built. There are times when generalizability and projectability are not the goals of the study, in which cases convenience panels can be very useful. They can be "cheap, quick, and good" by offering ease and speed of access.

Chapter 11 provides some brief expectations about the future. Although much has been written about technological expectations, this chapter also focuses on topics and opportunities that provide tremendous potential for better understanding consumers and doing so in a way that has enriching consequences for all.

Chapter 1

Leveraging a Consumer Panel

> There's nothing panel data can tell us that we don't
> already know from scanner data.
> *—Brand manager of a now defunct breakfast cereal*

Consumer panels are a unique tool that can enable a clever researcher to examine dynamic longitudinal changes in behaviors, attitudes, and perceptions. Consumer panels can also be an overly costly and excessive generator of unused data. The importance is knowing when they are most useful and when they are not.

Instead of being an encyclopedic, definitional overview, this chapter is intended to "make someone smart in 10 minutes." It begins by differentiating consumer panels from surveys, and it then discusses the major benefits, and drawbacks, of panels. Following this, the four key challenges for panels are described so that they can be considered in more detail in subsequent chapters.

To provide context as to how panels have evolved (and how they have stayed the same), a brief history of the origins of panels is provided, along with a description of major, full-service panel operators as of 2002. The chapter concludes with a description of the format for the rest of this book.

What Are Consumer Panels?

Across both online and offline services, the major characteristic that distinguishes consumer panels from one-time surveys is that panel respondents report on multiple occasions, rather than simply once. There are two basic kinds of consumer panels. In the first kind, respondents report essentially the same information repeatedly over some period of time. The chief examples of these kinds of panels are syndicated purchase panels that use store and home scanners, diaries, and the media use of panels such as those that measure television viewing. Other examples include panels measuring restaurant and home consumption of food, medical experiences and medical care, and time use. For ease of reference, we refer to these kinds of panels as *continuous panels*.

The second kind of panel consists of samples of prescreened respondents who report over time on a broad range of different topics. In the first edition of this book, these panels were excluded from our definition, but their use has become increasingly widespread and is worthy of discussion. The operators of such panels use the word "panels" to describe their services, but we should recognize that the two kinds of panels have major differences in how they are used, as well as in their benefits and disadvantages. To distinguish these panels from continuous consumer panels, we refer to them as *discontinuous access panels*.

Both kinds of panels come in all different forms. Panel studies can involve data collection at widely different intervals that vary anywhere from a day to several years between waves of interviews. Panel operators are continuously faced with the decision about how often panel members should be contacted and asked to report. Contacting the panel either too frequently or too infrequently may lead to reduced cooperation, an issue we discuss in Chapter 5. Panel data collection may be carried out in many different ways, including personal interviews conducted primarily by telephone; diaries and questionnaires using regular mail, e-mail, and the Web; or electronic methods such as "people meters" for television and scanners for home purchases.

Consumer panels share many of the same characteristics as panels of businesses, physicians, and other occupations. Business panels, especially those surveyed by the U.S. Bureau of the Census and the Bureau of Labor Statistics, are very important for measuring economic activity in the United States. Although this book limits itself to panels of consumers, either of households or individuals, most of the issues discussed are relevant for other kinds of panels.

With all panels, however, an important distinction needs to be made between static and dynamic panels. A static panel is one for which no effort is made to rotate panel members during the life of the panel. For example, a continuing study of the lifestyles and careers of students in the high school or college graduating classes of 2002 would be a static panel because every attempt would be made to retain the members of the class in the panel, and there would be no reason to rotate sample members for the purpose of the study.

In contrast, a dynamic panel seeks to rotate panel members, either because of concerns about panel fatigue or conditioning or to maintain the sample as representative of a particular population. Although one might think offhand that a sample would continue to be representative over time if it initially represents a particular population, in practice this does not happen. This might be true of a stationary population, but in practice we do not have stationary populations. Consider the U.S. population. People move, and the population shifts among states, new households are formed, some households dissolve because of death, divorce, or other reasons, and even if the household continues to exist, its composition may change. We discuss this issue in detail in Chapter 3.

Both static and dynamic panels have their advantages and disadvantages, and the type chosen depends on the particular problem. For example, some experimental designs, such as those testing the effects of various forms of advertising and promotion, need before-and-after data from the same households. In this case, static panels are preferable because they help hold extraneous factors constant. However, if a panel is being operated to provide estimates of purchases or uses of products, services, or media over time by different population groups, a dynamic panel is needed, because a key requirement is that the panel be representative of the total population.

A good example of a dynamic panel is the Current Population Survey conducted by the U.S. Bureau of the Census for the Bureau of Labor Statistics to measure unemployment. In any one month, this panel consists of eight replicating subsamples, selected in a staggered fashion, so that no household is interviewed more than eight times in the period of a year and four times in the following year. At the end of the twelfth interview, the subsample is replaced by a new subsample.

The Uses of Continuous Consumer Panels

The benefits of the two kinds of panels are quite different. For continuous consumer panels (sometimes called "full-time panels" or "static panels" because panel members remain relatively constant), the major benefit derives from the need to measure how actions in the marketplace change the behavior or attitudes of consumers. The following examples illustrate some of the uses of continuous panels. In Chapter 2, we present a more detailed discussion of panel uses.

1. The effect of a special offer can be measured through a before-and-after design using a panel approach. Samples of families might be interviewed initially to gather information on their purchases of soft drinks, possibly over several weeks to obtain a good idea of their "steady state" purchasing patterns. A special deal for a particular brand is then introduced, and the purchases of the same sample are monitored perhaps every week for three months. In this way, sampling variation is minimized, and both short- and long-term effects of the deal are obtained.

2. A static consumer panel of families with young children might be set up to monitor the acceptance of a new line of toys. In this case, no type of experimental treatment is involved. Rather, information is obtained, say, every month on the toy purchases of the families. In this way, data are compiled on the types of families that are buying any of the new toys, how soon the toys are purchased after they have been placed on the market, and how many of the toys are purchased by each family.

3. A dynamic consumer panel might be used to keep track of the purchases of frozen foods of one brand in relation to other brands. By obtaining such data every week for several years, very detailed information can be obtained on what sorts of families are purchasing each major brand and on the change in market shares of the different brands over time among different groups of consumers. Also, estimates can be derived of the extent to which purchasers remain loyal to different brands.

4. A continuous consumer panel may be used to obtain more detailed and reliable information on different types of behavior. For example, it has been demonstrated that data on consumer financial holdings are obtained much more reliably if this information is sought over a period of time, which allows the respondent to build up confidence in the validity and trustworthiness of the study. Similarly, information on medical care events is obtained much more accurately from panels than from one-time surveys.

5. A continuous consumer panel is the only means of obtaining information on a series of events extended through time. For example, reactions to the weekly episodes of a television program are best obtained by monitoring the viewing patterns of the same family and simultaneously getting the family's reactions to the different programs. In this way, it becomes possible to measure changes in program acceptance and to relate attitudes and behavior at one time to viewing and attitudes toward earlier episodes.

6. Only through continuous consumer panels is it possible to monitor changes in the behavior of particular cohorts. For example, the purchase habits of teenagers might be monitored over several years to ascertain how their purchase habits change as they move into different stages of life. By monitoring the behavior of peers at the same time, it becomes possible to distinguish effects due to history (i.e., changes in economic and social conditions) from effects due to the aging process.

It is possible to use a series of demographically identical, discontinuous access panels for the purposes of continuous tracking. This can be done by selecting demographically identical samples containing different panelists at predetermined intervals across time. These different groups of panelists can then be used separately in the separate waves of the panel. Because the sample is not static, traditional static panel analytics, such as measures of trial and repeat and brand switching, are lost. What is gained, however, is a means of obtaining other insights at a lower cost than would be required to maintain a continuous, full-time panel.

The Uses of Discontinuous Consumer Access Panels

The benefits of discontinuous consumer access panels are primarily related to reductions in the cost and time required to obtain market research information. Although these kinds of panels are used in a variety of ways, three uses are especially common: (1) screening for special populations (especially rare special populations), (2) evaluation of new product concepts and formulations, and (3) marketing and advertising experimentation.

The following examples illustrate some uses of discontinuous consumer access panels:

1. The Federal Trade Commission wants to determine whether purchasers of hearing aids were being deceived during the purchase process. Information on purchases of hearing aids had previously been obtained from respondents of one of the very large panels, so that a sample of several thousand people was available for surveying. To have obtained such a sample by a new screening of households would have been prohibitively expensive and would have made the study impossible.
2. A manufacturer of tennis racquets is considering alternative shapes for a new racquet that would make it easier to handle. Initially, sheets with pictures and a description of the new racquets might be sent by mail or e-mail to prescreened samples of respondents who play tennis. Any one respondent would receive only one of the alternatives, but the manufacturer could determine which racquet was preferred from the different samples. Alternatively, respondents might receive pictures of two racquets, with the order of the pictures randomized, and be asked for their preference between the two. At a later stage, respondents might receive the actual racquets for use testing.
3. Instead of a new product, a marketer might be considering a new advertising campaign for an existing product and might wish to choose among several alternatives that had been proposed by the advertising agency. Again, samples of each of the alternatives would be sent to relevant panel members for their evaluation. As in Example 2, members might be asked to evaluate a single advertisement or to choose from among multiple

advertisements. The testing could also be done by the advertising agency before a recommendation was made to the manufacturer. Similarly, panel members could be asked to evaluate different designs or layouts for a Web page or a brochure. In all cases, the objective is to screen different ideas or executions inexpensively by having a panel evaluate them singly or side-by-side.

Similar information could be obtained from one-time surveys but with greater difficulty and at greater expense. Two reasons for using discontinuous panels are because they can provide greater relevance and better quality. They are more relevant because respondents can be easily screened on the basis of prior questions (e.g., pet owners, users of denture cream, recent car purchasers). They are often of better quality because respondents are experienced and can be prequalified as panel members on the basis of the quality of their previous survey responses. In the next section, we discuss problems with discontinuous consumer panels that sometimes make one-time surveys the better alternative.

The Power of Causality, Control, and Disaggregation

Although one-time surveys and panel data can sometimes provide similar information as can continuous consumer panels, it is with less precision and often with a great deal of additional cost. For example, brand sales can be obtained from store scanner data. This is another form of panel data, though it is not a consumer panel. Whereas store scanner data provide excellent and efficient estimates of overall sales, these data cannot provide estimates of the types of people buying different brands, nor can they provide information on brand loyalty, brand switching, consumption rate, or market segmentation unless combined with some form of consumer panel data.

To a limited extent, some of the information obtained by continuous consumer panels could be obtained by one-time retrospective surveys. However, unless very carefully designed and pretested, such surveys would involve a great deal of strain on the memory of individuals, and the resulting data could be unreliable (see Chapter 5). In addition, understanding how and why attitudes and preferences have changed over a long period of time in a retrospective interview can be problematic. Although the general direction of these changes can be estimated, their magnitude is much more accurately estimated through the repeated sampling that is only possible with continuous panels.

In a similar manner, two separate samples could be used to measure before-and-after effects. However, doing so could introduce a considerable amount of sampling variation, with the result that any real effect due to the special deal or other treatment might be mistakenly ascribed to sampling variation. In addition, the cost of the study would usually be larger because two different samples would need to be selected and contacted.

Studying how attitudes or behavior of a cohort change over time is impossible without the panel approach. Consider a panel study of World War II veterans that investigates how their different experiences with the free samples they were given during the war influenced their subsequent buying habits. In this instance, it is essential that the same people be interviewed over time. This is also necessary if information is to be obtained on the true extent of change taking place in a particular population. In this sense, aggregates can be highly misleading, because the stationarity of aggregates over time does not necessarily mean no change on the part of the individual members of a population.

This is illustrated in Table 1.1, which shows how any aggregate purchase distribution can remain unchanged but conceal different patterns

Table 1.1
Two Scenarios that Show How Aggregate Purchases Do Not Reflect Individual Trends

TIME PERIOD 2		Purchase (Period 1)	No Purchase (Period 1)	Total
TIME PERIOD 1				
Scenario A: One-Time Purchasers	Purchase (Period 2)	200	0	200
	No Purchase (Period 2)	0	800	800
	Total	200	800	1,000
Scenario B: Two-Time Purchasers	Purchase (Period 2)	0	200	200
	No Purchase (Period 2)	200	600	800
	Total	200	800	1,000

among individual households. In both parts of this table, aggregate purchases of the product amounted to 20% in each time period. In Scenario A, this stationarity mirrors the stationarity in individual purchases, in the sense that the individual households either purchased or did not a make a purchase in both of these periods. That is, 200 people purchased in both Time Period 1 and Time Period 2, and 800 people did not purchase at all. However, in the lower part of the table, we see that, whereas the aggregate purchases were unchanged, substantial variations occurred in the purchase patterns of individuals. In particular, no single individual purchased in both Time Period 1 and Time Period 2. From the point of view of marketing strategy, these two purchasing patterns have different implications. Consumer panels enable us to determine which scenario is operating. Other methods, such as discrete surveys or panel data, do not.

What Are the Key Challenges for Panels?

Like most techniques, consumer panels, either continuous or discontinuous, have problems of their own. These problems are discussed in much greater detail in subsequent chapters, but it seems appropriate to summarize them here briefly. Essentially, a continuous consumer panel operation poses four problems: (1) gaining and maintaining cooperation, (2) information validity and reliability, (3) panel conditioning, and (4) record maintenance.

Gaining and Maintaining Cooperation

The first problem is one that can seriously affect the representativeness of a panel study. Even when panels are recruited by personal methods, the initial rate of cooperation can be as low as 50% and may be much lower if recruiting is done by mail, Internet, or the World Wide Web. Those who cooperate are more likely to be educated, in professional or clerical occupations, in middle- or upper-middle–income levels, and in the younger and middle age brackets.

As a result, a panel at the beginning of the operation may not be representative of the population from which it was selected. This is only the beginning of the problem, however. Attrition can be substantial. Approximately half the people that even consent to participate may drop out after the first two or three rounds, especially if they are asked to keep extensive written records. As a result, a panel operation can become increasingly unrepresentative of the population from which it originally came, something that could be a problem even for a static panel. Of course, panel operators take steps to reduce this nonrepresentativeness through the use of a variety of methods, such as selective recruiting and weighting the panel. These methods are discussed in Chapters 3 and 4.

Information Validity and Reliability

The second problem of sample representativeness is also the key problem for discontinuous consumer panels. Almost all these panels are recruited by mail with initial cooperation rates usually below 5%. As with continuous panels, there are also very high initial dropout rates. Operators of discontinuous panels make initial efforts to balance their samples for major demographic characteristics by selectively recruiting respondents from groups least likely to cooperate and by dropping from their panels respondents from groups that are overrepresented. It is often claimed by operators of such panels that the response rate to an individual survey is 70% or higher, but this refers to respondents who have already agreed to participate. As with continuous panels, the data from individual surveys are weighted to further control for major demographic biases.

Sample representativeness is also a concern when recruiting online panels. Critics argue that because online panels necessitate computer literacy and the means to access the Internet, it is biased against low-income groups and technological laggards. These concerns may be exacerbated depending on how the panel is recruited. Surfers who inadvertently stumble onto a site or are attracted by the lure of a lottery may be even less representative than those recruited through more deliberate or personal means. Yet, just as efforts are made to make offline panels more representative, so are many of these same efforts being used to make online research more representative.

It is important to realize that purpose defines precision. The representatives and precision required to determine which of six package designs is most appealing are different (and perhaps less important) than those needed to estimate the impact of a price change on market share.

Independent of the population being sampled is the reliability of the information obtained from panel members. For discontinuous panels, these problems are identical to those for conducting one-time surveys. Because many of the uses of the panel relate to attitudes and buying intentions, the only way to ultimately verify the quality of responses is to observe marketplace results. The extensive and increased use of discontinuous panels suggests that the responses obtained from these panels provide information that is sufficiently accurate for making marketing decisions.

For continuous panels, which are more often measuring behavior, shipment data can validate results, particularly at an aggregate level. Certainly the introduction of portable household scanner equipment and electronic meters for television viewing has increased validity, but even such equipment and meters do not prevent errors caused by respondents forgetting to use them. Many panels still rely on diaries. Although diaries significantly reduce reporting errors as compared with recall, reporting errors occur if panel members forget to make their entries or attempt to recall and record earlier behavior at the end of the recording period instead of at the time it occurred. This is especially a problem for behaviors that are infrequent and of low salience to respondents. This topic is discussed in Chapter 4.

Panel Conditioning

The third major problem that affects continuous panels, but probably not discontinuous ones, is the danger of conditioning effects, that is, the possibility that the behavior or attitudes of panel members will be influenced or contaminated by their participation in the panel. For example, respondents who keep diaries about visits to restaurants may become aware of the large amount of money they are spending on restaurant meals and either reduce the frequency of their visits to restaurants or switch to lower-cost ones. In a similar fashion, family members asked month after month about ownership of savings accounts may decide to open a savings account, even though they originally had no such intention.

Panel conditioning effects are both erratic and pervasive. They exist in some studies but do not seem to exist in others. As with panel mortality, methods exist for detecting and correcting such effects; these are covered in Chapter 5.

Record Maintenance

The fourth major problem of a continuous panel study is not so much methodological as one of the researcher's own making. There is the need for some systematic means of keeping easily accessible records on the activities of panel members and changes in the characteristics of these panel members over time. Because members of a panel are usually households or families rather than single individuals, there is the problem in a long-term panel study of keeping track of changes in the composition of these households and changes in their characteristics. A family member may leave the household, another may be born or move into it, a household may be dissolved, or a new household may be formed. In addition, the employment status and other characteristics of the individual members will change over time. All of these changes must be recorded so that the data can be used for analytical purposes when required. The attitudes and behavior of the panel members also must be recorded in such a way that the data are readily accessible, particularly so that analyses can be made on either a cross-sectional or a longitudinal basis.

Some idea of the magnitude of the problem can be obtained from the fact that, in many panel studies, a single round of data collection may provide information on 500 to 1000 variables. If a panel has 10,000 families, which is not unusually high, and information is obtained every month for, say, five years, the number of pieces of information could be as high as 600,000,000.

Fortunately, the capacity of computers has expanded so rapidly that the computers themselves are no longer the problem. The major problem was and remains the designing of computer systems that make storing and accessing the data straightforward. It is especially important for syndicated services to design systems that make client access to data fast and easy. This is discussed in Chapter 7.

A Brief History of Panels

Panel studies first appeared in commercial and social science research during the 1930s, shortly before World War II, a time when many of the market research techniques used today were being developed. In one of the first articles dealing with panel methods, Paul Lazarsfeld described the advantages of before-and-after interviews for measuring the effects of changes in behavior and particular types of stimuli. He described a panel for getting reader reactions to the magazine *Women's Home Companion* and discussed the use of panel techniques in England in studying what would now be termed lifestyles (Lazarsfeld and Fiske 1938). In a later article, he reported on the use of panels for measuring reactions to radio programs and pointed out, possibly for the first time, how the rate of response to a panel study tends to be influenced by the extent of interest in the subject matter (Lazarsfeld 1940).

Possibly the first study of buying behavior based on a continuous panel operation was carried out by Jenkins (1938), who followed the brand preferences of a sample of consumers under a grant from the Psychological Corporation. This study provided evidence of fairly high correlation between last-purchase questions and actual purchases reported at a later time.

Studies of voting behavior using the panel technique also started about this time but were apparently set up only to study individual elections (Lazarsfeld and Durant 1942; Roper 1941).

Another use of the panel technique that was developing about this time was testing food products. A large panel of housewives that was set up for this purpose by General Foods, and possibly by other food manufacturers as well, was reported to have been quite successful (Sellers 1942). It was about this time also that the Market Research Corporation of America, then called the Industrial Surveys Company, launched the first national continuous consumer purchase panel in October 1941 with an initial sample of 2000 families (Stonborough 1942).

In the decade following the end of World War II, the use of panel techniques multiplied rapidly. Consumer panels were organized to study buying patterns in New York City (Black 1948), to evaluate merchandise offerings (Quenon 1951), to gauge changes in readership interest and characteristics for magazines (Robinson 1947), and to follow radio listening (Dunn 1952; Sandage 1951; Silvey 1951). It was during this period that the use of automatic electronic devices for measuring consumer behavior was inaugurated, with the start of the Nielsen Audimeter for recording radio listening in conjunction with questionnaire techniques (Nielsen 1945). The Nielsen Audimeter evolved into the meter used to measure television viewing and later into the people meter.

The first discontinuous consumer panel was started by National Family Opinion in 1946 with 1000 households. Market Facts and the Home Testing Institute panels followed shortly thereafter. During this period, various studies also began on the methodology of consumer panels and the sorts of problems that might be encountered. Day (1948) investigated how responses might be improved for mail panels, and Shaffer (1955) studied the effect of alternative time periods for reporting panel data. More general operational problems of a continuous consumer panel were investigated by Ferber (1949), Quackenbush and Shaffer (1960), and the Industrial Surveys Company (U.S. Department of Agriculture 1952).

Interest in and use of consumer panels, both continuous and discontinuous, continued to mushroom in the 1960s and 1970s, as did research on panel methodology. One of the most popular consumer topics in that era, which still continues today, was the study of brand loyalty, something that could not be studied except by use of a continuous consumer panel. Possibly the first such studies were carried out by Brown (1952), who used data from the *Chicago Tribune* consumer panel. The widespread use of consumer panels was recognized by the American Marketing

Association with a publication evaluating the method (Boyd and Westfall 1960) and by the first edition of this book in 1979.

In more recent years, the developments discussed in the Preface have had major impacts on consumer panel operations and use. One of the developments that had the greatest impact on continuous purchase panels was the introduction of Universal Product Codes (UPC) for grocery products in 1973. The almost universal availability of bar codes on products quickly led to store scanner equipment, as well as portable devices that could read these bar codes and automated data collection procedures for most products. Nevertheless, diaries continue to be necessary to measure service use, consumption, and other events for which automatic collection procedures do not exist.

A second major technological development has been the enormous increase in computer power that has made collection, storage, retrieval, and analysis of panel data far easier and much less costly. This is discussed in Chapters 7 and 8. Although the World Wide Web has made new methods of recruiting panels and collecting data possible, significant sample quality issues remain to be resolved. Nevertheless, Web panels are already in wide use for discontinuous panels, and continuous panels measuring Web use have been established.

Finally, as we show in the next section, panel operations have become global for both continuous and discontinuous panels. This matches the increased globalization of clients. The development of panel uses and methods continues to be dynamic, and changes that cannot now even be anticipated are likely to occur in the twenty-first century.

Major Full-Service Panel Operations

Consumer panels are operated in almost every developed country in the world. In this section, we describe some of the larger full-service panels in operation at the time this book was written. This list is intended to indicate that panel activity is extensive, but the list is certainly incomplete, and information given here will change as the dynamic market research industry changes. Much of the information given here was taken from the ESOMAR Directory, Web sites of major panel suppliers, and telephone calls to these suppliers. These sites should be consulted for more recent information; their contact numbers and addresses are provided in Table 1.2.

By far the largest continuous panel operator is the ACNielsen Company, with a total of approximately 125,000 households in 18 different countries as of the year 2000. These panels primarily report

Table 1.2.
Selected Worldwide Major Panel Operators

Country	Firm	Started	Telephone	Web Address
USA	ACNielsen	1933	203-961-3330	www.acnielsen.com
USA	NFO Worldwide	1946	203-629-8888	www.nfow.com
USA	Maritz Marketing Research, Inc.	1973	636-827-1610	www.maritz.com
USA	Market Facts, Inc.	1946	847-590-7000	www.marketfacts.com
USA	NPD Group, Inc.	1953	516-625-0700	www.npd.com
USA	Opinion Research . Corporation Intl	1938	908-281-5100	www.opinionresearch.com
USA	Taylor Nelson Sofres Intersearch	1960	215-442-9000	www.tnsofres.com
USA	Roper Starch Worldwide, Inc.	1923	914-698-0800	www.roper.com
USA	Burke, Inc.	1931	513-241-5663	www.burke.com
USA	MORPACE International, Inc.	1940	248-737-5300	www.morpace.com
USA	Creative and Response Rsch Services, Inc.	1960	312-828-9200	www.crresearch.com
USA	Harris Interactive, Inc.	1956	716-272-9020	www.harrisinteractive.com
USA	Lieberman Research Worldwide	1973	310-553-0550	www.lrw.com
USA	Ziment	1976	212-647-7200	www.ziment.com
UK	BJM Research and Consultancy Ltd	1973	44-20-7891-1200	www.bjm.co.uk
UK	BMRB International	1933	44-20-8566-5000	www.bmrb.co.uk
UK	The Gallup Organization	1937	44-20-8939-7000	www.gallup.com
UK	GfK Marketing Services Ltd	1992	44-870-603-8100	www.gfkms.co.uk
UK	Harris Research	1965	44-20-8332-9898	www.mrsl.co.uk
UK	Information Resources	1992	44-1344-746000	www.unfores.com
UK	INFRATEST BURKE GROUP LTD.	1974	44-208-782-3000	www.nfoeurope.com
UK	Ipsos-RSL Ltd.	1946	44-20-8861-8000	www.ipsos.rslmedia.co.uk
UK	Isis Research plc	1973	44-20-8788-8819	www.isisresearch.com
UK	Martin Hamblin	1969	44-20-7222-8181	www.martinhamblin.co.uk
UK	Millward Brown UK Ltd	1973	44-1926-452233	www.millwardbrown.com
UK	MORI (Market & Opinion Rsch Intl)	1969	44-20-7222-0232	www.mori.com
UK	MVA	1968	44-1483-728051	www.mva-research.com
UK	ORC International	1938	44-20-7675-1000	www.opinionresearch.com
UK	The Research Business International	1981	44-20-7923-6000	www.trbi.co.uk

Table 1.2.
Continued

Country	Firm	Started	Telephone	Web Address
UK	Research International	1962	44-20-7656-5000	www.research-int.com
UK	Research Resources Ltd	1986	44-20-7656-5555	
Canada	Angus Reid Group, Inc.	1979	1-613-241-5802	www.angusreid.com
Canada	CF Group Inc. (ARC, Canadian Facts)	1932	1-416-924-5751	www.cfgroup.ca
France	B.V.A.	1970	33-1-30-84-88-00	www.bva.fr
France	CSA (CSA TMO Group)	1983	33-1-41-86-22-00	www.csa-fr.com
France	IFOP	1938	33-1-45-84-14-44	www.ifop.com
France	Ipsos France	1975	33-1-53-68-28-28	www.ipsos.com
France	SECODIP	1993	33-1-30-06-22-00	www.secodip.fr
France	MEDIAMETRIE	1985	33-1-47-58-97-58	www.mediametrie.fr
France	Research International	1952	33-1-44-06-65-65	www.research-int.com
France	SECODIP/Groupe SOFRES	1969	33-1-30-74-80-80	www.secodip.com
Brazil	IBOPE GROUP IBOPE Ad Hoc	1942	55-11-3066-1587	www.ibope.com.br
Brazil	INDICATOR Pesquisa de Mercado Ltda.	1987	55-11-3365-3000	www.indicator.com.br
Brazil	Instituto de Pesquisas Datafolha	1983	55-11-224-3933	www.datafolha.com.br
Brazil	MARPLAN BRASIL Pesquisas Ltda.	1958	55-11-3361-2033	www.marplan.com.br
India	Indian Market Research Bureau (IMRB)	1970	91-22-432-3636	www.imrbint.com
India	Indica Research Pvt. Ltd.	1994	91-22-265-1741	www.indica.com
India	MBL Rsch. & Consultancy Group Pvt. Ltd.	1987	91-40-335-5433	www.mblindia.com
India	ORG-MARG Research Ltd.	1961	91-22-218-6922	www.org-marg.com
Indonesia	PT AMI Indonesia	1996	62-21-521-3420	www.ami-group.com
Japan	Marketing Intelligence Corporation (MIC)	1960	81-424-76-5164	www.micjapan.com
Japan	NIKKEI RESEARCH INC.	1970	81-3-5281-2891	www.nikkei-r.co.jp
Japan	Video Research Ltd.	1962	81-3-5541-6506	www.videor.jp
Korea	Hyundai Research Institute	1986	82-2-737-2685	www.hri.co.kr
Turkey	Procon GfK Research Services	1997	91-212-216-21-91	www.procongfk.com

grocery, drug, and other household products using scanners and diaries. Nielsen Media Research, which is now a separate company, measures television viewing of more than 50,000 households in 26 countries using meters and diaries.

Information Resources Inc. (IRI), the major competitor of the ACNielsen Company, maintains two separate panels, each composed of approximately 55,000 households, for a total of 110,000 households in the United States, though the static sample used to measure within-household changes consists of 35,000 households. Through strategic partnerships, IRI provides its clients with panel information in 16 countries. Its major partner in Europe is GfK, a German panel operator. GfK operates a 12,000-household scanning panel, a fresh food panel of 5000 households, an individual panel of 10,000, and an impulse consumption panel of 4000 people.

The NPD group, which used to measure grocery and drug products using scanners and diaries, sold this service to the ACNielsen Company, but it still maintains a panel of 13,000 households in the United States that report on purchases of toys, clothing, and restaurant use. NPD and its partners operate continuous consumer panels in France, Germany, Italy, and the United Kingdom that consist of 22,000 households in total that report purchases of toys, restaurant use, and athletic footwear. They plan to expand this service to Asia and the Pacific Rim.

Taylor, Nelson, Sofres, a large British firm, operates continuous consumer panels in Great Britain (10,000 households), France (8000 households), and Spain (5000 households), as well as panels in Ireland, Portugal, Argentina, Taiwan, Romania, Bulgaria, Korea, and Thailand. Taylor, Nelson, Sofres cooperates with GfK and IHA to form Europanel, a service that provides information covering all of Western Europe. These household panels use a combination of diaries and in-home scanning equipment. Taylor, Nelson, Sofres also conducts continuous telephone panels to measure clothing and impulse purchases.

In Japan, Marketing Intelligence Corporation (MIC) has a continuous panel of 11,000 households that use portable scanners, plus additional household and individual panels for women's products, clothing, and over-the-counter drugs. Nikkei Research Inc. has a 3000-household panel that also uses scanners.

The major discontinuous panel operators in the United States are National Family Opinion, with a claimed total membership of 600,000 in its panels, Market Facts with 500,000 panel member households, and the NPD Group HTI (Home Testing Institute) Consumer Panel with 400,000 households in the United States and an additional 229,000 in

Western Europe and Canada. In Europe, the NPD Group is in partnership with Taylor, Nelson, Sofres and GfK Panel Services Consumer Research.

In turn, these European companies partner with the NPD Group for U.S. and Canadian studies. For example, the HTI panel is used to provide continuing data on athletic shoes and automotive products, but households are not surveyed more than once annually on these topics. These large panels are also used to prescreen respondents who meet the needs of particular surveys.

Discontinuous consumer panels are also found in most developed countries. Many of the operators of continuous panels also operate discontinuous panels. Thus, in Japan, the MIC operates a discontinuous panel of 100,000 respondents, and Nikkei Research operates a panel of 30,000 respondents in urban areas. Also in Japan, Util Inc. operates panels of 1000 housewives and 10,000 female Internet users, and RJC Marketing Research Inc. operates a panel of 20,000 households in eight major cities.

The Format of this Book

Figure 1 provides an overview of this book. Chapter 2 provides a wide range of examples that can help provide a context for understanding the flexibility of panels and providing ideas of new ways they can be used. It offers descriptions of panels, including some from academia, that have been making pioneering advances in the areas of consumption clusters, preference affiliation, affinity marketing, and usage frequency antecedents.

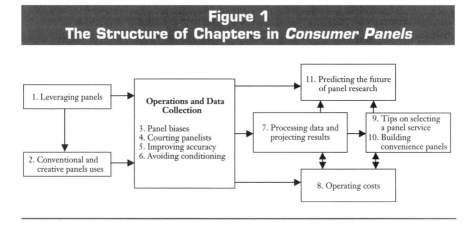

Figure 1
The Structure of Chapters in *Consumer Panels*

Chapters 3–5 focus on different aspects of obtaining the most accurate data desired. There are trade-offs among precision, speed, and cost, and these three chapters outline how to estimate and reduce sample biases (Chapter 3), recruit and compensate members (Chapter 4), and improve panel accuracy and reporting (Chapter 5). Once an accurate system for collecting data has been established, Chapter 6 examines how to keep it that way by minimizing the impact that conditioning has on biasing responses.

Organizing, processing, maintaining, and operating a panel is the focus of Chapters 7 and 8. It provides a bit of a behind-the-scenes view of the processing and economics of panel research to those who may be interested, but it is likely of greatest interest to managers.

Chapter 9, "Choosing a Panel Service," examines 12 common mistakes that can be made with panels and the opportunities for getting as much from panel research as is possible. Although this may appear managerial in nature, it provides a 12-point checklist that researchers can use to increase the quality of their services. Chapter 10 covers one of the most often asked panel-related questions from academics: How do I build a convenience panel?

Chapter 11 provides some brief expectations about the future. Although much has been written about technological expectations, this chapter also focuses on topics and opportunities that provide tremendous potential for better understanding consumers and doing so in a way that has enriching consequences for all.

Chapter 2

Conventional and Creative Uses of Consumer Panels

We used to only use panels for trend analysis and switching behavior studies. Now we're using menu planning to determine what other items people eat at dinner when they eat [our product]. This is helping us change the way we market.
          —*Brand director in* Fortune *500 company*

Sometimes our use of a tool is handicapped because of our limited imagination of what it can do or because of our lack of understanding of how much it can do. The initial goal of this chapter is to show the wide range of applications that panels can have for answering different types of research questions. The deeper objective, however, is to provide springboards for creatively using panels in ways that answer provocative new questions.

Panels are a subset of all surveys, but their uses are almost as extensive. The time has long passed when an all-inclusive listing of their uses would fit into a chapter. Because the major purpose of this book, however, is to describe how panels are operated for those who have already discovered their usefulness, a chapter is sufficient to illustrate some common and some clever uses of panels. As in other chapters, we distinguish between uses of continuous and discontinuous panels.

We start with some simple uses of continuous panels, not simply because the data are easy to obtain, but because the analysis of results is relatively easy. Following this discussion are some examples that use more advanced mathematical analyses, such as model construction, Markov processes, and multivariate methods. The chapter concludes with a discussion of the varied uses of discontinuous panels. We hope that the range of examples is broad enough to suggest the versatility of panels and their additional uses.

Consumer Purchase and Consumption Behavior

The chief use of continuous panels in marketing has always been to measure the purchase of nondurable consumer goods. Examples are found in many published sources (see the listing of references at the end of this book). Around the world, continuous consumer panels measure the purchasing of food and other grocery items such as paper products, soaps and cleaners, health and beauty aids including over-the-counter nonprescription drugs and other medical supplies, as well as other household products (see Exhibit 2.1). Clothing and athletic shoe purchases are measured in many countries, as are purchases of gasoline, tires, and other automotive supplies. Panels also measure toy purchasing, restaurant visits, and the buying of pet food and pet supplies.

Almost as important as purchase behavior has been the measurement of consumer media usage behavior. Most attention has been paid to consumer television viewing, but panels also measure print media, radio, and consumer use of the Web. There have been some efforts to combine information on purchase behavior and media use, but this is not something that is done on a continuous basis. Less often, panels have been used to measure information on how purchased products are used. This includes menu studies for which households report, for a limited time period (one or two weeks), all the meals eaten in the household and away from home, including snacks and all the ingredients used to make these meals. Generalizing from food, there have been other studies measuring use of other items and services, such as automobiles, public transportation, and vacation travel.

Continuous consumer panels have been used by governmental agencies to obtain detailed information on total consumer expenditures. In many countries, including the United States where the studies are conducted for the Bureau of Labor Statistics, respondents are asked to keep detailed purchase diaries for one or two weeks and are periodically asked for additional information on less frequently purchased durable goods. The increasing concerns about medical care and its costs have led to the use of household panels to obtain information on medical events and

Exhibit 2.1
Annual Panel Survey Used to Determine Brand Usage and Brand Switching Compared with Previous Years

Please have this CONSUMER PRODUCT SURVEY OF AMERICA No. 088

questionnaire filled out by the main grocery shopper in your household. Thank you.

INSTRUCTIONS:

Dear Fellow Shopper:

This quick survey is easy and will only take a few minutes. Here's all you have to do:

1) Let me know the products that you or other people living in your home may have used by marking a dark "X" in the appropriate boxes.

2) Please take into account products used by you and all other people living in your home.

3) If you get to a category that is not used in your home, just "X" the "DO NOT USE" box and skip it.

4) For each category, "X" as many boxes as apply.

EXAMPLE: in my family, we usually eat Campbell's or Lipton Soup, but we also used Progresso in the past 12 months. I would "X" boxes as follows:

SOUP

	Our Usual Brand(s)	Also Used In Past 12 Months
☒ WE DO NOT USE (Skip to next category)		
Campbell's	☒	☒
Healthy Choice	☒	☒
Lipton	☒	☒
Progresso	☒	☒
Other	☒	☒

URGENT: Please take a few moments right now to complete this survey. It's important. I appreciate your help.

Sincerely,

Laura

Laura David

P.S. Please note: It is extremely important that the information you provide be accurate.

SOUP

	Our Usual Brand(s)	Also Used In Past 12 Months
☒ WE DO NOT USE (Skip to next category)		
Campbell's	☒	☒
Healthy Choice	☒	☒
Lipton	☒	☒
Progresso	☒	☒
Other	☒	☒

ANTIPERSPIRANT & DEODORANT

	Our Usual Brand(s)	Also Used In Past 12 Months
☒ WE DO NOT USE (Skip to next category)		
Degree	☒	☒
Lady Speed Stick	☒	☒
Secret	☒	☒
Sure	☒	☒
Other deodorant	☒	☒

Which type of antiperspirant or deodorant is used most often by the female adult(s) in your household?

Aerosol	☒
Roll-on	☒
Stick or Gel	☒

DANDRUFF SHAMPOO

	Our Usual Brand(s)	Also Used In Past 12 Months
☒ WE DO NOT USE (Skip to next category)		
Head & Shoulders	☒	☒
Neutrogena T-Gel	☒	☒
Selsun Blue	☒	☒
Other	☒	☒

MAYONNAISE

	Our Usual Brand(s)	Also Used In Past 12 Months
☒ WE DO NOT USE (Skip to next category)		
Hellman's or Best Foods		
- Real	☒	☒
- Light	☒	☒
- Low-fat	☒	☒
Miracle Whip - regular	☒	☒
- Light	☒	☒
- Fat Free	☒	☒
Kraft Mayonnaise - Real	☒	☒
- Light	☒	☒
- Fat Free	☒	☒
Other	☒	☒

How many jars of mayonnaise or Miracle Whip type dressing are used in your household in a year?

6 or more	☒
3 to 5	☒
2 or fewer	☒

FOOD STORAGE BAGS (EXCLUDING SANDWICH)

	Our Usual Brand(s)	Also Used In Past 12 Months
☒ WE DO NOT USE (Skip to next category)		
Glad-Lock	☒	☒
Hefty OneZip	☒	☒
Ziploc - regular	☒	☒
- Slide•Loc	☒	☒
Other	☒	☒

PAPER TOWELS

	Our Usual Brand(s)	Also Used In Past 12 Months
☒ WE DO NOT USE (Skip to next category)		
Bounty	☒	☒
Brawny	☒	☒
Mardi Gras	☒	☒
Scott Towels	☒	☒
Sparkle	☒	☒
Viva	☒	☒
Other paper towels	☒	☒

1) How many days does it usually take to use an entire roll of paper towels in your home?

1 to 6 days	☒
7 to 10	☒
11 to 14	☒
More than 14 days	☒

2) Which paper towel sheet sizes do you buy most often?

Regular sheet sizes	☒
Select-a-size (Bounty)	☒
Pick-a-size (Brawny)	☒
Choose-a-size (Scott)	☒

PETS

Do you have cat(s) or dog(s)?

Cat(s) ☒ Dog(s) ☒

CAT FOOD

	Our Usual Brand(s)	Also Used In Past 12 Months
☒ WE DO NOT USE (Skip to next category)		
9 Lives	☒	☒
Eukanuba	☒	☒
Fancy Feast	☒	☒
Friskies	☒	☒
Hill's Science Diet	☒	☒
Iams	☒	☒
Other	☒	☒

DRY DOG FOOD

	Our Usual Brand(s)	Also Used In Past 12 Months
☒ WE DO NOT USE (Skip to next category)		
Alpo	☒	☒
Cycle	☒	☒
Eukanuba	☒	☒
Hill's Science Diet	☒	☒
Iams	☒	☒
Kibbles 'n Bits	☒	☒
Nutro Max	☒	☒
Purina - Dog Chow	☒	☒
- Fit & Trim	☒	☒
- O.N.E.	☒	☒
Other dry	☒	☒

FOOD SAFETY

1) Are you worried about the safety of the meats, fruits and vegetables you buy?

Very worried	☒
A little worried	☒
Not worried	☒

2) Are you worried about the experiments of scientists who are trying to improve our natural foods?

Very worried	☒
A little worried	☒
Not worried	☒

COOKIES & CRACKERS

	Our Usual Brand(s)	Also Used In Past 12 Months
☒ WE DO NOT USE (Skip to next category)		
COOKIES		
Chips AHoy!	☒	☒
Nabisco Grahams	☒	☒
Newtons (Fig or other flavor)	☒	☒
Oreo	☒	☒
Snackwell's	☒	☒
Other	☒	☒
CRACKERS		
Air Crisp	☒	☒
Premium saltines	☒	☒
Ritz	☒	☒
Triscuit	☒	☒
Wheat Thins	☒	☒
Other	☒	☒

How many packages of cookies and crackers are used in your household in an average month?

	Cookies	Crackers
6 or more	☒	☒
3 to 5	☒	☒
2 or fewer	☒	☒

HAND & BODY LOTION

	Our Usual Brand(s)	Also Used In Past 12 Months
☒ WE DO NOT USE (Skip to next category)		
Curel	☒	☒
Eucerin	☒	☒
Keri Lotion	☒	☒
Lubriderm	☒	☒
Neutrogena	☒	☒
Nivea lotion	☒	☒
Ponds Ultra Silk	☒	☒
Vaseline Intensive Care	☒	☒
Other	☒	☒

How many bottles of hand & body lotion are purchased in your household in one year?

5 or more	☒
3 or 4	☒
2 or less	☒

FACIAL TISSUE

How many packages of facial tissue does your household use in an average month?

2 or more	☒
1	☒
Less than 1	☒

EYE CARE

1) Does anyone in your household have any of the following eye conditions?

Dry, irritated, or gritty eyes	☒
Itchy, red allergy eyes	☒
Tired, strained eyes from computer use	☒
Astigmatism	☒
Presbyopia (need reading glasses)	☒

2) Does anyone in your household wear the following?

Eye glasses only	☒
Both eye glasses & contact lenses	☒
Overnight contact lenses	☒

CONTACT LENS SOLUTIONS & CLEANERS

	Our Usual Brand(s)	Also Used In Past 12 Months
☒ WE DO NOT USE (Skip to next category)		
AOSept or QuickCARE	☒	☒
Complete or Comfort Plus	☒	☒
Opti-Free or Free Express	☒	☒
ReNu or ReNu Multiplus	☒	☒
SOLO-care	☒	☒
Store brand	☒	☒
Any enzyme cleaner	☒	☒
Other	☒	☒

DENTURES

☒ WE DO NOT WEAR DENTURES (Skip to next category)

Has anyone in your household used a denture adhesive in the past 4 weeks?

Yes	☒
No - dentures fit very well	☒
- don't like feel or mess	☒
- other reasons	☒

EU-ILM10

Please turn to the next page

expenditures, though the chief sources of such information are still medical record studies.

Marketers' Uses of Continuous Panel Data

Both national purchase panels and test market panels are frequently used for monitoring trends, demographic profiling, brand-switching analysis, new trier–repeat buyer patterns, early predictions of test markets, and promotion evaluations. Although both panels are used to collect both types of information, national purchase panels are typically used more frequently to monitor trends, build demographic profiles, and conduct brand switching studies. Test market panels are disproportionately used to conduct new trier–repeat buyer patterns and make early predictions about test markets. Many of these uses of panels are described in detail subsequently.

Estimating Product Trends and Market Shares

It is clear that the most widely used information on the total market for a product comes not from consumer panels, but from store scanner data. However, there are limits to the usefulness of store scanner data. Store scanner data without household identifiers cannot provide any information about the characteristics of the purchasers, nor can it distinguish between household and nonhousehold purchasers. Also, for some product categories, there may be a significant percentage of sales through outlets that do not currently use scanners. Panels are one source of such information, though special audits of these outlets are also possible. The combination of store scanner data with consumer panel information obtained through using either diaries or home scanners provide the richest available information for marketers.

Panels measure purchasing through time of all brands of a product class. The manufacturer is therefore able to observe changes in its brand share and the brand shares of its competitors. The complexity of the distribution system for nondurable goods would otherwise make it impossible for the manufacturer to manage the inventory in its distribution pipeline or accommodate fluctuations in the demand for the product. By combining its own shipping figures with panel data, the manufacturer is able to determine when the pipeline is filling up and when it is emptying out and can adjust this production schedule accordingly.

Tracking Preference Changes Across Package Sizes, Flavors, and Types

Panel data provide information on flavors, sizes, and types of products purchased by consumers and can show how these variables change over time. It can be shown, for example, that the proportion of products that were purchased frozen rose sharply, while the proportion sold of fresh or canned products declined.

Among baking mixes, there have been substantial changes in flavor preferences through time, and most of the promotion of this product has been in the introduction of new flavors. The color of paper napkins and tissues, the presence of fluoride and other ingredients in toothpaste, the type of container for a laundry product and whether it is in dry or liquid form are other examples of differences in form or type that need to be considered when marketing a product and that are provided by a panel.

Information about the sizes of packages purchased is also important, because the manufacturer wishes to sell as much of the product in one transaction as possible, while the consumer seeks a convenient size. Such panel information can lead to larger sizes, as with laundry detergents, or to smaller, individual-serving sizes, as with some food products.

In addition to basic data on the percentage of purchases of a product class by various package sizes, panels provide information on the size of packages purchased by heavy and light buyers and differential package-size purchases by buyers of different brands. The data may suggest, for example, that new package sizes, either larger or smaller, would increase total brand sales or that an existing size could be eliminated with little or no loss in sales and reduced packaging costs.

Panel package size information is also useful in planning deals or other special promotions and as evidence to retailers that shelf space should be given or added for a new package size of a brand. In conjunction with menu census data, panel purchase information can segment package size by the uses and users within a household and thus indicate specific marketing strategies for different sizes.

Profiling and Prototyping Buyers

Panel data allows for the characterization of buyers by the amount of a product or brand they purchase over time. It is critical to distinguish heavy from light buyers, because a common generalization is that the top 20% of heavy buyers account for 80% of sales of a product or brand.

Table 2.1 gives an illustration of two brands with similar brand shares but whose buyers differ in the amounts they buy.

These two brands require different marketing strategies. Brand A would benefit from awareness-building programs to increase the number of households purchasing the product, whereas Brand B would benefit from a program that builds purchase frequency or amounts purchased at each time.

Consumers with varying characteristics purchase different products and brands. An example of such differences is seen in Figure 2.1. The

Table 2.1
Purchase Differences Across Buyers

	Brand A	Brand B
Volume share	20%	20%
Percentage of households buying	6%	12%
Purchases per buyer	5 times/year	3 times/year
Average size purchased	12 ounces	10 ounces

Figure 2.1
Market Profile of a Product

Differences in Consumption Rates by Characteristics

Below Average			U.S. Average	Above Average		
25	50	75	100	25	50	75

Eastern region
College education
Female under 35
"A" economic class
Cities 100,000+
1–2 person families
"B" economic class
Towns under 100,000

3–6 person families
"C" economic class
Female 45+
High school education
Towns under 100,000
Central region
Western region
6+ person families
Southern region
Farms

characteristics of the buyers of a product or brand are, of course, of vital interest to the manufacturer, and intuition may often be misleading. For example, when cake mixes first appeared on the market, it was thought that they would appeal to the employed wife who was too busy to start a cake from scratch. It turned out, however, that employed women continued to buy prepared cakes, but those women not in the labor force were greatly attracted to the mixes. This then dictated a change in promotional strategy on the part of cake mix manufacturers.

Demographic, psychographic, and lifestyle characteristics are important in the purchases of many brands, products, and services, and for many marketing activities it is useful to know what other products and brands are being purchased along with those being studied. Among demographic variables, important characteristics include (1) size of household, (2) household income and economic status, (3) presence of children, (4) education, (5) employment status and occupation, (6) ages of household members, (7) religious and ethnic background, (8) city size, and (9) geographic region. Lifestyle variables include such factors as price consciousness, innovativeness, hobbies, and leisure time activities, as well as media use.

Panels (both continuous and discontinuous) may obtain important classifying information that is difficult or impossible to obtain in a single interview because they have established rapport with their members. In addition, because the same classifying information is obtained on a periodic basis from the same families, these classifications can be compared over time and errors can be corrected.

Segmenting Markets

As is generally defined, market segmentation consists of dividing the market into more homogeneous parts that can be reached with different marketing mixes. Household characteristics, as just described, are one way of obtaining segments. Other methods are often even more powerful. These include segmenting by current usage (whether a product or brand has ever been used) and, if used, by the extent and frequency of usage, package size purchased, brand loyalty (discussed in greater detail next), and cross-brand and cross-product usage. Thus, a snack food manufacturer may wish to segment potato chip users by types of products purchased with chips such as dips, beer, and so forth. This information from consumer panels can lead to substantial increases in the effectiveness of the marketing mix, especially if information on shopping patterns and media usage is also available. References to methods of market segmentation, as well as other uses of panels, are given at the end of the chapter.

Estimating Geographic Sales Potential and Calculating Quotas

An important use of information about the characteristics of buyers of a product is setting sales quotas for small territories when scanner data for these areas are not available. For larger client regions consisting of a state or several states, store scanner data or the purchase behavior of the consumer panel sample in that region can be used to establish quotas, but costs of data collection make it impossible to have reliable direct data for all counties. The demographic characteristics of all U.S. counties are available on the Web from the Decennial Census conducted by the United States Bureau of the Census and from the large ongoing American Community Survey. Combining purchase and census data, it is possible to obtain estimates for the potential sales of a product in a county (Sudman and Ferber 1979).

A highly simplified example illustrates the process. A panel analysis of the characteristics of buyers of a product may indicate that income level, education level (no college versus some college), and city size (metropolitan versus suburban versus rural) are the demographic factors most highly related to the purchasing of the product. Table 2.2 shows the hypothetical purchase rates. By downloading the county characteristics from the Web, the tabulation of the quotas can then be easily performed.

Because the demographic characteristics used to explain the differences in purchase behavior do not correlate perfectly with purchasing (i.e., there are other unexplained factors), there will be residual error. This estimating procedure, however, is better than one that ignores all

Table 2.2
Household Purchase Rates (Purchases per Year) Cross-Classified by Purchase Characteristics

	Metropolitan Counties		Suburban Counties		Rural Counties	
	Over $75,000	$75,000 or less	Over $60,000	$60,000 or less	Over $50,000	$50,000 or less
No college	40	70	20	30	60	100
Some college	50	80	30	40		

consumer characteristics and uses only the number of consumers or that arbitrarily assumes that purchasing is directly related to income. For some products, consumption declines as income rises, as is shown in the hypothetical data in Table 2.2. It is important to note that the table is not and need not be symmetric. Income breakdowns differ by city size, and in rural areas, there is no education break.

Calculating Prices Paid and Store-Level Price Promotions

Store scanner data can be used to determine the volume of a brand that is sold at specific prices or when a deal or special promotion is in effect, but this is generally not enough to determine whether the deal was effective. A deal that causes a sharp increase in sales during the deal period may not have achieved its marketing objective. The question of who purchased the brand still remains. Did the deal succeed in attracting new buyers who continued to buy the brand after the deal period? Did it attract new buyers who went back to their old brands on the succeeding purchase? Or did the deal attract mostly those consumers who were already buying the brand but who saw the deal as a chance to stock up at a reduced price?

An extremely valuable use of panels is to determine pricing policies. A consumer panel provides data on the actual prices paid for a product, not merely the prices on the shelves. It is possible for the manufacturer to experiment in limited areas to determine the price elasticities of a brand so that profits can be maximized, if so allowed by competitors.

Estimating Brand Loyalty and Switching Behavior

A major aim of every manufacturer of frequently purchased nondurable goods is to establish a large group of loyal customers who will buy the brand all or most of the time. At the same time, the manufacturer is continuously trying to lure away customers from competitors and attract nonbuyers of the product to try the brand. The analyses of brand loyalty and brand switching are a vital part of a continuing marketing information system, and of course, such data can only be obtained from continuous consumer panels. One way of measuring competition between brands is to measure market share price elasticities, that is, to determine what happens to the brand shares of a brand as its price becomes higher or lower than that of other brands.

A wide variety of procedures for summarizing brand purchasing patterns and predicting future trends has been suggested. Earlier methods involved either Markov Chain analysis or the use of learning models.

Households generally found these procedures too simple because they did not take into account differential rates and quantities of purchases. Later studies have pointed out and attempted to measure the existence of multi-brand loyalty, which results from different household members having different brand choices within the product class, from individuals preferring more than one brand for variety, or from other reasons such as prices or store loyalty.

Brand loyalty and switching take on major marketing significance when there are major changes in the marketplace caused by new brands or by substantially altered price relations between brands. They are also critical when there are other major changes in the marketing mix, such as that which occurred when Crest toothpaste was first endorsed by the American Dental Association. When major disruptions occur, panels can measure the effects of the change after it occurs but unfortunately may be unable to predict in advance the number and characteristics of brand loyalists and switchers, either for the marketers of the new brand or for defensive action by marketers of existing brands.

It is intuitive that brand loyalty is highly related to store loyalty. Where a consumer shops limits the number of brands available. Inner-city consumers may shop at a small corner grocer in their neighborhood. Such a shopper will be constrained in the number of brands available to him or her, as well as by the availability of sizes. These results have important implications for manufacturers attempting to determine their optimum marketing mix. If store loyalty is a major component of brand loyalty, efforts aimed at the store management level take on even greater significance. Other aspects of shopping behavior are also important to both manufacturers and retailers. These are discussed in the next section.

Documenting Store Shopping Behavior

Closely related to the purchasing of specific products and brands is a consumer's choice about how and where to shop. This information, which is obtained from continuous consumer panels, is important to manufacturers in planning their promotional activities, but it is even more important to retailers. For example, panel data indicate that most heavy buyers of grocery products shop in several stores but that they spend more money in their primary store. Table 2.3 shows data on annual grocery expenditures of shoppers at Store 1 compared with other stores.

Combining shopping information with purchase information, the retailer can learn the effects of private labels, special deals, and the quality of meat and produce on store loyalty. Some panel results have indi-

Table 2.3.
Annual Store Shopping Behavior by Shoppers of Store 1

Store	Percentage Who Also Shop at Competing Stores	Annual Number of Trips	Dollars Spent per Trip	Total Dollars
1	100%	39	$46	$1,794
2	48%	35	$11	$385
3	86%	28	$26	$728
4	75%	29	$16	$464
5	44%	21	$ 8	$168

cated that, whereas loyal shoppers are attracted by private labels and disloyal shoppers by deals, the differences are generally small.

Another important finding is based on information about consumer purchases, shopping behavior, and menu preparation. It has been found that items most often bought in secondary stores (stores other than the store to which the consumer was most loyal) were the ones used to complete a dish or round out a meal menu. That is, shoppers were motivated to go to a secondary store because they had forgotten to buy something or because what they wanted was not available at their primary store. However, once at another store, they tended to spend almost as much on that visit as on a trip to their primary store. These results have obvious implications for both retailers and manufacturers. This is just one of many examples that illustrate that data about consumers, which are valuable in themselves, become even more valuable when combined with other data about the same consumer.

One desirable aspect of consumer panels is that they are able to obtain and report on purchases from all types of outlets, including door-to-door and now e-business, and to indicate the relative importance of the various outlets. This type of information not only is useful for manufacturers making distribution and marketing decisions, but also can aid salesforces as they negotiate with retail managers.

Test Marketing to Predict New Product Success

At any given time, leading manufacturers derive their greatest profits and sales from new products. Surveys have shown, however, that four out of five (some estimate even more) new products placed on the market fail. One of the chief methods for testing new product concepts and performance is through the discontinuous consumer panels we discuss later. At some point, when concept and use tests are encouraging, manufacturers will go into test markets to test the new product in the marketplace against the marketing activity of competitors. These test markets are critical but also very expensive in both money and time. Methods for rapidly determining the characteristics and buying patterns of purchasers of the new product can be of great value in reducing waste and distribution of unwanted products and in speeding up the decision of whether to introduce the product full-scale.

Store scanner panel data can give information on total sales of the product in the test markets, but this is generally insufficient. What is needed is information on the level of consumer interest, as measured by the number of new buyers who will try the new product at least once. Even more important for most nondurable goods will be estimates of repeat buying patterns, because repeat buyers will ultimately determine whether the product is successful. Also, it is critical to get these estimates of new and repeat buying as rapidly as possible.

To accomplish this, several models predicting new buyer penetration and repeat purchasing have been proposed. All these models depend on panel information from the early months of a test market, and the references to them are given at the end of this book. For simplicity, we discuss the first of such models, the Fourt-Woodlock basic model first introduced in 1960 but still widely used.

Fourt and Woodlock (1960) extrapolate the penetration of a new product (the number of new buyers that the product attracts) from observed periods to prediction periods. Their model assumes that the increments in penetration for equal time periods are proportional to the remaining distance to the limiting "ceiling" penetration. In other words, in each period the ceiling is approached by a constant fraction of the remaining distance.

Such a model is illustrated in Table 2.4 and Figure 2.2, in which the ceiling x is 40% and the constant of proportionality r is .3. In the first

Table 2.4
Simple x,r Penetration Model
x = 40%, r = .3

| Time Period | Increments in Penetration | |
	Formula	Numerical Example
1	$r(x - 0) = rx$	$.3(40) = 12$
2	$r(x - rx) = rx(1 - r)$	$.3(40)(.7) = 8.4$
3	$rx(1 - r)^2$	$.3(40)(.7)^2 = 5.9$
i	$rx(1 - r)^{i-1}$	$.3(40)(.7)^{i-1}$

time period, the number of new buyers is .3(40 – 0) = 12%. In the second time period, the number is .3(40 – 12) = 8.4%. Each increment is simply 1 – r times the preceding increment.

Ratios of successive increments in penetration, such as 8.4:12 or 5.9:8.4 in Table 2.4, are fast, simple estimates of 1 – r. These ratios can be averaged and applied to the last observed increment repeatedly to extend penetration as far as desired. Although this model turns out to be somewhat too simple, its basic properties remain usable.

More realistically, it is known that different buyers purchase a product class at widely variant rates. Experience shows that when buyers are grouped by purchase rates into equal thirds, typically the heaviest buying third accounts for 65% of the total volume, the middle third for 25%,

Figure 2.2
New Buyer Penetration—Assumed Model I (x,r)

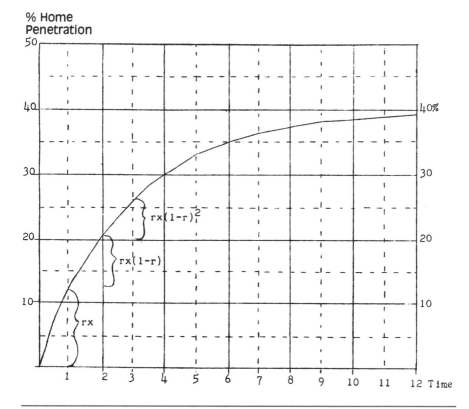

Source: Fourt and Woodlock (1960, p. 33).

and the light third for only 10%. This means that if transaction sizes are roughly equal, heavy buyers make 6.5 purchases and medium buyers 2.5 purchases for every 1 purchase by a light buyer, for an average total of 3.3.

If the original (x,r) model is applied to each third separately, the difference in purchase frequency will be enough to induce a large "stretch-out" effect in the decline of increments of penetration for all buyers combined. This effect is sufficiently pronounced that the penetration model can be improved for the purpose of predicting a year ahead by assuming that increments of penetration approach a small positive constant k rather than zero. This second model is illustrated in Figure 2.3, where total penetration approaches a line whose value at point t after i time

Figure 2.3
New Buyer Penetration—Assumed Model I (x,r,k)

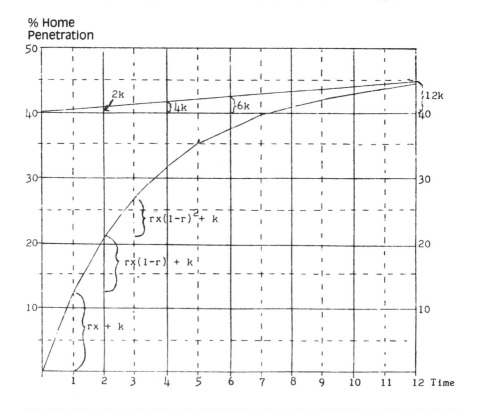

periods is $x_0 = ik$. Typically, k is a small number of the order of .2% of households per month, and the model is not very sensitive to small errors in k.

Predicting Repeat Purchase Behavior

The fraction of new buyers who have made a repeat purchase by the end of an observation period is necessarily an underestimate of those who will ever make a repeat purchase, for some new buyers will not have had an opportunity to repeat. The estimate of new buyers who will repeat can be substantially improved by omitting the most recent new buyers from the denominator of the repeat buying ratio estimate. Omission of those who purchased during the most recent one or two average purchase cycles works well empirically. The first new buyers of an item are typically heavy buyers of the product class. Their average purchase cycle is approximately one-half that of all buyers (compare 6.5 purchases with 3.3 for all buyers). Thus, for equal observation times, the average purchase cycle of repeat buyers to date will be a smaller fraction of the eventual average if the product is purchased infrequently. Such products will require omission of two average purchase cycles' increments of new buyers, whereas the omission of one may suffice for frequently purchased product classes.

In practice, the decision to use one or two purchase cycles can be guided by the trends in the two repeat ratio estimates that result. Typically, the trends converge as information accumulates. Similar theories hold for estimation of the proportion of second-time buyers who will make a third purchase, and so on. As might be expected, each successive purchase increases the probability of still another purchase.

Using these estimating procedures, a prediction can be made for the cumulative number of future purchases by new buyers and first-, second-, third-, fourth-, fifth-, and more than fifth-repeat buyers. These estimates are summed to give the final estimate, as indicated in Table 2.5. It may be seen from this example that errors of prediction for the various types of buyers appear to be offsetting. Underestimates of new buyers and more than fifth-repeat buyers compensate for overestimates of the other groups.

Estimating Brand Penetration with New Buyers

Parfitt and Collins (1968) and Ahl (1970) describe models for predicting brand shares for new brands for which total product class purchasing is assumed not to change when the new brand is introduced. Unlike the

Table 2.5
Estimated and Actual Purchases at End of Prediction Period (r,x,k model) (in thousands)

Buyer Type	Estimated Purchases	Purchases in Preliminary Period	Estimated Addition	Actual Addition
New buyers	8,141	6,021	2,120	2,544
First-repeat buyers	3,948	2,170	1,778	1,523
Second-repeat buyers	2,207	1,076	1,131	858
Third-repeat buyers	1,422	591	831	569
Fourth-repeat buyers	841	326	515	398
Fifth-repeat buyers	671	223	448	283
More than fifth-repeat buyers	2,214	627	1,587	1,711
Total Purchases	19,444	11,034	8,410	7,886

Fourt-Woodlock model, their definition of new buyer penetration is the cumulative percentage of the total product class volume accounted for by households that have tried the new brand. No matter when a family tries the new brand, its volume from the start of the measurement of the new brand is counted in the cumulative product class volume of users to account for buying rate differences between users and nonusers.

The repeat purchase rate is estimated as the users' product class volume that is accounted for by the brand in subsequent time periods after the first purchase. In this procedure, as a rule of thumb, the ultimate repeat level for most new products can be estimated after half the ultimate users have been active in five subsequent periods. The estimated brand share is then the product of the estimated cumulative volume trial percentage times the estimated ultimate repeat rate.

Massy (1969) developed STEAM (stochastic evolutionary adoption model) to account for differential purchase rates of individual households. His model makes a prediction for each household of future long-term rates of purchase of the new brand based on current rates of purchase of the product class, as well as trial and repeat behavior. These individual predictions are then summed to yield a prediction for the total population. Massy assumes that the probability distribution is of a compound Wiebull form, which requires the fitting of five parameter values from consumer panel data. After the parameters are estimated for current behavior, simulation methods are used to make predictions for each household.

A model that is simpler than STEAM was developed by Eskin (1973). Both the cumulative percentage of those who have ever bought and the cumulative percentage of repurchasing j times by those who have purchased j – 1 times are given by a geometric stretch function. The model requires estimating three parameters, a slope factor s that estimates how rapidly the curves approach the ceiling line, and parameters a and b that relate the ceiling line to time t by the simple linear function $y = a + bt$. The s parameters are estimated from all panel repeat purchase data by regression method. They are assumed equal for all repeat levels but not for the initial trial.

In the absence of evidence that the more complex models are superior to the simpler ones, we suggest using the simpler models unless they clearly fail to match reality. The Eskin model, which uses the framework of the Fourt-Woodlock model but estimates the parameters by regression procedures, appears to be a good first approach for most new product predictions. All the models assume that the remainder of the product class is not changing substantially during the period of the new brand's introduction. In some cases at least, this assumption is not met.

Although all the models may be applied to national and regional data, they are primarily used for test market data. The use of special panels in test markets is common. Any test panel will usually measure purchases of several products, even if there is interest in only one new brand. This is to prevent special attention being called to a specific product, because this could change overall usage (see Chapter 6 on conditioning). As with all test markets, extrapolation from test market results to estimates of the total population requires skill and experience. The errors introduced at this stage may be far greater than those made in estimating the model of penetration within the test market, but any additional discussion of extrapolation of test market results is beyond the scope of this book.

Measuring Advertising Effectiveness

With information on both purchasing and media exposure, it is possible, though difficult, to measure the short-term effectiveness of advertising. This may be done most readily for new product introductions for which the lagged effects of previous advertising do not influence current behavior.

Normally, manufacturers will set up field experiments to test advertising effectiveness, using panel data to monitor exposure to ads and purchase behavior. A control group that does not receive the ads is used for comparison purposes. In television advertising studies, split cable television allows a test ad to be shown to an experimental group while a different ad is shown to the control group. Similarly for print media, the use of split press runs allows different ads to reach the experimental and control groups. As in all tests, these groups are randomized in advance to minimize the effects of initial differences.

Without experimental designs, it is difficult to disentangle the effects of any one advertisement or promotional campaign from the effect of all concurrent and previous marketing activity. Nevertheless, some efforts have been made to use natural experiments. Therefore, an advertiser might advertise in a new medium, such as the Web, and observe the effects of sales on consumers who have Web access. Some efforts have been made to correlate brand switching at the individual level with opportunities to view advertising. McDonald (1970) found, for example, that consumers were 5% more likely to switch to than from a brand when, in the period between purchases, they had the opportunity to see two or more advertisements for the brand but that more than two exposures have no stronger effect. Similar saturation effects were found by Parfitt and McGloughlin (1968). Goodwin (1972) used Box-Jenkins time-series methods to suggest the longer range effect of media exposure to ads.

Assessing Home Menu Preparation

Consumer panels can provide information on the preparation and use of foods, as well as on purchase information. There have been several menu studies in the United States and elsewhere in which households keep records for one or two weeks of all meals prepared and served to individuals in the household, both in and away from the home.

The most important use of information on food preparation is in the development of new products or the modification of existing products to better meet the needs of the user. This may include changing the sizes of the packages to those amounts most commonly used in food preparation so that waste or spoilage is eliminated, or it may mean combining two products into a single, more convenient product. Using soup as an illustration, a menu census showed that many households combined a can of chicken soup with a can of vegetable soup to make a chicken–vegetable soup. This led to the manufacture of a chicken–vegetable soup in one can. The extensive home preparation of a menu dish presents the food manufacturer with opportunities to offer the same dish to the consumer in a more convenient prepared form.

Menu census data have been shown to be useful in advertising and promotion. Many new recipes and suggested uses of food products that have been featured in advertisements were derived from menu censuses

(Wansink and Gilmore 1999). Instead of menu censuses that obtain information on all food consumed, some uses have been made of special panels that obtain information on the use of one or two specific food and grocery products, such as butter and margarine, frozen orange juice concentrate, or paper products. Unfortunately, asking about only one or two products may cause special behavior by panel members. (This is discussed in detail in Chapter 6 on panel conditioning.)

Currently, menu studies are used by governmental agencies in many countries to measure the total caloric intake of individuals, as well as the intake of vitamins, minerals, proteins, and other food components, such as soy. It is also possible to measure the intake of certain food additives such as artificial dyes, sweeteners, or preservatives to determine what, if any, regulation of these additives is required.

Academic Uses of Consumer Panels

Because consumer panels provide rich data about individual behavior, they have been a rich resource for academics who study marketing and consumer behavior. Some of the findings, as described previously, have direct implications for marketing practices. Other studies enrich our understanding of consumer choice without having direct implications for practitioners. In this section, we briefly summarize some of these findings.

Determining Antecedents of Usage Frequency and Consumption Behavior

One of the most promising uses of panels is in studying how different marketing variables influence the usage or consumption rate of a product. Although previous studies have attempted to infer consumption rates on the basis of purchase–repurchase data, such an approach is plagued with causality problems (did the family eat more or was there a birthday party?) and measurement problems (was the product eaten all at once or over a period of time?). Panels help control these problems.

In one such study, Wansink and Ray (1996) examined how three different advertising strategies influenced the consumption volume for each of three different products: soup, gelatin, and cranberry sauce. The study benchmarked the average consumption rate of these products across each of 250 households. Each household then received advertising stimuli for two of the three products and was asked questions about the ads. The consumption of the consumers was tracked for the next three months. The resulting data showed how successful each of the ad strategies was in increasing overall consumption and in increasing consumption in specific instances, such as eating soup for breakfast or eating cranberry sauce with chicken.

Panel studies have long been used to study the eating habits of consumers. Research has focused on taste-specific satiety and on the cross-consumption elasticities of various food groups. With the recent interest in functional foods, interest also has been developing in understanding the profiles of people who responded most favorably to the Food and Drug Administration's (FDA's) "5 a Day" campaign to encourage consumers to eat at least five fruits and vegetables each day. Similarly, panels have been used by researchers to identify the psychological profiles of consumers who are most prone to eat soy. The eventual goal of the research is to track their eating and substitution patterns in an attempt to replicate this behavior in similarly predisposed consumers.

Because most marketing research has been focused on what consumers choose and not what they use, a recent series of studies has focused on the usage behavior that follows purchase. Panels have made this work possible by offering opportunities to track and record what happens behind closed doors. "Kitchen psychology," as it has been called, has most recently investigated how inventory levels of products influence usage frequency. Findings have shown that stockpiled products are consumed at a frequent level for the first three to six days after purchase, but their consumption then drops off dramatically if they are not made salient (Chandon and Wansink 2002). After a week has passed, most of these products have faded into the back of the refrigerator or cupboard and are no longer consumed at an accelerated pace.

Another recent inventory study used a panel to determine why people buy products they never consume. A frequent allegation is that marketing pressures (sales, coupons, and displays) are the primary suspects. The members of this panel were asked to find a product they bought but had not used, and they were then asked a series of questions about the product. It was discovered that 73% of the products were bought for recipes that were never made, guests that never arrived, or events that never happened. With marketing practices exonerated, subsequent samplings of this group were able to track what happened to the products after the households were made aware of them: 23% were consumed, 13% were given away to food banks, 21% were thrown away, and the remainder were kept (Wansink, Brasel, and Amjad 2000).

Consumption Clusters, Preference Affiliation, and Affinity Marketing

The Internet has brought about a greater ability to track consumer search patterns and purchase preferences across a wider range of product categories and services than ever before. This volume of data provides a range of possibilities to understand consumers on the basis of the clusters of products they prefer and purchase. These preference affiliations are a target of interest for academics who want to determine the extent to which preferences in one category can predict preferences in other categories. The use of continuous panels that track a wide range of purposes have been recently used to try to develop profiles of consumers and show how these profiles can be used to predict other purchase behavior.

In addition, recent studies of heavy users of consumer packaged goods have examined what personality variables are correlated with heavy usage of a particular brand or category. By cross-correlating this with heavy usage in other categories, researchers attempt to determine why these particular personality variables drive brand preference and category usage.

In some ways, this is related to the shopping basket analysis that is done with consumer products. Such a process typically examines coincidence and correlations between the purchase of various products in an effort to find patterns. The urban research legend of the "diaper–beer connection" is an example.

The unconfirmed legend is that an analyst of convenience store sales data saw a mysteriously high coincidence between diaper sales and beer sales but that this correlation existed only with sales made between 5:00 P.M. and 7:00 P.M. on weekdays. Qualitative interviews purportedly helped solve the mystery. These purchases were made by fathers who had been sent out after work to pick up some diapers. After making their diaper selection, they decided their effort was worth a toast.

Event Analysis

Another academic use of panels is to determine how a particular event—the Depression, the Vietnam War, a period of unemployment—may have influenced consumers. This would entail a calibration period before the event and the occasion to sample the consumers after the event. Often, however, the questions of interest do not occur until after the event has long passed. One such event is World War II. This war dramatically changed the consumption culture of the United States, yet little is known about how factors such as product sampling that occurred during the war influenced purchase preferences and consumption patterns following the war (Wansink 2002). Exhibit 2.2 shows a screening questionnaire that was used to recruit World War II veterans as panelists to study the long-term effectiveness of product sampling. This study examined the veterans and a demographically matched sample to determine how an experience in the armed forces differentially changed the long-term consumption habits of consumers. The ongoing survey of this population allows for follow-ups on important questions and hypotheses that became evident only after the first major sampling.

Marketers' Uses of Discontinuous Panel Data

Concept Testing and Test Marketing

A major use of discontinuous consumer panels is in the development and testing of new brands, products, and services. Long before these new products are test marketed in specific locations, there is substantial developmental work that goes into testing the product concept and, if the concept receives favorable consumer reaction, actual samples of the product for taste, usability, and general consumer satisfaction. Almost never would a new product be tested on a general population. There will be a limited population likely to be the target market for this new product. Such a target market will be identified by previous product usage or by other demographic or lifestyle variables. Discontinuous consumer panels that have prescreened large samples of the general population are efficient sources for locating such populations. The following are just a few of the kinds of special populations that are offered:

- Baby panels—Samples of new and expectant mothers;
- Health panels—Samples of persons with various ailments and the medication and treatments they use;
- Product purchase panels—Households that purchase or use specific products; and
- Demographic panels—Individuals or households with specific demographic characteristics, such as young adults or adults over 50 years of age, high income households, or individuals in specific occupations.

Advertising and Promotion Testing

Again assuming that a new ad campaign is aimed at a specific target market, a discontinuous consumer panel provides a prescreened sample for testing alternative advertisements and promotional offers using either mail or the Web. With the wide availability of VCRs, even television ads

Exhibit 2.2
Screening Questionnaire to Determine the Long-Term
Effectiveness of Product Sampling

Attention: This page (page 15) is for veterans.
If you are not a veteran, please turn to page 16.

Products and Samples

V14. What are the names of some of the companies that you remember making products that you used while serving during the War (e.g., Goodyear, Jeep., Prestone, etc.)?

a. _____   d. _____

b. _____   e. _____

c. _____   f. _____

V15. Were you given or sold products with brand names on them during your time in the Service? In the space below, please list the names of any brands that you remember being given or purchasing during your time in the Service, also please check whether they were free or whether you purchased them:

a. _____   ❑ Free   ❑ Purchased

b. _____   ❑ Free   ❑ Purchased

c. _____   ❑ Free   ❑ Purchased

d. _____   ❑ Free   ❑ Purchased

V16. Please answer the questions below rating how you felt about any free product samples that you received during your time in the Service.

	1 = Strongly Disagree 9 = Strongly Agree
a. Post-War use of these caused pleasant memories	1 2 3 4 5 6 7 8 9
b. Post-War use of these caused unpleasant memories	1 2 3 4 5 6 7 8 9
c. These gave me favorable impressions of their makers	1 2 3 4 5 6 7 8 9
d. Using these products convinced me of their quality	1 2 3 4 5 6 7 8 9
e. I still use these products	1 2 3 4 5 6 7 8 9

15

can be mailed to panel members to get their reactions. In the most typical situation, random subsamples of eligible panel members receive single different ads or promotional material. The ads or promotions that receive the highest favorability ratings are then adopted or tested further. In some cases, only a single ad or promotion is tested and compared with previous norms for the same product class. Sometimes panel members are each shown two or more versions and asked to choose the one they prefer. As a reminder, the advantage of panels over mall samples or telephone interviews is that the sample has been prescreened.

Packaging and Design Testing

As with ads and promotions, new product and package designs can be tested using panels. If the product is small enough, an actual package is usually preferred to a picture or video. For large durable products such as automobiles and washing machines, the test will consist of photographs and descriptive material. When photographs are used of products, both monadic and comparison tests can be conducted.

Investigations are being conducted to determine whether package and design testing can be feasibly done in the form of a Web-based test that is administered through the mail. In this version, people would be prescreened as to whether they are part of the target market and have a computer with Web access. In the materials they receive through the mail, they will be given a Web address and a password. This will enable them to view the packages or designs and to use Web-based advantages, which might include multiple angles, randomized order, and other features. Currently, these practices are not in widespread use, but as the population of Internet households becomes more representative of the population at large and as the cost and quality of Web designs drop, this method will be frequently used.

Developing User Profiles

When trying to facilitate the adoption of a product or behavior, it can be useful to know how segments of current users of the product differ psychographically, behaviorally, or attitudinally from segments of nonusers. Having this information can help identify predisposed segments in order to precisely target them. For example, knowing the ways in which consumers of soy products differ from nonusers helps determine more precisely the types of soy-related products that will be most successful in these segments and how these products need to be positioned.

Discontinuous panels are helpful in this regard for three primary reasons. First, they allow for any respondent prescreening that is necessary.

Second, they allow for the collection of a wide array of data that can be used to develop profiles. These data can be collected at once or on various occasions. Third, they allow for behavior tracking, which can be useful in determining what set of conditions or circumstances can foretell the onset of the target activity (such as product usage).

One such study was able to show that the type of soup a person preferred could generally be predicted by their personality (Wansink and Park 2000). The survey was conducted with prescreened soup lovers, and the results were able to generally profile the top five soups in the United States according to the personalities that most attracted them: vegetable soup—"The Better Homes and Gardener," clam chowder—"The Sophisticate," tomato—"The Affectionate Pet Lover," chicken noodle— "The Leisure Lover," and chili—"One of the Guys."

Attempts are also being made to determine the extent to which media preferences, primarily in the form of magazine subscriptions, can provide personality clusters that can predict consumption preferences across a wide range of products. For example, although it is not surprising that a person who subscribes to *Wine Spectator* may be more likely to buy a luxury car than a reader of *Sports Illustrated*, it would be useful to study whether knowing what other magazines this person subscribes to helps predict the type of luxury car he or she will buy (even before the person knows).

Brand Equity Research and Attitude Tracking

Attitudes toward brands, either of users or nonusers, can easily be obtained from discontinuous panels. Information on who uses a specific brand and how it is used can also be obtained, recognizing that usage information may be restricted by memory error (especially for products that are not highly salient).

Interest in brand equity research has led to an increased development of tools that are valuable for understanding a brand's equity. One such tool involves the in-depth analysis of brand fanatics. Brand fanatics are consumers whose consumption levels, dedication, or word-of-mouth generation is much higher than what could be expected from a typical loyal user. Although not representative of the population, these people provide a powerful opportunity to understand the magnified essence of the brand that contributes to its equity. Discontinuous consumer panels are important in these cases, because they enable these consumers to be located and screened and they allow for an in-depth analysis of the target brand and competing brands. A recent study was completed for a brand of cleaner that had only a 4% share of the market. By locating and analyzing fanatics of this brand, a better understanding of what characteristics needed to be emphasized and promoted became quickly and vividly clear.

Conducting Marketing Research and Trend Analysis

Continuous panels have also proved to be useful by companies that publish newsletters that are targeted to companies. These newsletters, such as The Shopper Report, regularly survey panelists on topics such as packaging, health foods, shopping behaviors, vacation expenditures, and so on. The resulting summary statistics and selected verbatims are then combined with focus group comments to round out an analysis of the particular issues for the upcoming newsletter. Discontinuous panels become invaluable for this research, because the trust and rapport that are developed over successive interactions help keep response rates high and provide the perception of accountability that can sustain data integrity.

Summary

In this chapter, we have briefly described most of the current important uses of consumer panels. These include market segmentation, measuring brand loyalty, outlet behavior, package-size usage, the effects of deals and other promotions, predicting the success of new products, media usage, advertising effectiveness, determining how foods are actually prepared and served, medical events and expenditures, and complete budget studies. Almost certainly, other uses already exist or will soon be found for this versatile research method.

Chapter 3

How Are Consumer Panels Biased?

How large would a panel have to be before it perfectly represented the U.S. population?
—President, neutriceutical division of a
Fortune 100 company

Nearly 300 million people. That's how large a panel would have to be before it perfectly represented the U.S. population. The seemingly sad fact of the matter is that no smaller sample will perfectly represent the actual population. The question then becomes: How can we reduce the number of people we need in a sample without increasing inaccuracy to an unacceptable level?

This chapter discusses the special sample design problems that face anyone who wishes to establish and maintain a consumer panel. To a large extent, the sampling methods used for panels are similar to those used for one-time surveys. A decision must first be reached on the universe to be measured. Then, among a large number of alternative methods of stratification and clustering, a method must be chosen that either maximizes the amount of information for a fixed cost or minimizes the cost of the required information. Finally, using random selection procedures, specific areas are chosen and the interviewer is given instructions on the procedure to use in contacting respondents.

Because the probability sampling methods most commonly used in the United States today are well described in sampling texts, they are not reviewed here. There are, however, two critical areas in panel sample design that are not covered in general discussions of sample survey methods:

1. Procedures for measuring and reducing sample biases due to noncooperation of respondents and
2. Maintenance of a panel through time.

These topics are, if anything, more important today than when discussed in the first edition. In addition, the stratification and clustering strategies for panels differ from those used for one-time surveys; these points are also discussed. Many of the sampling issues for discontinuous panels are similar to those for continuous panels, but when there are differences, we point them out.

After showing how offline and online panels are biased across various dimensions, this chapter demonstrates how to reduce some of these biases. Then, in examining the sample biases that occur, recommendations are given as to how to correct for these biases through sample balancing and ratio estimation. Last, effective panel maintenance policies are outlined, along with how they can be aided by using clustering and calculating sample variances. The general structure of the topics in this chapter is illustrated in Figure 3.1.

Sample Cooperation in Consumer Panels

No panel survey achieves full cooperation from its selected respondents. Government agencies generally get more than 80% cooperation in household surveys. Other high quality academic and nonprofit survey organizations with well-trained field staffs get household cooperation rates ranging from approximately 60% to 75%, depending on the nature of the survey. Many market research surveys get household cooperation rates of approximately 50%, and there is some evidence that cooperation

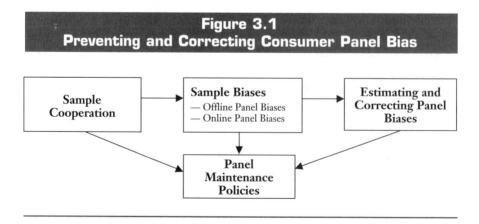

Figure 3.1
Preventing and Correcting Consumer Panel Bias

rates are continuing to decline for a variety of social and technological reasons. For periodic, repeated surveys, an additional 5% to 10% loss should be expected from the remaining sample on each subsequent interview unless major panel maintenance efforts are in place. Consumer panels that require households to scan their purchases or keep diary records generally have initial cooperation rates lower than those for one-time surveys, though if the effort is minimal, as for the Nielsen television meter panels, the initial rates may be as high as those achieved by the quality survey organizations. Scanner panels that require less effort than keeping a diary but more effort than a television meter report initial cooperation rates of approximately 70%. Nevertheless, there will be high initial attrition in any panel operation that requires respondent effort and some continuing attrition even with vigorous panel maintenance efforts. Most panels have continuing cooperation rates of less than 50%. Although the possibilities of sample biases are present in one-time surveys, it is clear that these biases are potentially more serious if the cooperation rate is less than 50% than if the rate is 80%.

The cooperation achieved is, of course, not independent of the recruiting methods used and the tasks required of the panel members. Yet even when substantial efforts are made to recruit and maintain panels, it is likely that cooperation rates will be below 50% for most continuing panels. The question arises of the value of geographic-based probability selection methods when less than half of the respondents will cooperate on a continuing basis. Some organizations have chosen to use less representative methods to reduce cost. Yet there is a good reason for using geographic-based probability selection methods: Where panel members live not only gives some indication of their socioeconomic condition, but also shows the range of outlets, products, and services that are available to them.

Operators of discontinuous panels typically recruit households by mail or, more recently, the Web using very large mailings from mailing list firms. Some operators of continuing panels also use mail recruiting for new test market panels or replacements or supplementary members for existing panels. Cooperation achieved in such mailings generally ranges from less than 5% to 25%. In most cases, large oversamples are invited initially so that the cooperators may then be balanced by demographic variables such as geography, household size, and other variables. Although the panels match the census data for the control variables, biases for other variables are almost certainly larger than for panels recruited by personal methods. These sample biases could lead to substantial errors if panel cooperation is related to actual consumer behavior. For example, suppose lifestyle is related both to willingness to cooperate on a mail panel and to the likelihood of buying a new product. Controlling for household size, geography, and education will not remove the sample biases caused by lifestyle.

As with all panels, we must depend heavily on previous experience with similar products. If a panel, regardless of the sampling method used, has been able to track these earlier products well, we would have greater confidence that the new product could also be measured by that panel. As a generalization, the flatter the demand for a product across market segments (i.e., the less variance), the less we would need to be concerned about sample biases. For such products, mail panels with loose sampling methods can provide extremely useful data at low cost.

Sample Biases in Offline Panels

During the past 50 years of panel research, more recent studies have given support, albeit with much more precision, to many of the findings of the pioneering panel studies. For example, Gupta and colleagues (1996) compared household panel results in the Sioux Falls, S. Dak., market area with store panel data in the same market for two products, laundry detergents and peanut butter. They found only minor differences in overall brand shares for detergents but that panel households purchased larger sizes of detergents, a finding that reflects the fact that panel households are larger (see Table 3.1). For peanut butter, the leading brand was well reported by panels, but there were large differences between store and household panel data for the next two brands. For peanut butter, no size differences were observed. There was no evidence of households being more price sensitive, and the price elasticities from the household data were similar to those from the store data.

Although there have been major changes in the U.S. distribution of demographic variables such as income, education, and women in the labor force, we believe that the panel biases have not changed greatly over time. In general, panel cooperation appears to be best in households with more than two members, with wives in the younger age groups, and with more education.

This is consistent with the largest scale study to date comparing cooperators and noncooperators in a national panel (see Table 3.1). Using the data from this 1959 University of Illinois study, it is also possible to compare the total composition of a panel with estimates of the U.S. population obtained from the Current Population Survey. This comparison, made in 1961, is given in Table 3.2. Previous comparisons by the

Table 3.1
Comparing Households that Join Panels with Those that Do Not Join

Characteristic	Percentage of Panel Cooperators (N = 4570)	Percentage of Noncooperators (N = 4588)
A. Household Size		
1 member	5.4	11.5
2 members	24.1	29.8
3 members	20.5	19.5
4 members	22.8	19.0
5 members	14.5	10.7
6 members	7.8	4.9
7 or more members	4.9	4.6
Total	100.0	100.0
B. Children under 6		
1 child	18.4	13.9
2 children	12.5	8.3
3 children	3.8	2.4
4 or more children	1.3	.9
No children	64.0	74.5
Total	100.0	100.0
C. Age of Female Head		
Nearer 20 years	8.9	8.4
Nearer 30 years	29.0	22.9
Nearer 40 years	28.6	24.8
Nearer 50 years	19.2	20.6
60 years or older	14.3	23.3
Total	100.0	100.0
D. Own Versus Rent		
Owners	77.8	74.0
Renters	22.2	26.0
Total	100.0	100.0
E. Type of Dwelling Unit		
One family	82.1	76.9
Two family	8.3	9.2
Apartment or three family	7.3	12.0
Other	2.3	1.9
Total	100.0	100.0
F. Female Head's Employment		
Employed	30.5	35.7
Unemployed	69.5	64.3
Total	100.0	100.0

	Table 3.1 Continued	
Characteristic	Percentage of Panel Cooperators (N = 4570)	Percentage of Noncooperators (N = 4588)
G. Mailed in Boxtops or Coupons		
Mailed in boxtops or coupons in last three months	19.3	13.2
Did not	80.7	86.8
Total	100.0	100.0
H. Price Consciousness		
More price conscious than average	41.2	32.8
Equal	35.0	34.8
Less price conscious than average	16.1	21.4
No opinion	7.7	11.0
Total	100.0	100.0

U.S. Department of Agriculture (1952) and other panels agree closely with these results (see Response Analysis 1976). Although these data are old, there is little evidence that the nature of panel biases has changed in recent years.

This study was based on initial classifying interviews that were obtained before households were invited to join the panel. Consequently, these comparisons do not show the effects of dropout families. It is clear that the characteristics shown are not independent. Nevertheless, it is useful to discuss them individually.

Household Size

Panels have difficulty recruiting small households. The greatest difficulty is with one-member households. Single individuals are less likely to be found at home and generally have less interest in such things as food purchasing than do homemakers in large households. Although keeping continuing records or scanning data is harder for homemakers in large households, this is offset by the greater interest that homemakers in larger households have in the behaviors being studied. Also, if the homemaker is unwilling to keep continuous records, the probability that some other person in the household will keep it increases with the number of adult household members.

Table 3.2
Comparing Characteristics of Household Panelists with the General U.S. Population

Characteristic	Percentage of Panel Households (N = 7500)	Percentage of All U.S. Households
A. Household Income (1961)		
Under $1,000	2.5	5.0
$1,000–$1,999	6.6	8.0
$2,000–$2,999	7.6	8.7
$3,000–$3,999	8.9	9.8
$4,000–$4,999	11.5	10.5
$5,000–$5,999	13.8	12.9
$6,000–$6,999	13.1	10.8
$7,000–$7,999	10.4	8.7
$8,000–$9,999	12.0	11.3
$10,000 and over	13.6	14.3
	100.0	100.0
B. Occupation of Head		
Professional, technical	11.2	9.4
Managers, proprietors	9.5	12.5
Clerical	9.3	6.2
Sales	5.4	4.7
Craftsmen, foremen	18.2	16.0
Operatives	16.8	16.0
Servants	5.5	6.1
Farmers	5.9	6.5
Laborers	2.3	4.4
Unemployed or not in labor force	15.9	19.2
Total	100.0	100.0
C. Education of Head		
0–8 years	30.3	37.5
9–12 years	46.5	44.3
13+ years	25.2	18.2
Total	100.0	100.0
D. Type of Household Head		
Male and female	85.8	87.4
Female only	13.5	10.0
Male only	.7	2.6
Total	100.0	100.0

There are two distinct types of one-person households: (1) women with a median age of 65+ with lower incomes and (2) men with a median age of 35 with mid-level incomes. One-person female households are usually easy to recruit and will stay on panels. One-person male households are more difficult to recruit and retain.

Age of Female Head

Women over 55 years of age are less likely to join a panel than are young or middle-aged women. This same tendency is seen in one-time surveys, in which older people have a higher refusal rate. When this study was conducted, age and education were strongly related, with older people having less education. Today, that relationship still exists, though it has been considerably weakened. Panel maintenance experience indicates, however, that older households, once recruited, are less likely to drop out of a panel. Women in the 25–34-year age group, who are most likely to join a panel, are also the most likely to drop out as a result of changing family circumstances, particularly a new baby, a move, or a change in employment status of the record keeper.

Own Versus Rent

Panel cooperators are slightly more likely than noncooperators to own their own homes. This is due mainly to differences in household size.

Type of Dwelling

Again owing to differences in household size, panel cooperators are more likely than noncooperators to live in single-family dwelling units.

Female Head's Employment

Women in the labor force are somewhat less likely than women not in the labor force to have the time or the interest to join an expenditure panel.

Mailed-in Rebates or Coupons

The mailing of boxtops or coupons to receive premiums or money shows a greater interest in home management, as well as some price consciousness. The process of filling in a form and mailing it is related to keeping written records and mailing them in as a panel member. It is therefore not surprising that panel members are more likely to mail in boxtops or coupons than are noncooperators (see Table 3.1).

Price Consciousness

A satisfactory measure of price consciousness requires observation of the actual purchase behavior of shoppers. Because this information is not available, the respondents were asked for a self-evaluation of whether they were more price conscious than average. More panel cooperators considered themselves price conscious than did panel noncooperators.

Household Income

There is fairly good agreement, as shown in Table 3.2, between the income distribution of panel households and all U.S. households, as estimated in the Current Population Report P-60 series. Although income levels have changed sharply since the end of World War II, this high level of agreement has been observed over time, and there is no reason to believe that income biases are greater currently.

Occupation of Household Head

There do not appear to be major differences between the occupations of heads of consumer panel households and those of all U.S. households, again as measured in the Current Population Survey.

Education of Household Head

As suspected, panel household heads have had more education than heads in the general U.S. population. Education within the household is clearly related to the ability and interest to keep written records. It is interesting to note, however, that the differences between the panel and the general public on this characteristic have been steadily decreasing as older, less educated people die and as the general level of education in the United States rises. Although there are no current comparisons available, we would speculate that education differences have continued to narrow, and the introduction of scanners, which has resulted in the reduction or elimination of writing, has also made education a less critical variable.

Type of Household Head

Table 3.2 shows that panels underrepresent households composed only of a single man. This difference would be more serious if these households were not such a small part of the total population.

Except for household size, most panel biases are small for demographic characteristics. The greatest differences between panel cooperators and noncooperators are in social–psychological characteristics, such as degree of organization and price consciousness.

Although dated, some additional comparisons between the Attwood Consumer Panels in Great Britain and Germany and general population samples show few or no differences in the readership of newspapers or magazines or in psychological or buying variables. Table 3.3 compares the reading of newspapers and weekly and monthly magazines for two consecutive years. The differences seen in one year are small and likely to be in the reverse direction in the other year, which indicates that the differences are probably due to sampling variability.

Table 3.4 compares the attitude scale scores of panel households in Great Britain and Germany to random samples. In Britain, the attitudes measured are rigidity in housework, traditionalism in housework, economy consciousness, and conservatism in shopping; in Germany, they are the last two and positive attitudes toward branded goods. On none of these scales are there any significant differences.

To summarize the rather limited and dated comparisons, both the U.S. and European experiences indicate that there are some biases in purchase panels, particularly in household size, age of female head, and education of household head. On many other demographic and shopping variables, panels are not substantially different from the general population. For scanner and other types of panels that require less effort from the respondent and achieve higher cooperation rates, the biases would be even smaller. In comparison with continuous and discontinuous panels recruited by mail under controlled conditions, the biases would be much larger.

Sample Biases in Online Panels

The question as to how well represented the general public is in online consumer panels is a contentious one. As with all surveying methods, self-selection biases are problematic. In 2002, online users tended to be better educated, more affluent, and younger than the average consumer. In addition, they tended to be male and have a greater willingness to respond to the survey's questions (Weible and Wallace 1998). Some of these differences can be problematic depending on the purpose of the panel.

Furthermore, as is explored in Chapter 4, the bias of online panels varies depending on the online method being used. Consider, for example, e-mail panels versus downloadable panel surveys. E-mail surveys are fast and simple, and they require relatively little setup time and the least

	Attwood Consumer Panel (Year 1)	General Population (Year 1)	Attwood Consumer Panel (Year 2)	General Population (Year 2)
Table 3.3 Comparing Readership Between Panel Households and the General British Population for Two Consecutive Years				
Characteristic				
Total Housewives in Great Britain	100%	100%	100%	100%
Dailies				
Daily Mirror	31	34	33	33
Daily Express	28	29	28	26
Daily Mail	18	15	18	15
Daily Telegraph	9	8	9	7
Daily Sketch	7	6	7	6
Daily Herald-Sun	9	9	8	9
Average readership	17.0%	17.2%	17.2%	16.1%
Sundays				
News of the World	37	38	36	37
People	37	37	37	37
Sunday Mirror	32	31	30	31
Sunday Express	27	27	27	25
Sunday Times	7	8	7	8
Sunday Telegraph	4	4	5	6
Average readership	21.2%	21.4%	21.0%	21.2%
General Weeklies				
Radio Times	37	37	36	33
TV Times	27	26	21	23
Reveille	10	13	10	12
Weekend	10	10	10	10
Average readership	21.0%	21.3%	19.1%	19.4%
Women's Weeklies				
Woman	38	40	37	39
Woman's Own	30	33	29	32
Woman's Realm	22	22	23	21
Woman's Weekly	18	16	19	14
Woman's Mirror	13	14	14	12
Average readership	24.4%	25.0%	23.8%	23.7%
Monthly Publications				
Reader's Digest	18	19	17	18
Woman and Home	14	11	15	12
Ideal Home	10	10	7.5	8
Everywoman	8	5	6	4
Vogue	7	12	5	10
Good Housekeeping	8	10	6	9
My Home & Family	8	5	4	4
She	6	6	6	6
Housewife	6	6	4	5
Woman's Journal	5	4	5	4
Average readership	9.0%	8.8%	7.6%	8.0%

Sources: IPA National Readership Survey, Attwood Consumer Panel.

Table 3.4
Comparing Attitudes Obtained from Surveys with Those Obtained from Panels

Attitude Scale	Average Score	
	Attwood Consumer Panel	Random Sample
Great Britain		
Rigidity in housework		
(1 = very, 5 = flexible)	3.53	3.46
Traditionalism in housework		
(1 = traditional, 5 = modern-minded)	2.98	3.00
Economy conscious		
(1 = very, 5 = not)	2.77	2.80
Conservatism in shopping		
(1 = very, 5 = not)	2.04	2.00
Germany		
Economy conscious		
(1 = very, 5 = not)	2.26	2.27
Conservatism in shopping		
(1 = very, 9 = not)	5.98	6.00
Positive attitude toward branded goods		
(1 = very, 5 = not)	1.42	1.52

Source: Attwood Consumer Panel, Great Britain and Attwood Institut für Marketanalyse, Germany.

user sophistication. They are ideally suited for internal audiences, such as employee groups, distribution partners, and beta testers. In contrast, downloadable panel surveys must be downloaded to an executable file on the panelist's own computer. These surveys result in further self-selection because of the download time and the necessary user sophistication and hardware requirements needed to download, complete, and upload these surveys.

The Best Sample Frame for Some Products and Some Subgroups

The representativeness of online panels of the general population of consumers is only important if we are actually interested in the general population of consumers. There are situations in which the population of interest—for example, people who purchase on the Internet—is best captured by an online panel. Presently, items that can easily be bought using the Internet are probably good candidates for online consumer panels.

These items include books, compact discs, airline tickets, magazine subscriptions, home banking, investment services, and computer software. In the future, these categories will likely expand to include high-tech equipment, travel services, training, boilerplate legal services, prestige real estate, mail-oriented luxury goods, specialty hobbies and crafts, technical employment services, and even some industrial equipment and parts.

Despite biases in relation to the general population, there are subgroups within the population that may be better represented through the Internet than through other methods. Teenagers, for example, have been an elusive group with respect to consumer panels prior to online consumer panels. (The number of children online is expected to rise from 5 million in 1998 to more than 21 million by 2002.) In addition, it is also effective with consumers who are single, affluent, and well-educated, such as physicians, lawyers, professionals, and working mothers.

All methods of obtaining research information have drawbacks, but there is a sizable concern that online panels tend to be psychographically biased toward progressive technology innovators and demographically biased toward younger, male professionals. Over time, as Internet services become as commonplace as telephone and television services, the self-selection biases that occur in online surveys will become less pronounced and the benefits more pronounced. Online surveys are able to attract respondents from previously elusive groups such as working mothers, professionals, and teenagers.

In general, successful online consumer panels will be possible as long as adequate representation of the target buying population can be ensured. In 2001, more than 125 million people—which is approximately two-thirds of the worldwide users of the Internet—live in North America. In the United States, more than 50% of households have Internet access, and 25% go online daily. This suggests that previous biases toward young, male professionals being the main Internet users are changing every day. As the number of Internet users increases over time, biases will decrease.

Methods of Reducing Online Biases

Although it is difficult to correct the bias that might exist between online users and nonusers, several methods are being experimented with to reduce the biases that might exist between those Web users who become panel members and those who refuse. For example, to make sure that panel members are, at the very least, representative of Web users, Javascript can be used to randomly sample site visitors. It can help obtain as representative a cross-section of site visitors as possible by avoiding oversampling of heavy site visitors.

A panel opt-in question is commonly asked of people who complete an online pre-panel interview. It briefly describes the panel and asks if people would like to take part. These people are then recontacted and asked to visit a related Web site. While there, all respondents are asked to complete the survey, which collects their demographics, Web usage, media use, and attitudinal information. The increased effort necessary to follow up and continue with the process helps increase the seriousness and validity of those who ultimately become part of the panel.

A weighting process can be used to extrapolate panel members' information on the basis of the entire adult U.S. Web population. Each panel member then becomes representative of a certain number of U.S. adult Web users. This is done by taking all the information from a survey and applying statistical weighting to the raw data.

In an effort to increase representativeness and counter concerns that online consumer panels are skewed, most reputable firms profile their members and send out online messages only to those they believe will be interested. The concern that panels are not representative of the general population and are skewed toward young, professional men is becoming less true as different segments of the population become better represented. As more cable wiring is placed in rural regions of the country and as wireless technology improves, the rural population also will become better represented within panels.

Estimating and Correcting Panel Biases

Sample biases need to be evaluated carefully when using a consumer panel. It should be remembered, however, that the importance of these biases depends not only on their magnitudes, but also on the correlations between these biases and the behavior or attitudes being measured. Surprisingly, there is little correlation between many of the things measured by consumer panels and biased sample characteristics. As an example, although there is a difference between the percentage of panel cooperators and noncooperators who mail in rebates or coupons, this does not influence the panel reports of purchases of cold cereals, because there is no significant relationship between cereal purchases and the mailing in of rebates or coupons.

We might wish to evaluate the effects of sample biases by observing the behavior of households that do not join a panel, but this is generally not possible. As is shown in Chapter 5, which deals with panel accuracy and recording, the data obtained from households in recall surveys are subject to errors that are larger than the biases being measured. The alternative, which is also not wholly satisfactory, is to examine the differences in behavior of panel members with different characteristics. Unless a characteristic is specifically considered, the biases that it causes in measuring behavior can never be ascertained.

Sometimes it is possible to validate the results of a panel by comparing it with outside data of sufficient accuracy so that sample biases can be measured. These comparisons generally show little or no effect on purchase behavior by any of the characteristic biases except household size. It is possible that, for behavior and attitudes other than grocery shopping, biases may be more serious. If biases are known, they may be compensated for by ratio estimating methods and maintenance procedures, which are described in the next two sections.

An illustration that nondemographic characteristics are not highly related to purchasing behavior was obtained from the unpublished University of Illinois study mentioned previously. Purchasing behavior of approximately 800 households was related to the two characteristics on which the panel was most biased and for which there were also some a priori reasons to suspect that purchase behavior would be influenced. These two characteristics were (1) whether they mail in rebates or coupons (in the last three months) and (2) whether they use a written shopping list.

Two product classes, regular coffee and frozen orange juice concentrate, were examined. These product classes were selected because they are frequently purchased and because chain private label brands are important. It was predicted that chain label brands would be purchased more frequently by the organized, price-conscious shoppers. An eight-week period was used, during which time 632 households purchased regular coffee and 459 households purchased frozen orange juice concentrate.

Although differences in purchase behavior can be observed in Table 3.5, these differences are not very large, and in some cases there are compensating errors. For example, shoppers who use shopping lists are more likely to buy nationally advertised brands, whereas those who mail in rebates and coupons are more likely to buy chain brands. Because both shoppers who use lists and those who mail in rebates are more likely to join a panel, these biases tend to cancel out each other. Again, it should be noted that the products and characteristics measured in the test were selected because large biases were expected. Most other grocery products and characteristics would show even smaller differences.

Table 3.5
Brand Share of Regular Coffee and Frozen Orange Juice Concentrate by Characteristics

| | | | Regular Coffee | | |
Characteristic	Total Buyers		National Brands	Chain Brands	Local Brands
Mailed in Rebates or Coupons (in last three months)					
Mailed in	202	100%	50.5%	12.9%	36.6%
Did not mail in	430	100%	55.8%	11.9%	32.3%
Used Shopping List for Groceries					
Always or sometimes	481	100%	55.5%	11.2%	33.3%
Never	151	100%	49.7%	15.2%	35.1%
Combined Characteristics					
Mailed coupons, used list	162	100%	50.9%	9.9%	39.3%
Mailed coupons, never used list	40	100%	43.8%	16.7%	39.6%
Did not mail coupons, used list	319	100%	56.6%	10.5%	33.0%
Did not mail coupons, never used list	111	100%	50.4%	14.8%	34.9%
All Households	632	100%	54.1%	12.2%	33.7%

| | | | Frozen Orange Juice | | |
			Five Leading Brands	Chain Brands	Other Brands
Mailed in Rebates or Coupons					
Mailed in	158	100%	50.0%	25.3%	24.7%
Did not mail in	310	100%	54.5%	20.6%	24.9%
Used Shopping List for Groceries					
Always or sometimes	352	100%	53.4%	21.3%	25.3%
Never	107	100%	51.4%	25.2%	21.6%
Combined Characteristics					
Mailed coupons, used list	133	100%	49.7%	22.4%	28.0%
Mailed coupons, never used list	25	100%	55.8%	28.1%	22.9%
Did not mail coupons, used list	219	100%	56.7%	20.7%	22.7%
Did not mail coupons, never used list	82	100%	48.3%	27.1%	24.6%
All Households	459	100%	52.9%	22.2%	24.9%

Another way of examining possible biases is to look at differences in purchase behavior between long-term (four or more years) panel members and the more recent members. For most product categories, there are no differences in either total amount purchased or brand shares. For a few products for which there is a dominant major brand that tends to be priced higher or price promoted less than the competition, the brand share of this dominant brand is lower for long-term panel members, controlling for age, income, education, household size, and geography. This indicates either that households remaining in panels longer are different in their purchasing in this special case or that some type of conditioning has occurred. (See Chapter 6 for a discussion of conditioning.) This discussion illustrates that sample biases may have some effect in special cases, though there are no observable general effects.

Still another method for measuring sample biases is illustrated by a report by Cordell and Rahmel (1962) of the ACNielsen Company. Here, the problem of recall error was not a factor because households were interviewed by telephone and asked whether they were watching television at that moment. Comparisons were made between those households that agreed to join the Nielsen panel and the total sample. The results are shown in Table 3.6. There appears to be a small positive cooperation bias in the Nielsen Panel; that is, cooperators are slightly more likely

Table 3.6
Percentage of Households Using Television Among Nielsen Panel for Cooperators and Total Sample

Time	Nielsen Panel Cooperators	Total Sample
Total all hours	45.3%	43.9%
Total daytime hours	29.2%	27.8%
10–11 A.M.	23.8%	22.1%
2–3 P.M.	25.1%	24.7%
5–6 P.M.	38.6%	36.7%
Total nighttime hours	61.4%	60.1%
7–8 P.M.	57.3%	56.8%
8–9 P.M.	63.8%	61.9%
9–10 P.M.	63.3%	61.4%
Sample size	18,843*	18,228

*The Nielsen panel sample includes substitute households recruited to replace noncooperators.

than noncooperators to watch television. The absolute difference is between 1 and 2%.

These examples do not guarantee that sample biases will never be important. For some kinds of behavior and attitudes that panels measure, sample biases may be large. The examples illustrate methods of measuring these biases and suggest that, even if sample biases exist, they need not necessarily affect the behavior being measured.

These results also help explain why continuous and discontinuous mail panels with low initial cooperation and large, unknown biases on some uncontrolled variables are able to provide satisfactory data in some cases. The low correlation between the sample biases and purchase or other behavior will often result in data that agree well with shipment or other outside validation data. In those cases when the sample biases of a panel are highly related to the specific behavior being examined, panel data that do not agree well with outside sources are typically not used.

Correcting Panel Biases Through Sample Balancing

One means of minimizing sample bias is to balance the sample by restoring it to the universe proportion of the demographics that were originally specified (or stratified upon). For example, if the initial return response from a panel underrepresented the proportion of men between the ages of 45 and 60, a second push would be made to increase the sample in this stratification. This increases accuracy by making the sample more representative of the target universe.

Although balancing is commonly done when initially recruiting panel members into a pool, it is not often done (via follow-up) for individual surveys or projects. As a result, 45- to 60-year-old men may appear to be representative in the general panel population but may not be as representative among the returned responses of a specific survey. This is because it is too time consuming and expensive to go back into the field for another round of data collection to balance the population. One solution is to oversample this population from the beginning. If it ends up being overrepresented in the final analysis, the extras can be trimmed out. In this case, it would be less costly to oversample from the beginning and not use some data than to have to return to the field to compensate for a lower-than-average response. This entails knowing what strata tend to provide historically poor response rates and compensating for this prior to the distribution of the survey.

Correcting Panel Biases with Ratio Estimation Methods

It will often be desirable to apply weights to panel results to obtain better estimates of universe totals. Panels frequently use household size and geography as controls. Household size is closely related to the quantities of food and other products purchased, and if no correction was made for the shortage of small households, the panel would consistently overstate quantities purchased. Geographic controls are also used because certain parts of the United States may have been oversampled deliberately so that special reports on these regions can be made.

The basic method used is simple, and computer processing speed makes the production of weighted data as easy as producing unweighted results. To compute weights, all panel households are first sorted into mutually exclusive and exhaustive cells or strata that are determined by the size of the panel household, its geographic location, and any other characteristics used in the weighting. As an example, a cell might consist of all three-member households living in non-metropolitan areas of a given state. The total number of U.S. households in this cell is estimated from decennial census data updated by current population surveys. The ratio (U.S. households in cell X ÷ panel households in cell X) is computed for every cell. These factors are then stored in the individual records for each household. Normally, each household in the same cell will have the same factor, but it is possible to make further fine adjustments if, on a continuing basis, some households do not return all of their records.

For computing reasons, the weights need to be part of the household record, because the data may be tabulated in many different ways. In addition to total U.S. reports, there may be reports by characteristics such as household income or age of female head. Here the households are no longer sorted by the control characteristics of household size and geography.

The number of strata or cells to use depends on the relative magnitude of sample biases compared with sampling variability. Increasing the number of cells tends to reduce sample biases but increases sampling variability. A rule of thumb has been to have an average of about 25 households in a cell, though some variance is allowed.

These weighting procedures are also used in discontinuous panels and are sometimes referred to as poststratification methods. Panels face the need to revise weights periodically as either the universe or the panel changes. Changing weights may introduce changes in data series. It seems better to make small changes in weights on a continuing basis, say annually, than to make large changes at long intervals. Large changes in weights may produce sizable changes in data that are artifactual and do not reflect real universe changes. (This topic is discussed in more detail in Chapter 7.)

Panel Maintenance Policies

The basic point to remember in maintaining a long-term continuing panel is that such a panel is dynamic and is not to be treated as a sample drawn for a one-time survey. Whereas individual households in the population change continuously because of new household formations, household dissolutions, and household moves, the aggregate or general characteristics of the universe change very slightly from year to year. A panel reflects these changes and can therefore not only remain continually representative of the universe, but also provide evidence on what changes are occurring. That is, it can track these changes if it is allowed to do so. To illustrate this, we describe four key changes in household composition: household moves, household dissolutions, new household formations, and panel member dropouts.

Let us take the first question, regarding what to do with families that move. People who are accustomed to working with a good fixed sampling frame become extremely uneasy when this geographic sample frame is discarded. Yet, in operating a panel, experience has shown that it is essential that families that move be followed when they move. This may perhaps be conceived of as a dynamic system that is frozen for just an instant to allow a sample to be drawn from it. The system is then released, and the motion of the sample represents the motion of the universe. If we made the mistake of sticking to a fixed sampling frame, thus dropping households that move out of the selected dwelling units and replacing them with households that move in, the following difficulties would arise:

1. It would be difficult to locate and include dwelling units that were built after the sample frame was designed;
2. It would be difficult to allow for shifts in population from some states to others, notably the population shift to the Southwest and West; and
3. Dropping families that move frequently would require costly and impractical methods to prevent obvious sample bias, because certain types of families (i.e., young, small households) are far more likely to move than are larger or older families.

Allowing a panel that is representative of the universe at a given point in time to move, that is, not dropping or replacing households when they move, contributes to a biased sample that is geographically correct at all times. There is a question of whether any original nonrepresentativeness of a panel affects its ability to represent moves in the universe adequately. Fortunately, there seems to be empirical evidence that a well-designed panel, even with some sample selectivity, does a good job of representing moves in the universe, because these moves do not appear to be highly correlated with willingness to join a panel.

For discontinuous panels and panels that are interviewed periodically, it is important to obtain the name of a close friend or relative who will always know where the respondent lives, so that movers may be traced between interviews. In addition, periodic mailings to respondents not only keep cooperation high, but also provide information on new addresses for movers.

If the interviewing must be done face-to-face, a respondent who moves to a new area where no trained interviewer is available will be lost from the panel. Frequently, however, it will be possible to get all or most of the required information from such respondents by long-distance telephone, mail, or the Web. In special cases, it may even pay to send an interviewer from the nearest area to the new location, even if the travel costs are considerable.

For some studies, a panel may be limited to residents of a specified geographic area, such as a city, county, or state. If a household moves within the area, it should be followed. If it moves from the area, it becomes ineligible and is dropped from the panel.

Accounting for moves, however, is not enough. Some method must be designed for continually rejuvenating a long-term panel by adding the appropriate number of new households and dropping dissolved households. The latter is quite easy to handle. The only necessity is that a careful watch must be kept on all moves a family makes so that any families that move into an established household rather than establishing a new household can be dropped from the panel. A situation in which all members of a household die at the same time is rare. Far more typical is the case in which, when the husband dies, the wife goes to live with some other members of her family. If she has been a panel member, she should be dropped at this time. There is, of course, no need to replace her in the panel with a new household.

A panel can also provide information on new household formations. Usually, households are periodically asked to report whether there has been any change in the number of adults or children living in the home and if anyone has moved away to set up housekeeping. The reason for moving away is also asked. By far, the greatest majority of these moves result from marriages and college. Family members who move away to set up housekeeping should be recruited with probabilities inversely proportional to the number of persons who will constitute the new household. (This is done so that all new households will have the same probability of being added, regardless of the size of the new household.) Thus, in the case of a marriage, half the split-offs are recruited. Again, empirical evidence has suggested that the panel adequately reflects the new household formations in the universe. This recruiting method constantly brings new, young households into the panel at the proper rate and at the time that the household is formed.

There are some changes occurring in panels that do not reflect changes occurring in the universe. Panel members occasionally drop from the panel after they have been recruited for reasons beyond the control of even the best-run panel. Personal situations such as illness in the family or the birth of a child are among the most common reasons for dropping. Although this dropout rate may be low, it can affect panel data unless methods for replacing these households are used. Two methods of handling this situation are available:

1. Oversample on the basis of past experience. That is, we might determine a profile of households that are dropout prone and oversample their profiles. In practice, it is not economical to maintain a large oversample whose data are not used, so most panels replace households when they drop out. However, some European panels have maintained oversamples.

2. In the replacement of households, the same kinds of noncooperation problems are found that occur with households originally selected. Typically, a replacement method specifies a list of addresses or telephone numbers that are contacted until a cooperating household is found with characteristics similar to that of the dropped household.

Reduction of the dropouts in a panel requires considerable effort and experience in the techniques of maintaining panel cooperation. Even though most panels find it important to compensate families with money or prizes, a continuing program of communication with panel families is equally essential to establish and maintain the high level of panel morale that reduces panel turnover.

The use of compensation and careful initial contact and training is especially important for less-educated respondents for whom keeping written records is a more difficult task. Most of these families, once past the initial learning of their task, become extremely loyal panel members.

Panel Clustering

How much clustering should there be in a panel sample? There is really no good reason for geographic clustering if households are recruited by telephone or mail and return their records by telephone, mail, or the Web. If, however, recruiting is done face-to-face, the cost of hiring and training interviewers would suggest using the same procedures for selecting primary sampling units (PSUs) and about the same number of PSUs as a survey organization would use for a series of one-time surveys. If the interviewing within the PSUs is to be done face-to-face, it is appropriate to note that they have the same kind of block-level clustering that would be used for one-time surveys. For panels recruited face-to-face that report by mail or the Web, there is no need for clustering within the PSU. Recruiting and replacing a household using face-to-face methods is such a lengthy process that clustering within the PSU does not really reduce travel costs.

Computing Sample Variances for Panels

The current procedures for computing sampling variances from complex samples using Taylorized deviations or replication methods of PSUs can also be used for computing variances for panel samples. For measures of change from one period to another, the units of observation are changes in behavior or attitude at the individual respondent or household level. These change measures are summed over PSU, as previously. Fortunately, even though there may be substantial sample biases that affect the estimates of behavior or attitudes at a single point in time, the estimates of change have been found to be subject to much smaller biases. Thus, total errors in estimates of change for panels, including both variance and bias, are far smaller than errors in estimates of levels at one point in time.

Consider, for example, a brand purchase volume estimate with a 10% relative bias and a 5% relative sampling error but for which the correlation between months is .6. Then, the total relative error of the estimate is

$$(.05^2 + .10^2)^{1/2} = 11\%.$$

The relative error of the estimate of change omits the bias, because it constant over the two periods. The relative sampling error is reduced because of the correlation between the two periods. The total error is

$$[(2 - 2r)\sigma^2]^{1/2} = [.8(.05)^2]^{1/2} = 4\%.$$

Summary

The lower initial and continuing cooperation with panels compared with one-time surveys makes sample biases a potentially serious problem. Fortunately, for many kinds of consumer behavior, especially purchase behavior and consumption behavior, the biases do not appear to cause major distortions in the results. This may be a somewhat optimistic appraisal of the effects of bias, as panel operators have probably ceased measuring product classes in which sample biases caused severe problems, so these cases are not reported.

Some improvement in data quality results from weighting procedures that can correct for major biases or deliberate sample disproportionality. Even if the effects on bias are not large, weighting the data smoothes out the variability caused by households that do not provide information for every period.

Long-term panels must use some procedure to prevent the aging of the panel relative to the general population. The recommended procedure in this chapter is to obtain new household formations and dissolutions from the panel itself, to follow movers, and to replace dropouts with other households that are similar in critical variables.

A consideration of optimum designs for panel recruiting suggests that if the recruiting is to be done face-to-face, then a limited number of PSUs should be chosen for recruiting. There is, however, little advantage to clustering within the primary areas, and if recruiting is done by mail or telephone, there is no need for any form of clustering.

Sampling error computations for panels are done in the same way as for other complex samples, recognizing that trend sampling errors are computed by measuring the change in behavior at the household level. The reduction in the trend sampling effort because of the high correlation in household behavior in successive periods is one major advantage of using a panel.

Chapter 4

Courting Panelists and Collecting Data

I can't believe so many respond to your panel solicitations [in the United States]. We Dutch are very private people, and it takes more than a letter for us to join a panel.

—Researcher from the Netherlands

There are four basic ways of recruiting panels: face-to-face, over the telephone, through the mail, or online. Although these methods get progressively less costly, there is a justifiable concern that they also get progressively less representative in the cooperation they elicit. Because panel recruiting is a large part of panel operations, it is important to highlight the details of all four recruiting options.

In this chapter, we discuss the procedures used to recruit panel members and the forms and other methods used for data collection. The major issues addressed in this chapter can be considered in the form of questions:

- Should panel members be recruited face-to-face, by telephone, by mail, or online?
- What compensation, if any, is required to obtain cooperation?
- What should be the frequency of data collection—weekly, monthly, or some other time period?
- How should the data collection form be structured?
- How do changes in the data collection form affect recording?

Through this chapter, we address the difficulties in getting completely accurate data. At the end of the chapter, we show some interesting data that compare the accuracy of panel data to that of survey data. The results show that panel data are, in general, far more accurate. Herein lies the good and bad news for panel data. Although difficult to obtain, the data reward the diligent researcher with accuracy.

Panel Recruiting

The choice of the recruiting method to use is a function of the concern about sample biases, which were discussed in the previous chapter, and the costs of the alternatives. As is true with one-time surveys, face-to-face methods are more expensive than telephone methods, and mail methods are even less expensive. There is substantial evidence, however, that cooperation by mail and online is far lower than that obtained in face-to-face recruiting for household panels. This exactly parallels the experience for one-time surveys. However, for some special populations or for special purposes such as test marketing, the cost advantages of mail may outweigh the sample biases and possibilities of data distortion.

In the United States, face-to-face recruiting is not commonly done except to generate a quick convenience sample from, for example, church or social groups. Yet this is still a widely used method in many countries in which people are not as forthcoming. Consider the Dutch researcher whose quotation began this chapter. In cases like this, the most representative panel of Dutch people might only be obtained through personal recruiting that is able to allay personal doubts and fears that could not be easily addressed in a letter or e-mail solicitation. Because of this, a reasonable amount of detail is provided in this next section. Much of it will also be generalizable to other recruiting methods.

Face-to-Face Recruiting

Even more than for one-time surveys, the recruiting of households or individuals to a panel requires great skill. The recruiter must be a combination of a survey interviewer and a door-to-door salesperson. High pressure techniques, however, are not desirable. Although it may be possible to obtain an initial agreement from households by such methods, these households also tend to drop out at a high rate. Aside from the recruiter selection and training discussed subsequently, the actual recruiting process generally takes the following steps:

1. The field representative introduces him- or herself and makes it clear that he or she is not selling anything but is gathering research and information.

2. An initial screening interview is conducted to obtain demographic and purchase behavior information about the household or respondent. It has been found that this initial interview helps build rapport between the respondent and the recruiter and facilitates the recruitment process that follows. In addition, it provides information on the characteristics of households that do not cooperate at a later stage for use in estimating the magnitude of sample biases.

3. After this interview, the household is invited to join the panel. Two principal motivations are given for participation. The first is the importance of the information, how it will be used, and why cooperation from all types of families is necessary. The second is the compensation that the household will receive for participating. (Compensation is discussed later in this chapter.) A third motivation, unstated but possibly most important, is a desire or willingness to agree to a request from the field representative with whom rapport has been established.

4. Unless there is an absolute refusal, the next stage is to explain the recording form to be used. For a consumer purchase panel, this would generally be done by taking items from the pantry shelf and entering them in the training diary. Another method is to take items from the initial interview and transfer them to the diary. The diary is discussed in detail to make clear what is to be included and what need not be entered. The importance of making entries immediately after the purchase or other event is stressed.

5. At the close of the training, the field representative leaves a diary and other training material for the household to use, as well as any material for other household members. This might include a government publication showing how panel data are used and a copy of a "memo to the public" explaining market and survey research. Finally, but perhaps most important, information is provided on compensation and/or gifts and how they are earned. This information usually stresses the increased compensation for regular and long-term cooperation. The field representative will always leave his or her address and a telephone number where he or she can be reached if the household has any questions.

6. Depending on the complexity of the data required and the frequency of data collection, a training call is scheduled at a later time. Experience suggests that after the household has something to record, the sooner this training call occurs, the more likely the household is to continue cooperating. The greatest loss in cooperation occurs between the initial agreement to cooperate and the completion of the first diary or record. A major reason for this loss is the household members' uncertainty about what is required and a concern that they will make mistakes and appear foolish in the eyes of the interviewer or others. Both at the initial contact and at the training call, the emphasis should be on cooperation, not on minor clerical mistakes.

7. Training and motivation continue during the first several record-keeping periods, though this is mainly by mail or telephone rather than face-to-face. Households that cooperate for three or four periods are unlikely to stop cooperating unless family conditions change.

8. One method sometimes used is to start with a short simple diary form and to introduce the full-scale diary only at the end of the training period.

Selecting Field Representatives

Although panel recruiting and survey interviewing are not identical tasks, the same observable characteristics are traditionally desirable:

1. Age—30 to 45 years.
2. Sex and marital status—married women.
3. Family status—no children under 10 years of age unless adequate provision can be made for their care during both the day and evening.
4. Education—two to four years of college desirable.
5. Experience—responsible position working with women. Interviewing experience desirable, especially if on surveys employing a probability sample design. No house-to-house selling and preferably no retail selling.
6. Appearance—neat personal appearance, conservative dresser.
7. Health—ability to work long hours and in various types of weather.
8. Personality—pleasing. Must like all kinds of people. Ability to carry on a conversation with all types of people. Not overbearing or too aggressive. Good listener. Persevering yet tolerant.
9. Availability—available to work nights, Saturdays, and Sundays.

There have been some attempts to predict the success of field representatives using personality tests, but these have not proved very useful. The crucial attribute is a pleasing personality, and the best method of judging this has continued to be a field supervisor's evaluation. Because the interview between the applicant and the field supervisor cannot fully indicate how well the applicant will do, a newly hired representative will generally recruit several households immediately after hiring and training. This will enable the field supervisor who accompanies him or her to get a better picture of his or her personality and ability. At this stage, the supervisor may decide that a mistake has been made, or as is more usual, the field representative may decide that he or she is not suited for the job or that the job is not suited for him or her.

Training Field Representatives

Although no two organizations use identical training procedures, the following description of methods used by the USDA National Consumer Panel is typical of many current training programs:

As part of the training program each field worker was required, first, to keep a diary for her own family for four weeks and to perform all the tasks expected of a regular panel member. These diaries were edited and the interviewers were advised in detailed letters of any mistakes that were found. Thus, each interviewer learned exactly what was expected of a panel member. She learned also that the task of keeping a diary becomes simpler and less time-consuming after a few weeks' experience. A comprehensive interviewer's instruction manual, which anticipated the field problems that would be encountered, was prepared and sent to interviewers for concentrated study. Each interviewer was required to master the instructions and to pass a quiz which required complete knowledge of all essential points in the manual. The quizzes were reviewed in the office and an individual letter was written to each interviewer indicating any points she should study further.

After recruiters have had a chance to study the training manual, some form of personal training takes place. This may be on a one-to-one basis between the field supervisor and recruiter or in group settings. At these training sessions, role playing is used extensively, with the recruiters playing their own roles and the role of the respondent being played by the field supervisor or others in the group. The final stage of personal training is done in the field, where the supervisor observes the recruiter and offers suggestions after the call on a household has been completed.

Step-by-Step Procedure for Contacting and Recruiting Families

The procedure for recruiting households to participate in a panel should advance along the following steps:

1. Selection of families;
2. Contacting the individual family: letters of introduction, personal calling cards, introductory remarks, proper interviewing climate, not-at-home calls, making future appointments;
3. Explanation of consumer panel: what the panel is and how it works, the individual family's responsibilities, time required, ease in reporting, use of diary forms, average number of entries, systematic entry, regularity of reporting, point payments, family cooperation, confidential nature of reporting;
4. Handling of special socioeducational families: illiteracy, linguistic difficulty, nationality, or race;
5. Forms to be left with individual family and explanation of each;
6. Answering objections and questions: Why was I chosen? I'm too busy and don't have the time. It looks like a lot of work. What I buy is nobody's business. I have never heard of your company, how do I know I'll get these premiums? We don't need any of these premiums. Someone else does most of the buying. My husband wouldn't want me to do this;
7. Detecting resistance or uncertainty: ascertaining the cause, setting the stage for future interviews, not giving the respondent an opportunity to give a definite refusal, systematic recording of conditions;

8. Training the family: answering questions about any subject already covered, explanation of diary mechanics, going through the diary form page by page, obtaining cooperation from all members in the household, recording difficult product classes, systematic diary keeping, regularity in reporting and late diaries, vacations, point system and bonuses, setting up next training call and its importance;

9. Closing the interview (whether respondent has accepted or not): forms to be left with appropriate comments, setting up next interview date; and

10. Communication of interview results to field supervisor: forms to be filled out and disposition of each, conference with field supervisor on future contact strategy.

Telephone Recruiting

Many of the procedures used in telephone recruiting are identical to those for face-to-face recruiting. The major difference is that respondents and recruiters cannot see each other. This makes it more difficult to train the family in diary-keeping methods, but there are some compensations. For example, it is easier to maintain close control and supervision over the recruiters, because telephone recruiting is conducted from a central location.

Although a pleasing personality is still the most important attribute of a successful recruiter, it is important that this be conveyed over the telephone. Some field representatives who are highly successful in face-to-face contacts are uncomfortable working on the telephone and perform poorly. Conversely, some people do far better on the telephone than face-to-face. Physical appearance and handicaps are of no real importance in telephone recruiting, but aggressiveness, drive, and the willingness to work hard are still important.

As with face-to-face recruiting, the process starts with an interview related to grocery shopping habits. Although the major purpose is to build rapport, the data are again useful for measuring sample biases. Within the interview, brief statements are made to start the recruiting process. Thus, after a few questions the interviewer says:

> By the way, Mr. or Ms. _____, I should have mentioned earlier that I am part of the consumer panel and that we are not selling anything. In fact, you might say that our work is just the opposite of selling and advertising. We represent you by telling the producers what people like you are buying and the kinds of stores and packages that you like best.

Later, the following statement is made:

> I hope that I remembered to tell you that our consumer panel is a member of the Better Business Bureau. Some people are interested in knowing that.

Finally, households are asked about future cooperation:

> Would you be willing to help by answering a *telephone* survey like this again?

> One other thing, Mr. or Ms. _____, that I would like to have you think about. More than 10,000 families all over the United States are keeping a short list every week of a few foods and products they buy. We *pay* these families with their *choice* of surprise gifts or cash for keeping their weekly lists. Their information is important to us because it tells which products, sizes, and packages are most popular. If you were asked to keep a short list of a few foods and household products that you buy, the same as our other families are doing, do you think you would consider doing it for us?

This final question is an effective screening device. It has been found that only a small percentage of the households that answer "no" to this question can be persuaded at a later date to join the panel.

Ordinarily, because of problems in training, households that are recruited by telephone are given a simple diary with only a few product classes. The diary is sent along with the other materials that an interviewer would leave on a face-to-face interview. These might include an initial gift, a "memo to the public" on market research, a reprint of an article showing government or industry use of panel data, quotes from the letters of current panel households, a letter of welcome from the panel director, and a filled-in diary with sample entries.

Typically, two days or so after the initial call, a second call is made to recruit and train the household. It has been found that the shorter the period between the calls, the greater is the likelihood that the family will agree to participate. This is supported by learning theories that suggest learning is facilitated by frequent reinforcement.

After this call, the first diary is returned to the panel through the mail. Following this, the recruiter makes another call to thank the household for cooperating and answer any further questions that the diary keeper might have. This call is made to reduce the high dropout rate that might occur if there was no additional contact.

Households that do not return a diary after promising to do so are called after a week in an effort to get them to return the first diary. If they agree to keep a diary on this call and again fail to return it, a second fol-low-up call is made. If no diary is received after this second follow-up call, they are dismissed.

After keeping a short diary for four or five weeks, households are transferred to a full-scale diary. The loss of households due to the trans-fer is small—only about 5%. At the time of transfer, another telephone call is made explaining that the household will be able to earn larger prizes for keeping the larger diary. A short second call is made for train-ing, but most households find that they have little difficulty with the longer form. Additional training calls are made by telephone in the few cases when they are necessary.

Recruiting by Mail

Although mail recruiting is inexpensive, the cooperation rates obtained are far lower than can be obtained by more personal methods. This is because no rapport is established with a field representative, and thus a desire to please the representative is not a motivating factor. In mail recruiting, the chief motivation is the compensation offered.

Mail recruiting generally starts with the same type of printed material used in personal recruiting, but diaries and instructions are not sent ini-tially. Instead, a classification quiz is sent to the household to obtain basic demographic information on household size, education, income, occu-pation, and so forth. Because of the low cooperation rate, it is necessary to balance the sample of respondents on several variables. A sample is provided in Exhibit 4.1.

It is generally estimated that, after this balancing, less than 5% of those initially invited will be recruited. In some cases such as short-term mail test panels, no balancing is attempted. Then, depending on the area selected, a higher fraction that ranges from 10% to 25% of those invited may be recruited initially.

As with telephone procedures, those households that agree to keep a diary are first sent a short diary with only a few product classes. At some point, a month or so later, they are transferred to a larger diary if required. Some panel firms skip this step and start immediately with the larger diary.

One situation in which mail recruiting can obtain high cooperation is in the sampling of new households formed by split-offs from existing panel households. This procedure was discussed in the last chapter as an efficient way of keeping a panel from aging by accounting for new house-hold formations. In this case, one of the members of the new household is familiar with the panel, has seen the prizes, and knows that keeping a

Exhibit 4.1
Recruitment Letter and Qualifying Questions for
Prospective Panelists

October 1996

SURVEY OF AMERICA

BMT   0132568
Naomi Williams
1234 Main St.
Sioux City, IA 51106-2703

If your address shown left needs any changes, please correct here.

‖‖‖‖‖‖‖‖‖‖‖‖‖‖‖‖‖‖

Dear Consumer:

Your household has been carefully selected to participate in this survey. In order for companies to truly understand what consumers want, it is important for them to know more than simply how much of a product is sold. They need to have a clear understanding of who is buying and why they are buying. This survey can help make it easier for us to understand your preferences and attitudes. You'll have a voice in how important products are developed and marketed. And, you'll also receive these bonus incentives:

◆ *$100,000 Give Away*
    You will be automatically entered in our cash sweepstakes and be eligible to win the $50,000 Grand Prize, $25,000 Second Prize or one of five Third Prizes of $5,000 each.

◆ *Valuable Coupons*
    When we receive your completed survey, you'll be sent a wide variety of high-value coupons, good for substantial savings on well known, national brands.

◆ *Special Promotions*
    Many companies like to send samples and test promotional ideas to special groups of people. You'll be a part of this select group by completing this survey.

◆ *Reduce Unwanted Mail*
    Buyer's Choice will help reduce unwanted mail in categories that don't interest you.

Thank you for your contribution to this important program. To be included in our final executive summary, you must return your survey by November 11, 1996.

Sincerely,

Liz James

P.S. Only a small number of households have been invited to contribute to this survey. Your completed response is very important to our findings.
P.P.S. Save your stamps. We have enclosed a postage paid envelope for your convenience.

diary is not difficult. An initial invitation letter with one follow-up letter to nonrespondents generally obtains as high or higher cooperation than can be obtained by personal recruiting.

Exhibit 4.1
Continued

BUYER'S CHOICE SURVEY OF AMERICA

BMT01-01

If you feel uncomfortable answering any of the following questions, simply leave them blank and continue on to the next question.

About your interests and activities

1. To help us understand your lifestyles, please indicate the interests and activities in which you or your spouse enjoy participating on a *regular* basis.

Home Life
01. ☐ Flower Gardening
02. ☐ Vegetable Gardening
03. ☐ Grandchildren
04. ☐ Home Decorating/Furnishing
05. ☐ Home Workshops/Do-It-Yourself
06. ☐ House Plants
07. ☐ Home Video Games
08. ☐ Home Video Recording
09. ☐ Watching Cable TV

Good Life
10. ☐ Attending Cultural/Arts Events
11. ☐ Cruise Ship Vacations
12. ☐ Fashion Clothing
13. ☐ Fine Art/Antiques
14. ☐ Foreign Travel
15. ☐ Gourmet Cooking/Fine Foods
16. ☐ Travel in USA
17. ☐ Wines

Investing & Money
18. ☐ Entering Sweepstakes
19. ☐ Casino Gambling
20. ☐ Moneymaking Opportunities
21. ☐ Real Estate Investments
22. ☐ Stock/Bond Investments
23. ☐ Mutual Funds

Sports, Fitness & Health
24. ☐ Bicycling
25. ☐ Dieting/Weight Control
26. ☐ Golf
27. ☐ Health/Natural Foods
28. ☐ Physical Fitness/Exercise
29. ☐ Running/Jogging
30. ☐ Snow Skiing

31. ☐ Horseback Riding
32. ☐ Walking for Health
33. ☐ Watching Sports on TV

Great Outdoors
34. ☐ Camping/Hiking
35. ☐ Fishing
36. ☐ Hunting/Shooting
37. ☐ Motorcycles
38. ☐ Recreational Vehicles
39. ☐ Waterskiing/Watersports
40. ☐ Power Boating
41. ☐ Tennis
42. ☐ Scuba Diving
43. ☐ Sailing

World & Environment
44. ☐ Community/Civic Activities
45. ☐ Current Affairs/Politics
46. ☐ Wildlife/Environmental Issues

Hobbies & Interests
47. ☐ Automotive Work
48. ☐ Avid Book Reading
49. ☐ Bible/Devotional Reading
50. ☐ Buy Pre-Recorded Videos
51. ☐ Coin/Stamp Collecting
52. ☐ Collectibles/Collections
53. ☐ Crafts
54. ☐ Electronics
55. ☐ Listen to Pre-Recorded Music & Programs
56. ☐ Needlework/Knitting
57. ☐ Our Nation's Heritage
58. ☐ Photography
59. ☐ Science/New Technology
60. ☐ Self-Improvement
61. ☐ Sewing

2. Using the numbers in Question 1, please indicate your 3 most important activities: ☐☐ ☐☐ ☐☐

3. Is there an active collector in your household of: (check all that apply)
1. ☐ Books
2. ☐ Coins
3. ☐ Dolls
4. ☐ Plates
5. ☐ Porcelains
6. ☐ Sports Items
7. ☐ Stamps
8. ☐ Die Cast Cars
9. ☐ Other Collectibles

About your family

4. Your date of birth: ☐☐☐ 19☐☐ 1. ☐ Male 2. ☐ Female
   Month / Year

5. Your current marital status:
1. ☐ Single
2. ☐ Engaged
3. ☐ Married
4. ☐ Divorced
5. ☐ Widowed
6. ☐ Separated

6. Has your marital status changed?
1. ☐ In the last 6 months? 2. ☐ In the last 7-12 months?

7. Spouse's Name: ☐☐☐☐☐☐☐☐☐
   Spouse's date of birth: ☐☐☐ 19☐☐
   Month / Year

8. Area Code/Telephone #: ☐☐☐ ☐☐☐ - ☐☐☐☐

9. Date of birth (month/year) of all other adults and children in your household:
Male Female Date of Birth
1. ☐ 2. ☐ ☐☐ 19☐☐ Month Year
1. ☐ 2. ☐ ☐☐ 19☐☐ Month Year
Male Female Date of Birth
1. ☐ 2. ☐ ☐☐ 19☐☐ Month Year
1. ☐ 2. ☐ ☐☐ 19☐☐ Month Year

10. Which group describes your annual family income?
01. ☐ Under $15,000
02. ☐ $15,000-$19,999
03. ☐ $20,000-$24,999
04. ☐ $25,000-$29,999
05. ☐ $30,000-$34,999
06. ☐ $35,000-$39,999
07. ☐ $40,000-$44,999
08. ☐ $45,000-$49,999
09. ☐ $50,000-$59,999
10. ☐ $60,000-$74,999
11. ☐ $75,000-$99,999
12. ☐ $100,000-$124,999
13. ☐ $125,000-$149,999
14. ☐ $150,000 & over

11. Level of education: (check highest level completed)
1. ☐ Completed High School
2. ☐ Completed College
3. ☐ Completed Graduate School
4. ☐ Technical School

12. What languages are spoken regularly in your household?
1. ☐ English 2. ☐ Spanish 3. ☐ French 4. ☐ Other

13. Which credit cards do you use regularly?
1. ☐ American Express, Diners Club
2. ☐ MasterCard, Visa, Discover
3. ☐ Department Store, Oil Company, etc.
4. ☐ Do not use credit cards

14. For your primary residence, do you:
1. ☐ Own Home?
2. ☐ Rent?
3. ☐ Live w/Parents?
4. ☐ Live in School Dorm?
5. ☐ Other?_____
6. ☐ Own Condo/Coop?

15. Is there a child/teen/young adult in your household who lives away from home? 1. ☐ Yes 2. ☐ No

16. If yes, is this person attending:
1. ☐ Boarding School? 2. ☐ College or University? 3. ☐ Military (between ages of 17 to 23)?

17. How long since you last moved to a new address?
1. ☐ Less than 12 months
2. ☐ 1 - 5 years
3. ☐ 6 - 10 years
4. ☐ More than 10 years

18. Please tell us how many pets you have.
1. ☐ None
2. ☐ Dogs ☐☐
3. ☐ Cats ☐☐
4. ☐ Birds ☐☐
5. ☐ Horses ☐☐
6. ☐ Aquariums ☐☐

19. Religious affiliation:
1. ☐ Catholic
2. ☐ Protestant
3. ☐ Mormon
4. ☐ Jewish
5. ☐ Muslim
6. ☐ Other_____
7. ☐ None

About your work life

20. Occupation: (check all that apply) | You | | Spouse
Professional/Technical | ☐ | 1. | ☐
Upper Management/Executive | ☐ | 2. | ☐
Middle Management | ☐ | 3. | ☐
Sales/Marketing | ☐ | 4. | ☐
Clerical/Service Worker | ☐ | 5. | ☐
Tradesman/Machine Operator/Laborer | ☐ | 6. | ☐

21. Are you or your spouse: | You | | Spouse
A Full-time Homemaker? | ☐ | 1. | ☐
Retired? | ☐ | 2. | ☐
College/University Student? | ☐ | 3. | ☐
Self Employed/Business Owner? | ☐ | 4. | ☐
Working from a Home Office? | ☐ | 5. | ☐
Working Outside the Home? | ☐ | 6. | ☐

22. In your household is there an: | You | | Spouse
Active Federal employee? | ☐ | 01. | ☐
Rank: GS1-3 | ☐ | 02. | ☐
GS4-5 | ☐ | 03. | ☐
GS6-10 | ☐ | 04. | ☐
GS11 & above | ☐ | 05. | ☐
Federal Wage Board Worker? | ☐ | 06. | ☐
Postal Worker? | ☐ | 07. | ☐
Retired Federal employee? | ☐ | 08. | ☐
Active Military member? | ☐ | 09. | ☐
Rank: E1 - E4 | ☐ | 10. | ☐
E5 - E6 | ☐ | 11. | ☐
E7 - E9 | ☐ | 12. | ☐
Officer | ☐ | 13. | ☐
Retired Military member? | ☐ | 14. | ☐

Travel and vacations

23. How much have you spent on travel for pleasure? | Last 12 Months | | Next 12 Months
$0 - $999 | ☐ | 1. | ☐
$1,000 - $4,999 | ☐ | 2. | ☐
$5,000 - $9,999 | ☐ | 3. | ☐
$10,000 + | ☐ | 4. | ☐

24. When traveling for pleasure, please indicate your destinations. (check all that apply) | Last 12 Months | | Next 12 months
Within Your State | ☐ | 01. | ☐
Rest of Continental US | ☐ | 02. | ☐
Hawaii | ☐ | 03. | ☐
Canada | ☐ | 04. | ☐
Alaska | ☐ | 05. | ☐
Mexico | ☐ | 06. | ☐
Europe | ☐ | 07. | ☐
Asia | ☐ | 08. | ☐
Pacific Rim | ☐ | 09. | ☐
Caribbean | ☐ | 10. | ☐
South America | ☐ | 11. | ☐
Other Foreign | ☐ | 12. | ☐

Recruiting Online

Many online companies have more than 500,000 active panel members. Buying an e-mail list and "spamming" the list yields around a 10% return. However, there is a much higher reported attrition rate of these consumers. Two of the more generally accepted methods of online recruitment include targeted e-mail solicitations and banner ad recruitment (including cross-links from other sites). Whereas the former is a more carefully selected analogue to the solicitations mentioned previously, banner ad recruitment has its own unique set of advantages and disadvantages.

One common strategy is to post panel invitation banners on Web sites that receive a large amount of traffic from their targeted panel prospects. These Web site visitors then can click on the banner and be immediately sent to a secure Web site to conduct a brief, prequalifying interview.[1]

To investigate what types of banner ads were most effective, a study by Tuten, Bosnjak, and Bandilla (2000) compared whether intrinsic appeal or monetary incentives were more effective at encouraging banner click-throughs. It was found that banner ads with intrinsic appeal (interesting cues, graphics, and punchy, high-content messages) generated significantly more click-throughs than did banner ads with extrinsic appeal (prizes, color, animation, size, and sound). The key recruiting question, however, is what is the resulting quality of respondents?

Successful recruitment requires knowing what type of message-related cues would be successful given the level of involvement of the panel member. Someone who is highly involved is able and motivated to think carefully about information in a message and will be more influenced by intrinsic appeals, such as message content. In contrast, someone who is distracted or unmotivated will be attracted to extrinsic appeals, such as repetition of an argument, an attractive spokesperson or celebrity, the number of arguments presented, pleasant sounds, colors, images, and pictures. Depending on the type of person being solicited for the panel, different banner ad strategies need to be used. It may be beneficial to have both types of banner ads to attract a larger group of people.

Recruiting for Replacement

The discussion of the methods used for initial recruiting holds, with only minor changes, for replacement recruiting. Because all panels try to control demographic characteristics, only those households with the needed characteristics are recruited. Although most panels use the same proce-

---

[1]To increase the assurance of representativeness among Web site visitors, banner ads can be placed on the site for every nth visitor. This ensures that the first 1000 people recruited for panel prescreening do not happen to be the 1000 people who happened upon that Web site from midnight to 3:00 A.M. the evening it was first launched.

dures for screening and recruiting of replacement households as they used for initial recruiting, some do not. For example, the National Consumer Panel was initially recruited by personal interview methods, but replacement recruiting is done by mail and telephone. The cost advantages of mail and telephone procedures are even greater for replacement recruiting, because finding a household with the proper characteristics may require extensive screening.

Panel Compensation and Retention

All continuing panels compensate their members in some way for participating. The compensation may be in the form of money or gifts or in another special form such as participation in lotteries. Although the primary purpose of compensation is to obtain continued participation in the panel, compensation also improves the quality and completeness of the reporting. According to our survey of panel operators, the amounts paid to households ranged from $20 to $135 a year. The median amount was about $55 per year, and the mean was only slightly higher. There seems to be no relation between the cost-of-living index and amount paid. The European panels pay as much or more than do American ones.

It is obvious that the compensation is low if it was considered as salary for work done. These rates, however, obtain good, long-term cooperation. It is evident that the compensation has symbolic significance for the household by indicating that they are doing something important and valuable.

Obviously, the same low rates cannot be used with panels of professional groups such as physicians. These groups expect substantially higher levels of compensation. One research group in Japan, for example, reported that it compensated physicians who participated in its panel US$845 per month.

Forms of Compensation

Compensation can take many forms. The most obvious is a cash payment for each record or group of records. The most common form of compensation, however, is gifts. In a previous survey of panel operators, 12 reported using gifts, 6 used money, and 3 used lotteries, which are legal in Europe but appear to present some legal problems in the United States.

The advantage of gifts over cash is that gifts may sometimes be purchased at reduced prices by the panel operators so that the perceived value to the panel member is greater than the actual cost. In addition, gifts act as a continuing reminder and reinforcer each time they are used or observed. The list of available gifts is usually described in an attractive catalog or brochure similar to the ones used by trading stamp companies.

There is little evidence that the form of the gift has any major impact on cooperation. Experiments at the Survey Research Laboratory of the University of Illinois, using cash and several different gifts, showed no difference in cooperation on a consumer expenditure panel. For long-term panels, however, it is evident that any form of compensation, in order to act as a reinforcement to cooperate, must be received periodically and not just at the beginning or end of a panel. For short-term panels, however, one or two gifts at the beginning and/or end may be sufficient. Most panel operators offer graduated payments to motivate respondents to report regularly and on time. Thus, households that do not return all diaries within a specified period have their compensation reduced sharply.

In recruiting online panels, one point of agreement is that people often join panels because of the potential of getting a reward. In some cases for business-to-business panels, incentives for a six-month involvement in the panel included a choice of high technology products, such as Palm Pilots or DVD players. For consumer panels, payments supplemented with sweepstakes seem to be more successful. One such incentive system involves a $10,000 sweepstake every panel round. The prize money is split among four winners so that each person receives $2,500. Having sweepstakes with lower monetary values but higher probabilities of winning helps improve response rates.

As noted in the recruitment letter in Exhibit 4.1, one form of incentive includes a $100,000 give away, in which timely respondents are automatically entered in cash sweepstakes and are eligible to win a $50,000 grand prize, a $25,000 second prize, or one of five $5,000 third prizes. A wide variety of high-value coupons for national brands are very attractive in recruiting and compensating panelists. Exhibit 4.2 is a recruiting letter that emphasizes cash and vacations but focuses on coupon compensation. It also reinforces personalization and decreases skepticism by providing a series of quotes or references from current panelists.

Effects of Compensation on Level of Reporting

Although the literature supports the use of intrinsic rewards, more companies rely on extrinsic incentives to entice people to join their panels and complete the surveys in a timely way. Many research firms believe that the results of surveys that use incentives are less biased. Without incentives, they have found that respondents are either incredibly

Exhibit 4.2
The Importance of Coupon Compensation

Consumer Product Survey of America

Consumer Research Center, Shopper's Voice, 1200 William Street, Box 1382, Buffalo, NY 14240-1382

You don't get a letter like this everyday...
so we hope you'll take just a few moments to participate!

Dear Shopper:

Here's a simple statistic that may surprise you:

> *80% of all NEW products that come to market fail in a few short years.* What's more, a significant percentage of the products you use today will simply <u>disappear</u> from the marketplace— never to return again.

Have you ever wondered what causes these failures? One fact may surprise you. Everything you buy, from laundry detergent to headache remedies, is <u>critically dependent</u> upon one thing to continue its existence. That thing is <u>your opinion</u>.

Surprised? Over the years, successful manufacturers have learned that your opinion is invaluable for quality improvements and long life for their products. <u>When you speak your mind, better products get to market</u>. The manufacturers are happy. Consumers are happy. And it really is that simple.

That's why it is so important for you to take a few moments right now to complete the enclosed survey. What's more, the companies who commissioned this study are willing to <u>reward you for your efforts</u>!

In return for completing this survey by November 3, these companies have assembled these bonuses for you:

1. **Receive Valuable Money-Saving Coupons!** These are not the meager cents-off coupons you get in the store or from a newspaper. These are special coupons prepared by the manufacturer specifically for limited distribution to select audiences. Many of the coupon values are as high as $1.00 or more - and there are packets of them waiting to be mailed to people who respond to this survey!

2. **Earn a Chance for $4,000 Cash or a Caribbean Vacation Cruise!** It's a great chance to win a great vacation for two...or a handsome windfall you can use for anything you want! Just get your survey in and you are entered!

3. **More Cash Prizes!** In addition to the Grand Prize, you're also entered for 10 separate cash drawings for $100! (See sweepstakes details on the back of this letter.)

4. **Exclusive Bonus Offers for Survey Responders Only!** Here's a program you want to be involved in! Manufacturers seek out groups like ours to send free product samples,

Please see over ...

interested in the topic or want to complain about something. Indeed, for customer satisfaction surveys, incentives such as cash or prizes actually discourage honesty. People feel guilty expressing their displeasure about a company and then getting paid by that same company. By using incen-

Exhibit 4.2
Continued

information, and valuable trial coupons. If you would like to be included in these offerings, be sure to check "YES" to the LAST QUESTION ON THE SURVEY!

Thank you for your time. I can assure you that the few moments you take to complete this survey will be <u>well worth your time</u>.

Sincerely,

Laura David

Laura David

P.S.   I have enclosed a postage-paid envelope which you can use to return your survey to me. But please remember, <u>I need your response no later than NOVEMBER 3</u>! I'd hate for you to miss out on the coupon mailings and sweepstakes, so won't you take a moment to complete the survey right now, while it's on your mind?

P.P.S. Below are a few notes from new friends who replied to one of my recent surveys

" *I want to say thank you for keeping your word and sending coupons to those who completed your recent consumer products survey ... The majority of coupons you sent to me, I use a great deal. I am most impressed with the dollar amount of the coupons - they are a real savings! I don't get coupons like this in my Sunday paper inserts! I'll be glad to participate in more of your surveys for these kinds of rewards any day!* "

P. W., Madison, ME

" *... thank you for the coupons and the report I received from you today. The coupon amounts and lengthy expiration dates are terrific! I also found the research report graphs very interesting. So many research companies either ignore you when you send in their questionnaires or send coupons with very small amounts. None send reports like yours! Keep up the good work and please keep me on the panel.* "

N. B., GFLD., MA

" *I wanted to tell you how impressed I was receiving your promised coupons for completing your recent survey. In past years I've done similar surveys for (company name deleted) but your coupons and samples were so much better. Your envelope had quality coupons and samples and I am so appreciative. I hope to receive more surveys ...* "

C. D. , Bethesda, MD

" *I just received your Consumer Products Survey 'Results' and coupons in the mail. Of all the surveys I've been a part of, yours was certainly handled the most professionally. Thank you for the very generous coupons you sent, most of which I immediately used. It was a pleasure to be a part of your survey. I would be more than happy to participate in any future surveys you may have.* "

J. T., Livingston, LA

tives, the belief is that those people who would have filled out the survey anyway will participate, as will those who need to be coaxed.

When panel members keep written records, compensation should improve the quality of record keeping by conveying to the respondent an obligation to devote effort and care to providing the requested information. The relatively sparse data available support this expectation.

In a study conducted by the Survey Research Laboratory at the University of Illinois (Sudman and Ferber 1974), households that received compensation reported higher levels of expenditures than did households that received no gifts, as is shown in the inflation-adjusted figures in Table 4.1. The differences increased each week, from 9% the first week to 18% the second week to approximately 60% in weeks 3 and 4. This would suggest that compensation becomes increasingly effective in improving the quality of record keeping for longer time periods.

To summarize, compensation in sufficient amounts is necessary to ensure initial and continuing cooperation, as well as quality of reporting. Although there is no evidence that the form of the compensation is critical, the amount is. If households perceive that the compensation is far too low, the dropout rate will increase substantially and reporting will suffer. Yet there appears to be a threshold. When a reasonable minimum rate is reached, however, there is no indication that either cooperation or reporting will improve further with additional compensation.

Panel Maintenance, Relationships, and Retention

In addition to compensation, most panel operators stay in contact with panel households through individual correspondence, telephone calls, personal visits, and newsletters. The effect of these contacts is difficult to measure, because the dropout rate of households that have been in a panel for more than a few periods is very small. Online companies have the means to consistently stay in contact with the panels. Of the 11

Table 4.1
The Impact of Panel Compensation on Reported Weekly Expenditures (Number of Reporting Households in Parentheses)

Week	No Gift	Some Gift	Summary and Comparison of Purchases	Large Stationary Holder	Flag or Book
1	$248 (85)	$270 (327)	$282 (97)	$272 (105)	$258 (125)
2	$214 (42)	$256 (207)	$244 (57)	$226 (74)	$284 (76)
3	$188 (20)	$284 (120)	$288 (37)	$280 (41)	$282 (42)
4	$121 (7)	$198 (46)	$192 (13)	$152 (16)	$230 (17)
Average	$224 (154)	$262 (700)	$266 (204)	$252 (236)	$266 (260)

offline panels we are familiar with, 4 use mail contact, 4 use personal contact (telephone or face-to-face), and 3 use both.

It appears that the personal contacts are less frequent and used only if mail contacts are ineffective. Many of the contacts are to correct errors or omissions in the diary records. Some organizations send notes of congratulation (and sometimes special gifts, such as a silver spoon) when a new baby is born into the household. Notes of sympathy are sent when there is an illness or death in a panel family. This is not done solely for altruistic reasons; these are times when a household is more likely to drop out.

Periodic newsletters are used for instruction as well as for maintaining cooperation. They may contain information on panel families and how panel data are being used. Exhibit 4.3 shows how a company might maintain contact with a brief monthly newsletter.

Part of this retention is based on building relationships and being able to relate to members to the degree they want. This is of greatest importance to online panels that want to differentiate themselves from database e-mail spammers. To help panel members identify with an otherwise faceless panel operator, many companies use a fictitious representative such as Janet Hall, Liz James, or Carol Adams. Like Betty Crocker, these fictitious representatives provide a point of contact and "answer" panelists' questions.

People are involved in panels for many reasons. Some like the coupons and the lottery possibilities of winning money. Others like to believe they are making a difference and having a voice. Even others simply like filling out panel surveys in the same way people like to complete crossword puzzles. How curious are panelists about the results of the questions they answer? If the survey is of great interest to consumers, a strong show of goodwill would be to send summarized results of selected topics. How important is it for us to follow up panel surveys by providing the topline results for curious panelists?

We conducted several studies at the University of Illinois to examine this. Following the surveys sent to panelists, we asked them whether they would be interested in receiving the basic results of the study they had completed. We varied the level of involvement required of them to receive the results. If they wanted to receive the results, members of the first group had to merely check a box on the questionnaire that requested they be sent the findings. The second group had to enclose a self-addressed (but not stamped) envelope, and the third group had to enclose a self-addressed, stamped envelope.

Exhibit 4.3
Monthly Newsletter Used to Thank and Maintain Contact with Panelists

Home Testing Institute
P.O. Box 9351
Uniondale, NY 11553

January 2001
Panel Talk

Dear Panel Member,

Welcome to the Winter Edition of HTI Panel Talk! Inside, you'll find many fun things for you to do and read. There's the birthday puzzle where you'll find out which of your favorite stars were born in January. You'll also see some interesting facts about a couple of January's most talked about topics: the frigid weather and the Super Bowl. Don't forget that you are automatically entered into our Winter Drawing when you return your completed mini-questionnaires. Details on what you can win are inside too.

Thank you again for being an important part of the HTI panel family. Good luck with the Winter Drawing and have a Happy New Year!

Janet

January 2001 Winter Drawing

When we receive your completed mini-questionnaires on time, you will be entered into our Winter Drawing, with a chance to win one of these great prizes:

GRAND PRIZE: TWO WINNERS
You will win your choice of any prize from our gift catalog valued up to **$500**. Examples of prizes include a Sony 20" Trinitron TV, a Brother Laser Printer, or a Hedstrom Swing Set.

SECOND PRIZE: TWO WINNERS
Will win a choice of any prize from our gift catalog valued up to **$250**. Examples of prizes include a Sony Hi-Fi Stereo VCR, Leyse 11-Piece Cookware set, or a Casio Personal Digital Organizer.

THIRD PRIZE: FIVE WINNERS
You will win your choice of any prize from our gift catalog valued up to **$100**. Examples of prizes include a George Forman Grill, Patton 52" Ceiling Fan, or a Dirt Devil Broom Vac.

All winners will be notified before April 2001.

GOOD LUCK!

Congratulations to our October 2000 Fall Drawing Winners

Grand Prize Winners
L. Lassabe, CA
C. Weitzel, IN

2ⁿᵈ Prize Winners   *3ʳᵈ Prize Winners*
M. Springer, IN   *M. Odato, PA*   *S. Goldtrap, IL*
A. Towne, TN   *R. Harris, PA*   *R. Simmons, TX*
                J. Breckenridge, MO

January Birthday Puzzle

Do the puzzle to see which actors were born in January! Each number is a code representing a letter. For example, notice below that "55" is the code for letter "K". Write in a "K" wherever else you see "55" in the puzzle. The actor's first initial and last name are on the left. A movie he starred in is on the right.

Actor:

K C O S T N E R
55 27 96 74 15 81 45 50

_ _ _ _ _ _ _ _
98 81 45 17 40 34 81

_ _ _ _ _ _ _ _
40 28 20 35 74 96 81

_ _ _ _ _ _ _ _
28 87 34 27 55 40 34 81

Movie:

J F K
89 57 55

_ _ _ _ _ _ _ _
15 87 45 74 15 20 81 28

_ _ _ _ _ _ _ _ _
35 50 34 73 45 87 45 34 50 15

_ _ _ _ _ _ _ _
87 96 96 74 20 45 50 74

If you think it's cold where you are then consider that the coldest recorded temperature in the U.S. was -79.8° in the mountains of Northern Alaska on 1/23/71. As far as the 48 mainland states are concerned, the all-time recorded low was -69.7° in Montana on 1/20/54. If you want a guarantee of warm weather in the U.S., go to Hawaii, where the record low is 12° atop the Mauna Kea Mountain. Since Hawaii couldn't come close to a negative temperature at 13,770 ft., you shouldn't have to worry!   Source: www.usatoday.com

Put these states in order of lowest recorded temperature.
(a) Alabama   (b) California   (c) Idaho   (d) Vermont

All answers are on the bottom of the next page

SUPER BOWL

Over 800 million people in 188 countries across the world, including some 130 million in the U.S., will watch the Super Bowl on TV this January. Many of these people, however, will wish they were at the game instead. That's a big change from the first Super Bowl back in 1967. For that contest, only 61,946 people attended, leaving more than 30,000 seats empty in the Los Angeles Coliseum. Even more amazing is the fact that tickets to that game would have cost you a mere $6 - $12 dollars. The lowest face value on a ticket to last year's game was $325. Advertising expenses have changed too. A 30-second commercial in 1967 cost $42,000, whereas last year, the same length commercial ran $2.2 million. The Super Bowl has grown in other ways as well. It is now the second largest day of food consumption in the U.S.

 Can you guess which day is first?
(see answer below)

Sources: www.canoe.ca, www.CBS>SportsLine.com

ANSWERS TO QUESTIONS

▶ Thanksgiving is the biggest day of food consumption in the U.S.

▶ (c) Idaho, which hit -60 degrees on 1/18/43 was the lowest of the group. It's followed by (d) Vermont (-50; 12/30/33), (b) California (-45; 1/20/37), and (a) Alabama (-27; 1/30/66)

▶ P. Newman/The Sting, M. Gibson/Braveheart, G. Hackman/Hoosiers

To estimate panelists' interest in the data, we aggregated across different panels and different topics (shopping, food consumption, travel, meal preparation, leisure activities, health behavior, and so on). For the members that only had to check a box to get the results, we found that only 37.4% wanted to be informed about the results of the survey they completed. If they were required to enclose a self-addressed envelope, only 3.3% wished to be sent results. If the envelope had to be stamped, this number dropped to 1.4%.

Clearly, panelists' interest in receiving summary results depends on their interest in the topic. Whereas many shopping and consumer-related behaviors perhaps do not arouse passion or curiosity, other behaviors that are of personal or professional interest do. For example, a panel study that has been tracking consumption behaviors and product loyalties of 1400 veterans of World War II (Wansink 2002) typically results in 23% of them enclosing self-addressed envelopes with each wave of the panel survey they return. Similarly, when panels focus on people of a specific profession, these people frequently wish to receive copies of summary findings. In both of these cases, spending the money to send findings can offset some (but not all) of the money otherwise spent on premiums and other incentives.

From a practical, relationship-building perspective, any type of contact that keeps panelists feeling informed, valued, and connected is important. If sending panelists some brief summaries of this information accomplishes this at minimal cost, it is worth doing. Exhibit 4.4 does a nice job of thanking consumers, answering their questions regarding the most recent survey, and providing some basic results they might find interesting.

Frequency of Data Collection

Theoretically, the frequency with which data are collected should have no impact on the reporting of events if all entries are made immediately after the event. In practice, however, some panel reporters do not make their entries immediately but at some later time. To the extent that reporters depend on recall, the frequency of data collection becomes important. If recall is used, the shorter the period is, the less likely that purchases or other events will be forgotten. However, increased frequency raises the cost of data collection, especially as postage becomes a significant fraction of the total cost. The weekly mailing of diary records also requires greater effort on the part of the respondent compared with

Exhibit 4.4
Summaries of Results that Are Reported to Panelists

Shopper's Voice

1200 William Street, Box 1382, Buffalo, New York 14240-1382

Dear Panel Member,

Please accept my sincere thanks for taking part in our Consumer Products Survey over the last couple of months. Thanks to you and your fellow panel members, it was a great success.

I also want to thank those who wrote a letter about the survey. Your comments are very helpful and much appreciated. I read all of your letters, and my staff and I are trying to reply to as many questions as we can. Some questions were asked so frequently, in fact, that I thought all our panelists might be interested in the answers...so I've included them on the next page.

At Shopper's Voice we truly appreciate the time you spend helping with our research studies. As a token of our appreciation, we also want to share some general results from our most recent survey. See pages 3 and 4 of this letter for a brief report from our study. I hope you find it interesting.

Once again, thank-you for your time and your help.

Respectfully,

recycled paper

Laura David
Research Director

P. S. I've also enclosed a few coupons that I hope will save you some money on your next trip to the store. We are grateful to the fine companies who provided them as an extra "thanks" for your help with the survey.

P. P. S. You will receive more coupons and samples over the next several months. Some companies who support our survey couldn't get all their coupons and samples ready in time for this envelope. They will mail them to you directly from their offices as soon as they are ready.

```
Coupon Expiration Dates
Look closely, some of the enclosed coupons may have much
longer expiration dates than regular coupons.
```

CCL-BU-12   OVER

Questions from Panel Members' Letters

When will the Caribbean Cruise and Cash Prize winners be selected and notified?
For the survey you completed, a random draw will be held on January 9, 2001 from all completed surveys received on or before the contest closing date. All the winners will be contacted shortly thereafter, by telephone or by registered mail.

Congratulations!
I know that you will join me in congratulating A. Riley of Chester, NH...the $4,000 grand-prize winning panel member in our most recent draw.

Congratulations also go out to the 10 lucky panelists who won $100 cash prizes.

C. Valen ....Nederland, CO.	P. Coleman ....Laurel Hill, FL.
P. Fitchett ....Cheriton, VA.	J. Lubragge ....Broomall, PA.
H. Grace ....Winder, GA.	E. Brown ....Cleveland, OH.
T. Lawson ....Los Alamitos, CA.	K. Williams ....Albertville, AL.
G. Jordan ....Pikesville, MD.	E. Ehrenberg ......Haverton, PA.

Why don't you ask questions about food allergies?
Frankly, that's a very good idea. Fortunately, most of us do not suffer from many severe food allergies. However, for those who do, it's an extremely important and threatening problem. Thanks to your letters, we have come to appreciate just how many people are affected by food allergies of one type or another. Research is now under way that will help manufacturers learn more about the special needs of these consumers.

Why not get rid of coupons and just lower the price?
Most of my clients are manufacturers, and manufacturers cannot legally set the prices you see in the store; they are set only by the retailer and therefore are beyond the control of manufacturers. By sending you a coupon, manufacturers are bypassing the retailer and giving you the money directly. This is the only way they can be absolutely sure you will get the savings on their product.

Why did you ask such personal questions?
The "personal questions" we ask are merely a tool which helps us place you and your family into smaller subgroups. Different products and brands appeal to different groups of people. Sometimes the age of the household members makes the difference, sometimes it's the number of males or females, and sometimes it is the income level of your household.

Surveys like ours help manufacturers understand these differences. This is the basic information they need to develop improvements to their products, as well as to design totally new products for the marketplace.

Research Report Extract

The following information was compiled from our most recent survey. I hope you find it interesting.

Survey issue :
How much do we spend on groceries in an average week?

Survey results

Survey issue :
How many households buy certain categories of grocery products?

Survey results :

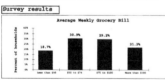

Survey issue :
Which health and nutrition concerns are important to us?

Survey results :

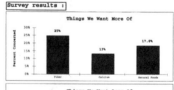

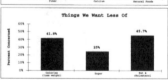

Survey issue :
How many households have at least one person actively involved in the following hobbies?

Survey results :

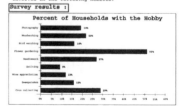

monthly or less frequent mailings and, thus, increases the possibility that some diaries will not be returned or will be mailed late.

The solution that has been adopted by most panel operators is to vary the frequency of data collection by type of product. Information on frequently purchased products such as food, groceries, and drugs is usually collected on a weekly basis, whereas information on less frequently purchased items such as clothing and other textiles is collected monthly. Our data on panel operators (Table 1.2) indicate that 12 collect some information weekly and 6 collect information monthly. For special groups, such as physicians and farmers, or for groups involving nonpurchase behavior, such as media viewing or political attitudes, less frequent periods may be used.

The classic work comparing reports of purchases as noted in weekly versus monthly diaries is by Lewis (1948). In the half century that has followed, no evidence has been presented to disprove his findings. He found a 19% increase in the number of purchases reported weekly as compared with monthly when two panels were compared for a three-month period. These results (Table 4.2) are based on diaries of the same size and that include the same product classes.

It should be stressed that frequency of data collection is only one of the factors that influence reporting. Other important factors are the type of diary used and the length of the diary, which are discussed in the next

Table 4.2
Number of Purchases Reported Per Month by Households Using Weekly and Monthly Diaries

Item	(1) Weekly Diaries	(2) Monthly Diaries	Ratio (1)÷(2)
Detergent	4.3	3.9	1.10
Bar soap	3.4	2.6	1.31
Coffee	3.9	3.1	1.26
Hot cereals	1.3	1.0	1.30
Cold cereals	3.0	2.9	1.03
Butter, margarine, or oil	5.6	4.7	1.19
All-purpose flour	.9	.6	1.50
Cake and ready-mixed flour	1.3	1.1	1.18
Baby food	2.6	.9	1.37
Frozen food	1.3	1.7	.76
Total groceries	26.2	22.6	1.16
Clothing and accessories	10.3	8.0	1.29
Yard goods and house linens	1.7	1.6	1.06
Grand total	38.3	32.2	1.19

section. Thus, recording in a short monthly diary might be more complete than in a longer weekly diary.

One reason for a separate monthly diary for textiles and clothing or other special products is that panel operators found that these items tended to be forgotten in a weekly diary stressing food and groceries. Although separate weekly diaries of clothing and textile purchases would probably produce more complete reporting than monthly diaries, it would be both costly and burdensome on the panel reporters to require that they send in two separate forms each week.

Diary Forms and Panel Cooperation

Journal Versus Ledger

Several different diary formats are possible. One format arranges entries by the order in which the events occur; this is called a journal diary, corresponding to the financial journal used in business bookkeeping. Another format arranges entries by the type of outlet at which the purchase is made. This outlet diary is intended to improve the level of reporting by associating purchases with the trip to an outlet. Entries may also be arranged by product or event categories. This product diary is also called a ledger diary because it corresponds to business ledgers.

For purchase behavior, all current panel operators use a product (or ledger) diary rather than a journal or an outlet diary. Exhibit 4.5 provides dated but illustrative pages from a ledger diary. As is apparent from this illustration, diaries make it easier to obtain the specific details required for different product classes, for example, to determine the flavor of soft drinks, the color of paper towels, or whether toothpaste is fluoridated.

Panels do vary, however, on the formats used within a product category. Thus, some panels use rather broad categories such as men's and boys' or women's and girls' apparel, whereas others subdivide these into subsections with headings for coats, suits and dresses, pants, shirts, pajamas, underwear, socks, and so on.

Even more important, the evidence suggests that ledger diaries act as reminders to the record keepers and thus improve the completeness of reporting. The MRCA National Consumer Panel reported approximately 3% more purchases in a ledger than in a journal diary (Sudman 1964b).

In other experiments (Sudman and Ferber 1971), not only was the level of reporting higher in ledger diaries than in journal or outlet diaries, but willingness to participate in a panel was greater (Tables 4.3

Exhibit 4.5
Journal vs. Ledger Forms Images

Page 13

FRUIT and SOFT DRINK MIXES, CARBONATED BEVERAGES, SOFT DRINKS

STORE TRIP NO	BRAND	PRODUCT DETAILS		DEAL CODES	

FRUIT DRINK MIXES, SOFT DRINK MIXES, ADE MIXES — POWDER OR LIQUID CONCENTRATE

DEAL CODES:
1 Newspaper Coupon — 6 Free Product/Bonus Size Package
2 Magazine Coupon — 7 ¢ Off on Label
3 Mail Coupon — 8 Store Special
4 Coupon From Prior Purchase of Same Item — 9 Other Special Offer
5 Coupon From Other Purchase

(Enter Powdered Breakfast Drink Here)

5432-60 POWDERS, CRYSTALS, TABLETS (DRY) (1)

WRITE IN FLAVOR OR KIND (Orange, Grapefruit, Lemonade, Lemon Lime, Fruit Punch, Grape, Root Beer, Ice Tea Flavor, etc.)

PRESWEETENED? Check One — With Sugar Only / With Artificial Sweetener Only / With Artificial Sweetener and Sugar / Not Presweetened

Check HOW PACKAGED? — Regular Can / Regular Jar / (Envelopes) / Other—Describe (Cannister, Bag of Envelopes, etc.)

IF ON PACKAGE WRITE IN UNIVERSAL PRODUCT CODE | QUAN-TITY | WEIGHT (SIZE) | PRICE PAID EACH | TOTAL | IF SPECIAL OFFER ENTER CODE AND VALUE OF DEAL / ¢ CODE / VALUE

LIQUID CONCENTRATES (2)

CARBONATED BEVERAGES, SOFT DRINKS CANS OR BOTTLES

Write FLAVOR (Cola, Orange, Lemon Lime, Ginger Ale, etc.)

Does label say "Sugar Free", "Low Calorie" or "Diet"? Yes / No

Container (✓) One — All Glass / All Plastic / Plastic Wrap Coated Glass / Metal Can

Are Bottles or Cans Packaged Together? If Yes How Many Per Pack? (✓) I NO

Check (✓) Taken? — Return / No Deposit (No Return)

Where Taken? (✓) — Consumed at Place Purchased / Brought Home / Taken Elsewhere

STORE TRIP NO 5585

"Ozs each bottle or can" Do not include deposit

Purchased At Grocery, Supermarket, Food Store (1)

Purchased At Beer, Wine, Liquor Store (2)

Purchased at Gas, Service Station (3)

Purchased At Any Other Place (4)

*On label, in the glass neck or bottom, or stamped into the can

and 4.4) as well. It can be seen in Table 4.3 that 55% of contacted households kept four weekly product diaries, whereas only 24% kept four journal diaries. Because there was no initial difference, it must have been eas-

Exhibit 4.5
Continued

PAPER PRODUCTS, PLASTIC BAGS

Page 18

STORE TRIP NO	BRAND	PRODUCT DETAILS	DEAL CODES
			1 Newspaper Coupon 6 Free Product/
			2 Magazine Coupon Bonus Size Package
			3 Mail Coupon 7 ¢ Off on Label
			4 Coupon From Prior Purchase of Same Item 8 Store Special
			5 Coupon From Other Purchase 9 Other Special Offer

PAPER TOWELS, All-Purpose Cleaning Cloths

INCLUDE PURCHASES MADE FOR TRIPS, PICNICS, ETC.

TOILET TISSUE

FACIAL TISSUE

BE SURE TO INCLUDE ALL PURCHASES MADE BY FAMILY MEMBERS FOR USE AT WORK OR ON BUSINESS TRIPS, etc.

PAPER NAPKINS

INCLUDE PURCHASES MADE FOR PICNICS, BARBECUES, TRIPS, ETC.

PLASTIC BAGS - FOOD STORAGE, TRASH, GARBAGE

(Include: Heavy Weight/ Super Weight

(Do Not Include Paper Or Wax Bags)

---

ier for households to keep the product diaries. Note that the differences in cooperation became larger week by week.

Households using product diaries reported 12% higher purchase expenditures over the four weeks, as can be seen in the inflation-adjusted

Exhibit 4.5
Continued

Page 19

HAIR CONDITIONERS, HAIR COLORINGS, SHAMPOO, TOOTH PASTE, TOILET & BAR SOAP

STORE TRIP NO	BRAND	PRODUCT DETAILS	DEAL CODES
			1 Newspaper Coupon 6 Free Product/Bonus Size Package 2 Magazine Coupon 7 ¢ Off on Label 3 Mail Coupon 8 Store Special 4 Coupon From Prior Purchase of Same Item 9 Other Special Offer 5 Coupon From Other Purchase

HAIR CONDITIONERS and CREME RINSES TO BE USED WHEN HAIR IS WET

(EXCLUDE COLOR RINSES)

	Check TYPE of Product	Formulation as shown on label (Write in — Regular, Extra or Super Hold, Extra Body, Oil Free, etc.)	Copy from Label Type of hair to be used for? (Write in — dry, normal, bleached, fine, short, etc.)	Is Product Scented?		Enter AGE(S) of ALL INTENDED USERS (Write in)					QUANTITY	WEIGHT LBS. OZS.	PRICE PAID		IF SPECIAL OFFER ENTER CODE AND VALUE OF DEAL (¢)
	Conditioner / Creme Rinse / Creme Rinse With Conditioner			IF Yes Write In Scent or Fragrance (Herbal, Orange, Lilac, etc.)	Yes | No	IF Female AGE | AGE		IF Male AGE | AGE | AGE					EACH	TOTAL	CODE | VALUE
9155 (Brand)															

HAIR COLORINGS, TINTS, DYES, BLEACHES, PEROXIDES, LIGHTENERS, ETC.

	Copy From Label Data NAME, TYPE and KIND (Hair Color, Bath Creme Formula, Hair Color Lotion etc.)	Write in COLOR and NUMBER if any from Label (Fawn Brown No 77 Auburn Silver Brown No 73 Midnight Gloss, etc.)	Enter AGE(S) of ALL INTENDED USERS									
			IF Female AGE | AGE | AGE			Write in Male AGE | AGE | AGE						¢
0051 Brand												

HAIR SHAMPOO

	Copy from Label all Words for TYPE of HAIR and SUGGESTED USE (For Fine Hair for Added Body, for Dry Hair for Dandruff, etc.)	IF SCENTED Write In Scent or Fragrance (Herbal, Orange, Lilac, etc.)	Enter AGE(S) of ALL INTENDED USERS									
			IF Female AGE | AGE | AGE			Write in Male AGE | AGE | AGE						¢
6154 (Brand)												

TOOTH PASTE, POWDER, POLISH

	Check FORM	Contains a Fluoride?	If Tooth Paste or Powder has Special Flavor shown on label (Mint, Spearmint, etc.) Write FLAVOR	BUYER		To be Used by ALL Tooth brush Users?					
	Paste / Gel / Powder / Polish	Yes | No		IF Male Write AGE	IF Female Write AGE	(√) Yes | No					¢
6053 (Brand)											

TOILET SOAP— HAND, FACE and OTHER CAKE and BAR SOAP

	Check Size		PLACE(S) OF INTENDED USE Check as Many as Apply				
							¢

figures in Table 4.4. For some product categories, however, the journal diary was superior. (We show in a later section that the location of products in a product diary influences the completeness of reporting.) In a study of reporting of medical event usage diaries, the same results were found (Sudman, Wilson, and Ferber 1976). Here, households using ledger diaries reported 3% more medical events than households using journal diaries did, though there was no difference in the level of cooperation by diary form.

To summarize, with their advantages of increased detail, easier processing, and more complete reporting, ledger or product diaries should be used for expenditure studies. One exception to this rule are studies of television viewing and radio listening or use of time. In these cases, the forms are always broken into small time segments.

Online-Based Panels

There are three basic options available for online panels: e-mail surveys, HTML, and downloadable surveys. All three have their benefits and drawbacks. Currently, various studies are underway to determine which one best balances accuracy with cost. Some broad generalizations are noted for each.

E-mail surveys are often the fastest and simplest of the three methods, and they require relatively little set-up time. Even a novice user can create and send e-mail questionnaires and analyze results using one of several available off-the-shelf e-mail survey software packages. However, because e-mail is limited to a flat text format, questionnaires cannot typically include skip pattern logic, randomization, or thorough error checking. They are ideally suited for internal audiences (e.g., employee groups, distribution partners, beta testers).

HTML hypertext language is used to show links to a Web page from another page or e-mail message. Usually, they are shown with a different

Table 4.3
Effect of Diary Forms on Panel Cooperation

Extent of Cooperation	Journal Form	Outlet Form	Product/Ledger Form
Agreed to keep diary	88.5% (131)	87.3% (260)	85.1% (138)
Kept at least one diary	78.6% (131)	81.5% (260)	83.6% (138)
Kept at least two diaries	55.3% (96)	69.3% (192)	75.8% (99)
Kept at least three diaries	45.9% (63)	56.2% (130)	68.2% (66)
Kept four diaries	24.0% (27)	47.1% (70)	55.2% (29)

Notes: Percentages are the number of families keeping a given number of diaries as a percentage of those asked to keep a diary for at least that length of time. Base figures, in parentheses, are derived by summing across weeks. Thus, the base of 96 households that kept at least two journal diaries is the total number of households asked to keep that type of diary for two, three, or four weeks.

color text that can be clicked on by the person who is browsing or reading the message to go to the Web page. HTML form surveys offer the flexibility to create more complicated surveys with skip patterns, randomization, and grid-style rating questions and may even include complex graphic images and sound. These surveys require substantially more programming time to create, but the advantages in questionnaire design flexibility and data control often outweigh any marginal impact on cost and set-up time.

Downloadable survey applications help the researcher create an interactive environment for those being surveyed. With these surveys, the respondent downloads an executable file to his or her own computer rather than complete the survey on a host Web site. The program then takes respondents through the questionnaire and can include complex skip and rotation logic. The construction, flow, and content of downloadable surveys are only limited by the creativity of the survey researcher. Disadvantages include the expense of creating these pro-

Table 4.4
How the Form of a Panel Diary Influences Reported Expenditures

Product Group	Journal Diary	Outlet Diary	Product/Ledger Diary
Dairy	$ 3.85	$ 3.45	$ 3.62
Meat and fish	$ 7.02	$ 6.60	$ 7.52
Fruits and vegetables	$ 2.08	$ 1.88	$ 1.78
Bakery	$ 1.83	$ 2.22	$ 2.21
Canned, frozen, packaged	$ 5.86	$ 5.86	$ 5.48
Liquor, soft drinks	$ 1.88	$ 2.26	$ 2.60
Cigarettes	$ 1.71	$ 1.29	$ 1.75
Food eaten away	$ 4.66	$ 6.45	$ 6.33
Auto supplies	$ 6.90	$ 9.19	$ 12.01
Hardware	$ 4.11	$ 3.08	$ 3.56
Drugs	$ 2.04	$ 1.60	$ 2.02
Stationery or toys	$ 7.24	$ 3.97	$ 6.80
Personal care	$ 2.44	$ 3.08	$ 3.42
Housing payments	$ 29.16	$ 27.03	$ 36.91
Clothing	$ 7.80	$ 8.57	$ 8.63
Furniture	$ 4.08	$ 11.66	$ 10.95
Medical care	$ 4.27	$ 4.58	$ 4.14
Personal service	$ 6.38	$ 3.84	$ 4.97
All other	$ 22.05	$ 14.37	$ 16.15
Total	$125.36	$120.98	$140.85
Base	187	457	228

grams, the time required to make them, and the time it takes to distribute interactive questionnaires. These surveys result in further self-selection because of the download time and the necessary user sophistication and hardware requirements to download these surveys. Also, there is the problem of allaying the fears of users from opening programs with viruses within their personal systems that must be addressed.

Length of Diary Form

With the costs of recruiting and maintaining a consumer panel, panel operators would like to get as much information as possible from each panel household. Unfortunately, as the length of the diary increases, some product classes are reported less completely.

Returning to the MRCA National Consumer Panel, half of the households were given a new diary that was approximately 20% shorter than the 36-page diary then in use, which included more than 100 products. The new test diary resulted in an increase of approximately 10% in the level of reporting in the ledger diary but, as might be expected, had no effect on the experimental journal diary (Table 4.5). An examination of specific products showed that there were large increases in those known to be underrecorded, whereas items already recorded completely were unchanged. In all cases, the increased reporting was considered an improvement.

These same results would not have been found if the diary had initially been substantially smaller. In an experiment with the Attwood Panel, the accuracy of recording was unaffected by whether there were 30 or 50 products.

Table 4.5
Number of Purchase Entries Per Week by Type of Diary and Indices of Total Purchase Entries (Long Ledger, Current Diary = 100)

Type of Diary	Purchase Entries			Indices of Purchase Entries		
	Short Diary	Long Diary	Combined Diary	Short Diary	Long Diary	Combined Diary
Ledger	27.6	24.9	26.2	110.5	100	105.2
Journal	25.3	25.4	25.3	101.6	101.7	101.7
Combined				106.1	100.8	

Summary

The recruiting, grooming, and nurturing of a panel is costly but critical. Despite new technologies, the quality of a panel still depends on a representative sitting down and earnestly and sincerely completing a diary that is neither confusing nor fatiguing. To find that person, motivate that person, and maintain that person's interest and focus remain important functions regardless of the medium.

Chapter 5

Improving Panel Accuracy and Reporting

To paraphrase a great advertiser (John Wannamaker), I know half of the results I get are not accurate, but I don't know which half.

—Panel researcher

ertain factors that influence and bias accuracy, such as the length of a survey, are not surprising. What is puzzling, however, are factors that influence accuracy and cause biases of which we are not aware. In this chapter, we show that accuracy can unknowingly vary across products and what can be done to improve it.

We first outline the sources of reporting errors and show how accuracy can be assessed and measured. Following this, five studies are described that show how small changes in workload influences accuracy, and another five are described that compare various types of diary records with survey recall. Knowing what is causing mysterious variations in responses will go a long way toward increasing accuracy and reducing the frustration of the panel researcher quoted previously. Figure 5.1 illustrates how reporting errors arise and how they, along with changes in the instrument, influence the ability to assess reporting accuracy.

What Are the Sources of Reporting Errors?

We have conducted some studies in which the accuracy of diary reporting was validated against client shipment data. A regression model was

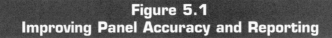

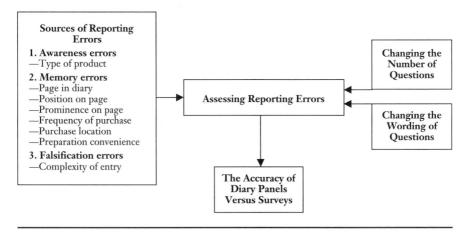

Figure 5.1
Improving Panel Accuracy and Reporting

Sources of Reporting Errors
1. Awareness errors
—Type of product
2. Memory errors
—Page in diary
—Position on page
—Prominence on page
—Frequency of purchase
—Purchase location
—Preparation convenience
3. Falsification errors
—Complexity of entry

Assessing Reporting Errors

Changing the Number of Questions

Changing the Wording of Questions

The Accuracy of Diary Panels Versus Surveys

developed to explain accuracy as a function of diary characteristics. Diary characteristics need to be related to the various reasons for recording error, which can be classified as follows:

1. The record keeper is not aware that the purchase was made by another household member.
2. The record keeper is aware of the purchase but forgets to enter it in the diary.
3. The record keeper enters it in the diary but errs on some detail of the purchase owing to either a memory or a recording detail.
4. The diary is deliberately falsified, either by omission of purchases or by inclusion of imaginary purchases or purchase details.

These different types of errors can generally be classified as awareness errors, memory errors, and falsification errors. They can often be traced to specific underlying causes, as shown in Figure 5.1.

Because the record keepers are usually the homemakers, meal planners, and grocery shoppers, they should be more aware of grocery items than of drugs, personal care, or miscellaneous items that are more often purchased by other household members.

In learning which product purchases are to be entered in the diary, record keepers study the diary from front to back. Their memory of what they have seen is unknowingly influenced by the "law of proactive and retroactive inhibition."[1] Because of this law, products in the back of the diary should be affected by proactive inhibition, whereas those in the middle are affected by both proactive and retroactive inhibition. We would expect the fewest memory errors for items in the front of the diary and the most errors in the middle. For the same reason, we would expect that, in general, products at the top of a page would be better remembered than those in the middle or at the bottom of the page.

Several other hypotheses were formulated about accuracy of reporting, as follows:

- Learning is related to the strength of the stimulus. Products listed in larger type should be noticed more often and remembered better.
- Complexity of entry is related to the possibility of deliberate omission.
- Owing to reinforcement, the more frequently the item is purchased, the better it will be remembered.
- Purchases made during major shopping trips, likely to be to chains, are more likely to be remembered than are purchases of a few items to small neighborhood stores.
- The record keeper's favorable attitudes about a product will improve his or her memory. Convenience of preparation is one of the factors determining favorable attitudes toward a product.

Assessing Reporting Accuracy

A multiplicative model was developed that related recording accuracy to the eight error factors. Recording accuracy for the ith product was defined to be the ratio[2]

$$A_i = \frac{\text{National Consumer Panel recorded purchases}}{\text{Manufacturer shipment data corrected for nonhousehold usage}}.$$

Corrections for nonhousehold use were made using sources independent of National Consumer Panel Reports. These sources included recall surveys of nonhousehold usage, manufacturer estimates of nonhousehold usage, and industry and U.S. Department of Agriculture and Department of Commerce estimates of nonhousehold usage.

The eight factors examined for their relation to recording accuracy were classified into groups to sort the 72 products into approximately equal groups for each factor (see Table 5.1).

---

[1]This law states that retention of learned material is a function of activities occurring prior and subsequent to the original learning.

[2]It is important to note that this ratio is numerical and has no units of measure attached.

The general form of the multiplicative model considered was

$$\hat{A}_i = B_o \prod_{j=1}^{m} x_{ij}B_j,$$

where

$\hat{A}_i$ = the fitted accuracy of recording for the ith product;

x_{ij} = 1 if the ith product has property j;

x_{ij} = $1/B_j$ if the ith product does not have property j (so that $x_{ij}B_j$ = 1);

m = total number of properties in a given combination (17 for the combination selected);

i = 1, 2, ..., 72 products; and

B_j = parameters to be estimated.

For computational purposes, the following logarithmic equivalent of the model was used:

$$\text{Log}\hat{A}_i = \text{log}B_o + \sum_{j=1}^{m} \text{log } x_{ij}B_j.$$

Note that if the ith product class does not have property j, log $x_{ij}B_j$ = log 1 and log 1 = 0. If the ith product class has property j, log $x_{ij}B_j$ = B_j. The coefficients of log B_j are all either 0 or 1.

For each of the eight factors believed to affect recording accuracy, the B_j for each of the following groups was arbitrarily assigned as 1.00 to reduce the complexity of computations required:

■ Front page in diary
■ Top half of top page
■ Main or side listing
■ Heavy purchase of product class by National Consumer Panel households per month
■ Heavy percentage of product purchased in chain stores
■ Food
■ New, convenience item.

A total of 44 combinations was tested. The combination finally selected was the one that gave the best prediction, though there was not much difference between the selected combination and the first few runners-up. This decision resulted in eliminating the percentage purchased in chain stores and convenience of item preparation as variables. For this best combination, the percentage of the variance in coverage explained by the model (i.e., the coefficient of multiple determination, the square of the multiple correlation coefficient, or the R^2) is 75%.

Determining the Values of Parameters

Table 5.1 shows the values of the B_j's using the least-squares criterion. In general, these values agree with the hypotheses that were based on experience in areas other than panel operations. Recording is less accurate for

Table 5.1. Estimated Effects of Variables on Accuracy of Recording	
Item	All Products
Diary page number	
3–7 (front)	1.00*
8–26 (middle)	.89
27–34 (back)	.91
Complexity	
Easy (0–1 check boxes)	1.00*
Medium (2 check boxes)	.91
Complex (3 or more check boxes)	.87
Product class purchases per month in a panel of 6000 households	
Over 2000	1.00*
Under 2000	.92
Type of product	
Food	1.00*
Nonfood, grocery	1.00
Nonfood, nongrocery	.056
Prominence of entry	
Main or side (1/8 inch heavy type)	1.00*
Subtype (1/16 inch heavy type)	.86
Position on diary page	
Top half of top page	1.00*
Bottom half of top page	.87
Top half of bottom page	.99
Bottom half of bottom page	.95
Percentage of product class purchased in chain stores	
60–100%	—
0–59%	—
Convenience of product preparation	
New, convenient—frozen foods, baking mixes, dry bleach, etc.	—
Old, semi-convenient—canned food, breakfast cereals, etc.	—
Non-convenient—all other, such as flour, fresh fruit, etc.	—
Constant term	1.07

*Arbitrarily assigned as 1.00.

products in the back of the diary and least accurate for products in the middle, though the difference between products in the back and the middle is slight. Accuracy declines as complexity increases. Infrequently purchased and nongrocery products are less accurately recorded than are frequently purchased grocery products. The more prominently mentioned products are more accurately recorded, and products at the top of a page are recorded better than are those at the bottom. It must be remembered that these results were obtained from a specific panel sample using a specific diary format, so they may not be directly applicable to all panels.

The values shown for nongrocery products must be interpreted cautiously. There are only five products in this category, because the National Consumer Panel Weekly Diary is heavily oriented toward food and grocery products. The training of panel households in keeping a diary also stresses food and grocery products.

As examples of how the model operated, two product classes are shown in the following example. Cake mix is a typical grocery item, whereas shoe polish is a product not purchased very often.

Example 1: Cake mix	Description	Factor
Diary page:	13	.89
Complexity:	Easy	1.00
Product class purchases per month in a panel of 6000 households:	4400	1.00
Type of product:	Food	1.00
Prominence of entry:	Main	1.00
Position on diary page:	Top half of bottom page	.99
Constant:		1.07

A_i = Estimated accuracy of recording = (.89)(.99)(1.07) = 94%.

Example 2: Shoe polish	Description	Factor
Diary page:	34	.91
Complexity:	Easy	1.00
Product class purchases per month in a panel of 6000 households:	1250	.92
Type of product:	Nonfood, nongrocery	.56
Prominence of entry:	Main	1.00
Position on diary page:	Bottom half of top page	.87
Constant:		1.07

A_i = Estimated accuracy of recording = (.91)(.92)(.56)(.87)(1.07) = 44%.

Verifying Results

Because the 72 products examined here were not a random sample of any universe but were those products for which information was available, it did not seem wholly appropriate to observe only measures of variance to indicate the reliability of the method. The model was later tested, however, on all products not included in the original model for which shipment information had become available. The results were generally encouraging.

Table 5.2 shows these results for 15 products (Sudman 1964a). To avoid disclosure of confidential information, only product type is shown and product names are designated by letters. The empirical model appears slightly biased downward; the average difference is 2%, which is small relative to the standard deviation of 6%. Both these values seem satisfactory, considering the possible errors in the shipment data.

Table 5.2
Comparison of Estimated Accuracy of Recording for 15 Product Classes Not Included in Model

	Estimated Accuracy of Recording		
Type of Product	Shipment Date (%)	Empirical Recording Model (%)	Difference Date (%)
1. Food	100	92	8
2. Food	100	94	6
3. Food	90	82	8
4. Nonfood, grocery	86	87	−1
5. Food	85	86	−1
6. Nonfood, grocery	85	75	10
7. Nonfood, grocery	85	77	8
8. Food	81	80	1
9. Nonfood, grocery	80	80	0
10. Nonfood, grocery	78	76	2
11. Food	75	76	−1
12. Food	72	82	−10
13. Food	62	67	−5
14. Nonfood, nongrocery	53	44	9
15. Nonfood, nongrocery	45	47	−2
Mean	78.4	76.3	2.1

$$s = \frac{[\Sigma(A_j - \hat{A}_j)^2]^{1/2}}{15} = 6.0\%.$$

Source: Sudman (1964a, p. 18).

Does the Location or Position Within a Diary Matter?

It is clear from the results of the mathematical model that only some of the diary characteristics can be manipulated. One that can be manipulated by panel operators is position in the diary. Those products that are considered most difficult or important, for whatever reasons, should be placed early in the diary. Whatever products are given favored positions, however, will mean that some others will have less desirable ones.

In the National Consumer Panel experiment discussed previously, one of the manipulations was to divide the diary into three product sequences:

1. Food first, laundry second, utility and miscellaneous last.
2. Laundry first, utility and miscellaneous second, food last.
3. Utility and miscellaneous first, food second, laundry last.

The results were in agreement with those of the mathematical model; all products benefit from being put early in the diary, and items in the middle are reported poorest. These results are given in Table 5.3.

Although no major changes were ultimately made in the diary sequence, a new diary was introduced that rearranged some items that had been out of sequence. This had occurred over the years because of the introduction of new product categories and an unwillingness to rearrange the diary to fit these new products into their proper place.

Table 5.3
Indices of Purchase Entries by Type of Product and Position in Diary (Product in Front Section = 100)

Type of Product and Diary	Product in 1st Section	Product in 2nd Section	Product in 3rd Section	Product in 2nd or 3rd Section
Ledger Diary				
Food	100	91.6	96.3	93.8
Laundry	100	99.6	98.5	99.0
Utility	100	84.7	98.0	90.9
Combined	100	91.9	96.7	94.3
Journal Diary				
Food	100	100.6	100.3	100.4
Laundry	100	96.7	89.8	93.1
Utility	100	114.9	98.2	105.9
Combined	100	101.8	98.8	100.3

Source: Sudman (1964b, p. 71).

Putting these new products into their proper location improved their reporting substantially. It also led to a policy of leaving empty space in the various diary sections so that new products could be added in their proper places rather than put at the end of the diary (Sudman 1964b).

How Can Changes in Question Wording Influence Accuracy?

There is a need to change diary forms periodically because of the introduction of new products, types, and flavors, as well as changing client interests. Because the major benefit of panels is their ability to measure change, it is important that the effects of small changes in the diary be measured so that these effects will not be confused with real-world changes. This is done by introducing any diary change into only a subsample of the total panel. Then the basic measures of the effect of a diary change are the number of diary entries per product class and per diary.

To measure the effect of a diary change, we can set up the following simple model:

Let X_B = number of entries per diary made by the experimental group in the period before the experiment begins;

X_A = number of entries per diary made by the experimental group during the experiment;

C_B = number of diary entries made by the control group in the period before the experiment begins;

C_A = number of diary entries made by the control group during the experiment; and

D = difference due to diary forms.

Then,

$$D = (X_A - X_B) - (C_A - C_B).$$

A decision must be made on the size of the experimental and control subsamples. Although a 50–50 split is optimal for measuring the magnitude of the change, smaller experimental subsamples are sometimes used if there is a concern about keeping the existing data series stable during the experiment. For example, the National Consumer Panel is divided into four subsamples containing 50%, 25%, 15%, and 10% of the households. Although a diary change is generally tested on the 50–50 split, it is also possible to test on other subsample combinations. From this control program, in effect for many years, the following generalizations have emerged:

1. Adding or deleting a check box or changing the wording within a check box will not measurably affect the level of recording. For example, a new column was added to the dentifrice section of the diary to pick up fluoride toothpastes versus powders and to allow for dentifrices with more than one additive. There was no significant change in recording.

2. Changing a product heading, especially the specific listing of a type that had been previously included under "Other," may measurably change the level of recording. Thus, the main listing "Polishes, Waxes, and Cleaners" was divided into two main listings: "Waxes, Polishes, and Cleaners for Floors, Furniture, Kitchen Cabinets, Woodwork, etc." and "Automobile Waxes, Polishes." No change in recording occurred for the floor polishes; the added section for auto polishes, however, resulted in a doubling of the recorded purchase entries for those items.

3. Moving a product listing from one page to another will temporarily reduce the level of recording. For example, the "Frozen Fruit and Dessert Pies" section was moved from the top of one page to the middle of the page facing it to make room for another product. An announcement of this change appeared in the monthly newsletter to panel households and produced no change in recording the first month. Apparently, purchasers during the first month saw the announcement in the newsletter of the changed diary location. During the next two months, recorded entries by the group receiving the experimental diary declined 14%. Evidently, purchasers in these two months did not see or remember the announcement in the newsletter and were not able to find its new location. In the next three months, however, recording returned to the old level, suggesting that by then it had been rediscovered at its new location.

4. Special reminders in the diary, such as stickers or inserts, result in temporary improvement in the level of recording but not necessarily in long-term changes. For example, a special postcard was sent to the experimental group reminding members to list purchases of soft drinks. In addition, diaries for the next two months had yellow stickers on their covers to remind households again about soft drinks. During these three months of special reminders, recording of soft drink purchases rose 30% in the experimental group. In the next two months, recording was still up but only by 15%. In the third month, the increase was down to 9%, and after that month, recording of the experimental group returned to the normal level.

How Can Changes in the Number of Questions Influence Accuracy?

Panel households not only keep continuing records of purchasing but also fill out special questionnaires from time to time on such subjects as appliance ownership and media receivership. Simple questions on ownership have no effect on recording of purchases, but a special survey might influence continuing record keeping.

This section describes three major changes in workload due to special surveys. None of these three surveys changed recording behavior substantially, though it had been feared that they might.

The Menu Study

In one of the most comprehensive menu studies to date, MRCA's National Consumer Panel was used to obtain information on how food was prepared and consumed in U.S. homes. Four thousand panel households kept records for two weeks, listed every ingredient of every meal prepared in the home, and reported who in the household ate what. Because the menu study was by far the most difficult reporting assignment ever asked of the panel households, three pretests were conducted to determine whether there would be any effect on National Consumer Panel diary reporting. Comparisons were made between 50 experimental households and 50 control households in each pretest. Records of diary reporting were obtained for the four weeks preceding the menu study, the two weeks of the study, and the six weeks after the study.

The results were somewhat surprising. They showed that rather than a decrease, which had been feared, the menu study would, if anything, slightly increase reporting of food items during the two weeks of the study. This could have been caused by an increase in purchasing due to the stimulation of the menu study or to an increase in purchases recorded. Because only a small group of panel households was to keep this record at any time during the year, the overall effect on continuing data was expected to be less than 1%. There was no reason to expect that particular food products would be affected more than others because of the generality of the menu study stimulus. A slight decrease was observed in the reporting of nonfood products during the two weeks of the study. Again, this indicated an expected difference of less than 1% to continuing data. The results of these pretests were confirmed during the full-scale menu census. There were no indications of any measurable changes in product class recording.

Auto Diary Effects

A subsample of 1500 MRCA National Consumer Panel households kept a special monthly diary of purchases of gasoline, oil, and auto repairs. To determine whether this added workload affected recording of purchases in the weekly diary, comparisons were made with a control group of other car owners that did not keep an auto diary during this period. The statistic measured was total coded weekly diary entries. An analysis of the results indicated virtually no effect on recording of weekly purchases due to the auto diary.

Media Diary Effects

A large-scale media study was conducted for the Magazine Advertising Bureau (MAB) of the Magazine Publishers Association using the MRCA National Consumer Panel (Magazine Advertising Bureau 1960). A pilot test with 1500 National Consumer Panel households was conducted for seven weeks during the winter of 1959. The MAB pilot study was designed to investigate several areas dealing with the accuracy of media measurements obtained from the MRCA National Consumer Panel. In addition, there was some concern that keeping detailed media records would reduce the accuracy of recording in the regular purchase diary. Comparisons were made of the reported products purchased by households that kept media records and products purchased by the remaining panel households. Again, no important differences were observed.

Special Contacts with Panel Households

In this section, we discuss the effects that special contacts with panel households have on recording. Although many such contacts occur between panel operators and panel members, most are not tested in a controlled experiment. Data are available, however, for tests conducted by the MRCA National Consumer Panel to determine whether a series of indirect reminders to households would stimulate their reporting. The following reminders were tried:

1. Contest quiz,
2. Inventory quiz,
3. Purchase quiz, and
4. Store shopping record insertion in diary.

The contest quiz asked families to go through the diary and write down the names of all the product classes in the diary. Special compensation was awarded for filling out this form completely. The thought behind this quiz was to remind families of diary product classes that they might have forgotten.

The inventory quiz asked for a record of products actually on hand in the home. Twenty products were listed, mainly those that were underreported. Again, the purpose was to remind households of product classes in the diary.

The purchase quiz asked for recall of who selected products in the household. The objective was, again, specifically to remind households that selected products were in the diary.

The store shopping record was an insert added to the front of the diary that asked households to list each trip to a food store and give the amount spent. The objective was not to remind households of specific items, but to ensure that the diary was opened after each shopping trip.

Three hundred households participated in these training tests. The three quizzes were rotated among all of the families in six different sequences to balance possible order effects. The store shopping record was kept by 150 households for three months, with the other 150 households as a control group.

Reporting on selected food and nonfood products was computed by product class purchases per month. The balance of the panel acted as a control group for the 300 households.

The quizzes had no long-term effect on reporting, though there was possibly a short, initial effect. The store shopping record, however, measurably increased recording, and it was made a part of the new diary. These results again confirmed earlier tests that showed that periodic training had no discernible long-term effect on diary recording.

The Mortality of Heavy Users

A notable study by Buck and colleagues (1997) examined the accuracy of panels in fairly representing heavy users. It is generally believed that the effort of keeping a purchase or consumption diary is related to how much a household purchases or consumes the target product. In general, heavy users are taxed a bit more than light users or nonusers. The possibility thus exists that households with the highest buying levels are more likely to leave the panel ("too much work") than are households of whom less is demanded.

In a 76-week study of 1889 homes across 52 different products, it was found that there was a higher mortality bias associated with heavy buyers than with light or nonbuyers. On the basis of the numerical data the study presented, it is possible to estimate that the impact this effect may have on pick-up levels may range at approximately ½% per year.

How Accurate Are Diary Records Compared with Survey Recall?

Although previous studies have shown that survey recall data tend to overstate purchases (Drayton 1954; Lansing, Ginsburg, and Braaten 1961; Metz 1956; Neter and Waksberg 1961), another significant error in recall data has not been studied fully. This error is the tendency to recall the names of well-known brands when, in some cases, the actual purchase may have been of a lesser-known brand. As a point of illustration, consider the consumption survey in Exhibit 5.1.

Exhibit 5.1
Discontinuous Panel Survey to Estimate Consumption
Volume in Categories and Situations

How many times in the past <u>YEAR</u> did you...

Eat anchovies	_____ times
Eat luncheon meats	_____ times
Use Tabasco Sauce	_____ times
Buy Hamburger Helper	_____ times
Grill out	_____ times
Buy Spam	_____ times
Buy Jell-O	_____ times
Eat grapes	_____ times
Eat horseradish	_____ times
Eat ostrich	_____ times
Eat Brocolli	_____ times
Use Bon Ami cleaner	_____ times
Eat M&Ms	_____ times
Buy <u>canned</u> cat or dog food	_____ times
Buy <u>dry</u> cat or dog food	_____ times
Drink a coke in the morning	_____ times
Eat pizza for breakfast	_____ times
Eat cereal for a night snack	_____ times
Eat cranberry sauce & chicken	_____ times
Eat Jell-O as a snack	_____ times
Used bleach as a cleaner	_____ times

Thanks again for helping us.
We appreciate your concentration.

How many times in the past <u>MONTH</u> did you...

Eat yogurt	_____ times
Eat pork	_____ times
Eat beef	_____ times
Eat chicken	_____ times
Eat lamb	_____ times
Eat dessert after dinner	_____ times
Take vitamins	_____ times
Drink a glass of milk	_____ times
Eat 5+ fruits/vegetables in one day	_____ times
Eat canned fruit	_____ times
Eat frozen vegetables	_____ times
Eat a hot dog	_____ times
Eat tomatoes	_____ times

Sophisticated market researchers have long been aware of this tendency, but its magnitude is probably larger than most would suspect. Leading nationally advertised brands often have their brand shares doubled in recall surveys as compared with diary records, whereas chain brands are almost always understated substantially. Methods are available for improving recall data through screening questions and other aids to the respondent's memory, but these are not often used, perhaps because the magnitude of recall error is not realized.

Suggested Hypotheses

Some preliminary comparisons of diary recording and recall for a small sample of panel households and products suggest three hypotheses for refining this relationship:

1. The status of the brand will affect the degree of difference between diary recording and recall.
    a. The brand shares of the best known nationally advertised brand will be overstated the most on recall surveys.
    b. Brand shares of other nationally advertised brands will be overstated on recall surveys.
    c. The brand share of the leading chain brand will be understated more than other chain brands on recall surveys.
    d. Brand shares of other chain brands will be understated on recall surveys.
    e. Brand shares of local brands will be understated, but less than chain brands, in recall surveys as compared with diary recording.
2. The type of product will affect the degree of difference between diary recording and recall.
    a. Differences will be greater for products purchased less frequently.
    b. Differences will be greater for products that are consumed after purchase (e.g., bread) as compared with those that are more durable (e.g., scouring cleanser).
3. Changes in brand shares obtained by recall surveys will lag changes reported in diaries.

A simple measure of the discrepancy between recall and diary recording is the ratio of brand shares on recall to brand shares on diary recording. This ratio is the basic statistic examined here, but the actual brand shares on recall and diary recording are also shown.

It is possible to consider the following hypotheses in the light of elementary psychology:

1. The more a brand is advertised and noticed, the more likely it is to be remembered and mentioned, regardless of the question.
2. The emotional content of a brand image will affect brand mentions. There may be guilt feelings connected with purchasing low-price brands, because the shoppers may feel that there is a positive relationship between quality and price and that they are in some way depriving their families of the best. In addition, advertising may give a brand a quality image.
3. The accuracy of recall has an inverse relationship to the length of the period of recall.
4. Respondents may tend to recall their usual behavior during a period rather than a specific act. This may result in recall lagging actual behavior.

Testing the Hypotheses

It was possible to obtain additional information to test these hypotheses. Information was available on brand shares of 31 food and 11 nonfood grocery products in the Chicago metropolitan area from the *Chicago*

Tribune Consumer Panel. Information was also available from the *Chicago Sun-Times–Chicago Daily News* Consumer Analysis for the same area. The *Tribune* Panel used diary recording; the Consumer Analysis is a recall survey.

Four reasons, other than differences in forms, suggest themselves as possibly responsible for some of the differences between the two services: sampling variability, differences in sample characteristics, conditioning, and differences in brand preferences related to frequency of purchase. None of these, however, appears to have any significant effect.

Brand Differences

The results in Table 5.4 enable us to test the hypotheses pertaining to brand differences. Each brand category is distributed by the size of the ratios of recall brand shares to diary brand shares. An even simpler summary is to observe that the median values of the ratios for the group are in the order hypothesized.

The brand shares of the best known nationally advertised brands are overstated the most. Brand shares of other nationally advertised brands are also overstated. The brand shares of the leading chain brands are understated the most. Brand shares of chain and local brands are also understated, with local brands understated less than chain brands.

Brands are classified as follows:

1. Advertised brands are those found in the Trade Name Index of the *Standard Advertising Register.*
2. Chain brands are those manufactured by or for the four leading chains in Chicago: Jewel, A&P, National, and Kroger.
3. Local brands are all other brands.
4. The best known nationally advertised brand is the one that had the highest brand share among nationally advertised brands in the *Chicago Sun-Times–Chicago Daily News* Consumer Analysis Survey.
5. The leading chain brand is the one that ranked highest among chain brands in the *Chicago Tribune* Consumer Panel reports.

The way in which the best known nationally advertised brands and the leading chain brands are defined could introduce a regression effect, but additional evidence suggests that the differences observed are not due to this. In all but five cases, the leading chain brand was an A&P brand, which agreed with the known leadership of A&P in private label products. During the four-year period, there were only three products for which the leading chain brand changed.

Similarly, over the four-year period, there were only four products for which the best known nationally advertised brand changed. In addition, though exact advertising figures for Chicago are not available, most of the best known nationally advertised brands also appear to be the most heavily advertised in the Chicago area. If there still remains a slight regression effect, it would not change the conclusions of this section but might tend to overstate the differences between the best known and other nationally advertised brands, as well as the differences between the leading and other chain brands.

Table 5.4
How the Ratios of Recall Brand Shares to Diary Brand Shares Vary by Brands

	A. Nationally Advertised	
Ratio	Best Known Brand	Other Brands
Under 1.01	6	16
1.01–1.10	6	5
1.11–1.20	2	7
1.21–1.30	1	2
1.31–1.40	4	2
1.41–1.50	4	4
1.51–1.60	2	1
1.61–1.70	1	0
1.71–1.80	5	0
1.81–1.90	3	0
1.91–2.00	3	0
Over 2.00	5	5
Total sample	42	42
Median	1.45	1.10

	B. Other Brands		
Ratio	Local Brands	Other Chain Brands	Leading Chain Brands
Under .11	1	4	0
.11–.20	1	0	4
.21–.30	1	1	5
.31–.40	4	4	8
.41–.50	6	2	7
.51–.60	6	3	2
.61–.70	9	2	2
.71–.80	2	3	1
.81–.90	3	1	0
.91–1.00	2	1	0
Over 1.00	5	1	2
Total sample	40	22	31
Median	.62	.50	.38

Product Differences

The 42 products investigated in these comparisons were grouped into three categories:

     1. Grocery, nonfood;
     2. Food, staples; and
     3. Food, perishable.

This final category consisted of the following eight items: bacon, bread, butter, frankfurters, frozen fish sticks, frozen orange juice concentrate, frozen vegetables, and margarine. The data show a clear relation between the durability of the product and the degree of difference between recall and diary recording. To simplify the analysis, a single measure of this difference has been adopted, namely, the ratio of recall brand share to diary brand share of the best known nationally advertised brand. This measure is shown in Table 5.5.

Table 5.5 shows that the median ratio for the three product categories declines from 1.83 for perishable foods to 1.54 for staple foods to 1.05 for nonfoods. It seems clear that the more durable the goods, the less subject recall is to memory error. This is further confirmed by studies of appliances, automobiles, and other hard goods.

For the grocery items, only small differences are observed in prices per unit, and there is no relationship between durability and prices. This suggests that durability rather than price improves recall, at least for grocery products.

Table 5.5 also ranks each product by its estimated frequency of purchase, with the least frequently purchased product ranked first. The results are mildly surprising. Recall accuracy seems to either increase or remain stable as purchase frequency declines. This contradicts the initial hypothesis that suggests an inverse relationship between frequency of purchase and the ratio of recall to diary recordings.

In retrospect, we see that most heavily advertised grocery products are probably also the most frequently purchased. In any event, there is certainly some correlation between frequency of purchase and the strength of "brand image." The products are observed in their three categories separately, because we already know that the durability of the product influences recall. The results of Table 5.5 are strongly confirmed by the four years of data.

Changes in Brand Shares

The hypothesis that changes in brand shares obtained by recall would lag changes reported in diaries is not supported by the data in Table 5.6.

Table 5.5
Ratio of Recall: Diary Brand Share for Best Known Nationally Advertised Brand by Type of Product and Purchase Frequency

Rank by Frequency of Purchase	Product	Ratio of Recall: Diary	Rank of Ratio*
A. Nonfood			
1	Dry bleach	.90	2
2	Liquid floor wax	1.37	10
3	Dry starch	1.00	5
4	Liquid starch	.88	1
5	Scouring pads	1.05	6.5
6	Scouring cleanser	1.05	6.5
7	Paper towels	.98	4
8	Waxed paper	1.08	9
9	Paper napkins	3.57	11
10	Liquid bleach	1.06	8
11	Toilet tissue	.98	3
Median		1.05	
B. Perishable food			
1	Frozen fish sticks	.83	1
2	Frankfurters	1.72	2
3	Bacon	1.79	3
4	Frozen orange juice concentrate	2.89	8
5	Frozen vegetables	2.57	7
6	Margarine	1.83	4
7	Butter	2.00	5.5
8	Bread	2.00	5.5
Median		1.83	
C. Staple foods			
1	Canned luncheon meat	1.17	4
2	Instant potatoes	1.44	10
3	Vegetable shortening	1.80	18
4	Tea	1.77	16.5
5	Dry milk	1.31	6
6	Pancake and waffle mix	1.42	9
7	Hot cereal	1.15	3
8	Fruit cocktail	1.95	21
9	Saltine crackers	1.37	8
10	Salad and cooking oil	1.26	5
11	Syrup	1.90	19
12	Rice	.64	1
13	Canned peaches	2.38	23
14	Instant coffee	1.03	2
15	Canned tuna	1.90	20
16	Peanut butter	1.77	16.5
17	Canned corn	2.23	22

	Table 5.5 **Continued**		
Rank by Frequency of Purchase	**Product**	**Ratio of Recall: Diary**	**Rank of Ratio***
18	All-purpose flour	1.45	11
19	Cake mixes	1.34	7
20	Catsup	1.58	14
21	Canned milk	1.47	12
22	Regular coffee	1.68	15
23	Cold cereal	1.54	13
Median		1.54	

*Least frequently purchased product has rank 1.

These changes in brand shares from the previous year are observed for each brand during the four-year period. Comparisons between diary and recall indicate whether the two series agree on a change in brand share from the preceding year. These comparisons are made for concurrent changes, recall lagged, and diary lagged, as follows:

Change	Diary	Recall
Concurrent	$t_n - t_{n-1}$	$t_n - t_{n-1}$
Recall lagged	$t_n - t_{n-1}$	$t_{n-1} - t_{n-2}$
Diary lagged	$t_{n-1} - t_{n-2}$	$t_n - t_{n-1}$

Shorter period comparisons, such as month-to-month or quarter-to-quarter, may indicate a lead–lag relationship masked by annual data. However, for the annual data, there is no evidence that changes in recall are useful predictors of future changes in purchase behavior.

Web studies need to be done to validate how an online method of data collection influences reporting accuracy. Some argue that there would be higher quality responses and fewer response errors because there is a reduced social effect due to a greater degree of online anonymity. This presupposes that a computer-entered questionnaire is more anonymous than one completed by hand. Although intriguing, this position is often balanced with some consumers' fears that electronic data are more easily accessed by unintended people.

Summary

Although much is known about how to recruit and collect data from panels, there is a continuing concern about the trade-offs between cost and

Table 5.6 Agreement Between Diary Recording and Recall on Changes in Brand Share			
Type of Comparison	Number of Comparisons	Number of Agreements	Percentage Agreements
Concurrent	283	178	63%
Recall lagged one period	188	99	53%
Diary lagged one period	188	110	59%

accuracy. The better methods are also more expensive, so that the proper balance of cost and quality will depend on the uses of the panel data. Answers to the questions raised in the introduction of this chapter and Chapter 4 can be briefly summarized as follows:

1. Although face-to-face methods are the most expensive, they are still a popular method for recruiting panel households (particularly overseas) because of the increased cooperation achieved. Telephone and mail methods are also used, however, especially for panels of special populations and for test marketing purposes.
2. All panels compensate their members. The median value of the compensation was about $55 per year in 2001. There is no evidence that the form of the compensation—money, lottery, or gifts—is important.
3. Both weekly and monthly diaries are widely used, but weekly diaries are used for frequently purchased food, grocery, and drug items, whereas monthly diaries are more likely to be used for less frequently purchased items such as clothing and textiles. The evidence suggests that all else being equal, data collected more frequently will be reported more completely.
4. Ledger (product) diaries are used almost universally because they obtain needed details, are easier to process, and also get better cooperation and more complete reporting from panel members. There are some problems with ledger diaries, however. As they become longer, reporting becomes less complete for items in the middle and back of the diary.
5. A desire for additional information about the purchase may result in less complete reporting, because accuracy declines as the complexity of the entry increases. The use of the UPCs and home scanners or wands may be of great value to U.S. panel operators.
6. Products at the top of a page are better reported than are those at the bottom, more prominently mentioned products are more accurately recorded, and frequently purchased grocery products are more accurately recorded, at least in a diary that stresses grocery products, than are infrequently purchased grocery products or nongrocery products.
7. Changing a product heading, especially the specific listing of a type that was previously listed under "Other," may increase the level of reporting.

Moving a product listing from one page to another will temporarily reduce the level of recording. Special reminders result in temporary, but not long-term, increases in reporting level. Adding or deleting a check box or changing the wording will not measurably affect the level of reporting.

8. Increasing the workload of panel families for short periods by having them fill out questionnaires or keep menu, media, or other diaries has no effect on reporting levels for the main diary.

9. Leading nationally advertised brands have their brand shares overstated an average of 50% on recall surveys as compared with diary records, whereas chain brands are almost always substantially understated. With all the possible sources of error in panels, they are still far more accurate than recall surveys in providing information on quantities and brands purchased.

Chapter 6

The Accidental Conditioning of Consumer Panels

We always worry about that Hawthorne effect with our panels. You know, it's where the survey starts influencing behavior instead of recording it. Like the guy who says, "Gee, I never thought about taking vitamins until that survey reminded me."

—Panel researcher

How big should our concern be about panel conditioning? Sometimes it should be large; sometimes it shouldn't. It is important to know when we are conditioning a panel and how it is influencing them. That is the objective of this chapter.

When we talk of conditioning, we refer to any unintended factors or stimuli that influence a panel in a way that biases its response or behavior. We use stimuli in a very broad sense to include all contacts between the panel operators and the panel households. These include initial recruiting contact, training (personal, mail, or online), diary keeping, compensation, newsletters, all other mail (including Christmas and holiday cards), e-mail, and personal contact. It will be convenient to classify stimuli into three time-related categories:

1. Recruitment-related conditioning, which results from initial contacts with the households up to and including the return of the first diary;
2. Short-term conditioning, which includes all stimuli in the first year of panel; and
3. Long-term conditioning, which includes all stimuli occurring after the first year of panel membership.

All three forms of conditioning are examined in this chapter, and recommendations will be made as to what options we have in avoiding them or remedying them after they have occurred. The bulk of the chapter is spent on the various types of short-term conditioning.

The Big Picture of Conditioning

The Hawthorne effect that our panel operator feared at the beginning of the chapter can manifest itself in many different ways. Put another way, there are very broad ways that various stimuli or interventions by a panel operator can influence a panel. For example, factors that might influence purchase behavior include the following:

1. Change in type of store shopped (chain versus independent),
2. Change in number of shopping trips per unit of time,
3. Change in total expenditures per unit of time,
4. Change of brand purchased (national versus private label),
5. Change in package size of products purchased,
6. Change in price paid per unit quantity of selected products, and
7. Change in expenditures per unit of time for selected products.

For other types of behavior, similar changes might be possible. Thus, keeping diaries of medical behavior might cause an increase or decrease in routine visits to physicians or other medical providers, a shift in the type of services obtained, or a change in the use of certain medicines or treatments. A time-use diary might cause a shift from a passive use of time, such as watching television, to a more active use. In addition to changes in behavior, there might also be changes in attitudes and beliefs that could lead to future changes in purchase behavior.

It seems unrealistic to expect major changes in the behavior or lifestyle of a household because one or more members are keeping limited records. Indeed, none of the research on conditioning has yet indicated that major changes occur. Subtle short-term changes have been observed and are discussed in this chapter. Yet, even here, the data are incomplete. This lack of data is not due to an unawareness of the need for such information but rather to the formidable problems of obtaining it.

The evidence described in the chapter indicates that special studies focusing on usage or opinion about a specific product or event can change behavior as reported in a diary. In contrast, the changes observed due to keeping a diary purchase record of many products or events have not been significant or systematic. They tend to be small and in different directions for different households. The net effects measured to date have not proved to be significant. Although this may result from the insensitivity of the tests used, it suggests that major changes due to conditioning through regular diary keeping are unlikely.

Researchers must be sensitive to possible conditioning effects, and they can reduce these effects by using a more general diary. That is, if a diary is used for testing a new product, it should obtain information on several product classes so that attention is not focused on only the new product class. With proper safeguards, conditioning effects are not a major problem in the use of panels.

Recruitment-Related Conditioning

Currently, only anecdotal information exists on a household's behavior, which is immediately influenced when it accepts an invitation to join a panel. Efforts to obtain information on a household's behavior using recall techniques have been unsatisfactory. The first studies merely compared a household's recall of purchases in a period prior to joining the panel with purchase entries in the diary after joining. As shown in Chapter 5, memory errors are so significant that they make any simple comparisons with measure conditioning unsatisfactory. A more sophisticated recall approach also failed. The design called for obtaining recall purchase information from all households contacted on an original survey call. The same recall information was to be obtained three months later from both panel cooperators and noncooperators. A measure of immediate and short-term conditioning was to be obtained by observing the differential change in recall among panel households compared with the change among noncooperators. Implicit in this design were two assumptions:

- Recall of panel cooperators and noncooperators would be equally correct (or incorrect), or at least changes of recall accuracy would not differ between cooperators and noncooperators between the initial and final survey call.
- Survey information could be obtained on a second call from all or most households not joining the panel.

Unfortunately, neither of these assumptions proved correct when the actual study was conducted. No useful measure of conditioning was obtained for the following reasons:

- Panel cooperators gave much more complete information on the initial survey call than did the noncooperators and gave even better information on the second call, because keeping the diary records evidently improved recall of purchasing.
- A substantial number of panel noncooperators who answered the initial survey calls refused to answer subsequent calls.

Because experience has indicated the problems in measuring conditioning by recall techniques, other approaches might include the use of observational methods or other outside validation. To our knowledge, such studies have never been attempted.

The Three Forms of Short-Term Conditioning

In this section, we discuss three types of short-term conditioning: (1) differences in behavior between the initial period of diary keeping and the second and later periods, (2) differences in behavior caused by special stimuli, and (3) other differences in the first year. Substantial evidence of conditioning exists for the first two types, but no evidence of conditioning exists for the last.

Differences in Behavior in Initial Period

Almost universally, panel operators have observed that in the first week or period of keeping a diary, households report higher levels of behavior or expenditure than they do in the second and subsequent periods. These examples are just a few that might be cited:

- In a U.S. Consumer Expenditure Survey conducted by the U.S. Bureau of the Census with 23,000 households, a diary record of food and beverage expenditures was kept for a two-week period. Expenditures in the first week were 10% higher than those in the second week. There was no evidence that this was due to any category differences. Indeed, the same results were seen for all the food and beverage categories.
- In work conducted by the Survey Research Laboratory in Illinois as a pilot study for the U.S. Consumer Expenditure Survey, expenditures in the first week were 8% higher than in the second week. Because this study also asked some households to keep records for three and four weeks, it could be observed that third-week expenditures rose again, whereas fourth-week expenditures dropped sharply.
- In a study conducted by the Survey Research Laboratory on the use of diaries in reporting medical events, a sample of Illinois and Wisconsin residents kept records for three months. The total number of events reported was 14% higher in the first month than in the second and third months. There were no differences between the last two months.
- In our study discussed in Chapter 3, purchase behavior was measured on ten products over an eight-week period. Expenditures in the first week were 20% higher than the average for the eight weeks; for the second week, expenditures were 8% below average. For weeks three through eight, results were just about average—stability had been reached.

Alternative explanations have been advanced for these results. One is that the diary has caused an actual, though short-term, increase in purchase behavior or other activity; that is, the diary acts as a reminder or stimulant and changes behavior. Another explanation is that panel membership changes the timing of behavior but not the level; that is, purchases that would normally have been made in the second or later period are made in the initial period owing to the stimulus of record keeping. This explains the drop from week one to week two and then the rise again in week three observed in several experiments on food purchasing.

Another explanation involves fatigue or ending-period effects. This explanation suggests that the most correct reporting is obtained in the initial period and that accuracy is reduced in later periods, particularly just before the end of the record keeping.

The evidence is clear that reports of level of expenditures or behavior differ from the first to later periods, but there is little evidence of any other types of differences. A comparison of where households made their purchases indicated no difference in the percentage of purchases in chain stores between the first and the eighth week. Nor did the same study reveal any evidence of changes in the percentage of deal purchases or in the percentage of purchases of nationally advertised brands.

One exception was observed in the U.S. Consumer Expenditure Study (though the differences were not statistically significant). There was a 7% increase in the percentage of purchases of large package sizes of food and grocery products between the first and later weeks. This finding has not appeared in other studies.

The evidence suggests that there is little that can be done to prevent the observed differences between the first and later periods. The remedies must be in the analytic procedures used. In the most common case of using a panel for measuring long-term trends, the usual solution by panel operators is to omit the initial period and consider it a training period (Chandon and Wansink 2002). Beyond this first period, nothing else is done to adjust for conditioning.

For short-term panels, the most common tendency seems to be to combine all the data and avoid any attempts at trend analysis. Some of these examples indicate that in a two-week study, the combined period is better than either the first or the second week separately. Some efforts have been made to adjust the data by omitting the first and the last two or three days of the study. This is useful for consumption-related studies (Chandon and Wansink 2002) but less useful for purchase-related studies because actual day-to-day shopping behavior by day of week makes this procedure impractical.

Differences in Behavior Caused by Special Stimuli

There is conclusive evidence that special stimuli can result in major changes in reported purchase behavior. Two examples are discussed, one dealing with soft drinks and the other with citrus products. These studies suggest that it is possible to influence household purchase reporting over a short time period with the following:

- A specific reminder to enter purchases of that product,
- A study of the usage or opinion of a specific product, and
- A diary that only requires information about one product.

Unless the special stimulus is maintained, its effect eventually dies out. The length of time that it takes the effect to fade away depends mainly on the strength of the initial stimulus.

The Postcard Reminder Study

A postcard reminder was sent to a subsample of panel households to test whether reporting of soft drinks and automobile waxes would be changed by reminding them to record all household purchases in those categories. The content of this postcard is shown here:

After talking with quite a few panel families recently, we found that some of them were not entering all their purchases of SOFT DRINKS and AUTOMOBILE WAXES, POLISHES & CLEANERS because these products were bought by *other members of the family* and *not* by the person keeping the Diary.

We want to be sure that YOU know that all purchases made by ANYONE IN YOUR FAMILY should be entered! So please read the rest of this card, fill out the bottom of it, and send it back TODAY!

1. SOFT DRINKS include both carbonated and non-carbonated beverages such as "pops," colas, root beer, soda, bottled water, sparkling water, ginger ale, etc.

THESE PRODUCTS SHOULD BE ENTERED ON PAGE ____.

2. AUTOMOBILE WAXES, POLISHES, & CLEANERS SHOULD BE ENTERED ON PAGE ____.

How many different persons in your home bought these products during the last month?

	Check one for EACH PRODUCT			
	No One	One Person	Two Persons	Three or More Persons
Soft Drinks	❑	❑	❑	❑
Automobile Waxes, Polishes & Cleaners	❑	❑	❑	❑

In addition, a special yellow sticker was attached to diaries, again reminding these households to enter soft drink purchases. These stimuli had the immediate major effects of increasing reported purchases of soft drinks by approximately 30%, but this effect faded quickly. Table 6.1 shows the results by month.

These increases were practically all due to an increase in the percentage of households buying. No significant change in volume per buying household was observed. It should also be noted that the only statistic that could be measured was reported purchases. It is not clear to what extent the reminders changed purchase behavior. It is clear, however, that a very specific stimulus caused a sharp, albeit brief, response.

The Citrus Usage Study

How does the reporting of citrus product consumption influence the purchase of citrus products? To determine this, half of the households in a panel reported on their usage of citrus products, while the other half acted as a control group. The effects of this special usage record on reported purchasing were measured for the following citrus products:

Orange products
1. All orange products combined
2. Canned orange juice
3. Frozen orange juice
4. Fresh oranges
Lemon products
1. All lemon products
2. Canned and bottled lemon juice
3. Frozen lemonade
4. Fresh lemons

Table 6.1
Increase in Reporting of Soft Drinks of Experimental Sample Relative to Control Sample

Month	Stimulus	Change in Reported Purchases
1	Postcard reminder (late in month)	0
2		+28%
3	Sticker reminder in diary	+37%
4		+26%
5		0
6		0
7		0

When people reported their buying habits, substantial increases were observed on all product classes. The details are shown in Tables 6.2 and 6.3. Table 6.2 shows the changes in total volume per diary. Table 6.3 shows the changes in the percentage of households buying. Average amounts per buying households do not appear to have changed significantly.

These results are in agreement with the soft drink study results. They show a rapid decline in responses to the stimulus during the second month. No additional comparisons were made, so it is not known how

Table 6.2
Increase in Purchase Reporting of Citrus Products by Citrus Usage Diary Households Relative to Control Sample

Product	Percentage Increase in Mean Amount per Diary Reported Purchased	
	1st month	2nd month
Total orange products	+16%	+ 2%
Canned juice	+ 7%	0%
Frozen juice	+ 6%	+ 2%
Fresh oranges	+55%	+34%
Total lemon products	+35%	+ 7%
Bottled lemon juice	+45%	+11%
Frozen lemonade	+32%	0%
Fresh lemons	+32%	+ 8%

Table 6.3
Increase in Percentage of Households Reporting Buying of Citrus Products by Citrus Usage Households Relative to Control Sample

Product	Percentage Increase in Percentage Households Reported Buying	
	1st month	2nd month
Total orange products	+16%	+3%
Canned juice	+23%	0%
Frozen juice	+10%	+15%
Fresh oranges	+41%	+15%
Total lemon products	+29%	+14%
Bottled lemon juice	+34%	+10%
Frozen lemonade	+ 9%	0%
Fresh lemons	+39%	+21%

rapidly the responses faded after that, but we could guess that, four to six months later, all was back to normal.

Tables 6.2 and 6.3 suggest that the effect on the reporting of fresh oranges and lemons was somewhat greater than that on canned and frozen citrus products, and the larger stimuli faded less rapidly. It is evident from this study that the same, or very similar, stimuli may cause widely varying responses for different products, depending on the household's previous purchase behavior and frame of reference for the product. It is thus not possible to predict very well a priori what the effect of a special stimulus will be. Controlled tests are required, as discussed in Chapter 5.

These results are also supported by a study in the United Kingdom (Buck et al. 1997). A reasonable concern was that joining a panel would cause consumers to shop more broadly, including warehouse stores and discount stores, because of the heightened salience of how much they were spending on groceries. The concern was unmerited. Of the 240 households that completed the 24-week test period, there were no differences in the number and type of stores at which they shopped.

Other Differences in the First Year

Some researchers have speculated that keeping diary records could sensitize households over time and make them better shoppers or more concerned about their behavior in other areas. Although this would be a benefit for the household, it would introduce new biases into trend comparisons. A continuing analysis of panel data, however, reveals no evidence of this form of conditioning. The data do not conclusively prove that there is no conditioning, but they indicate that any conditioning effects must be very small relative to real changes in the environment.

A panel study in the 1950s compared the buying behavior of a new group of panel households in their first four months of panel membership with the buying behavior of the existing panel. (The results of the study were reported in the discussion of differences between the first and second week of membership.) Looking at the total four-month period, there is no evidence of any change in total quantities purchased, in purchases from independent versus chain stores, in purchasing nationally advertised or chain brands, in average price paid per unit quantity of product, or in average package size.

A recent panel study showed the same stability with one exception. In each of the first three months of panel membership, the average household made 2.7 trips per week for grocery shopping. This figure dropped to 2.6 trips per week in each of months four through six. Although this difference is not significant by any of the usual statistical tests, it indicates that if there is any conditioning toward more efficient shopping, it is of the order of magnitude of approximately 4% or less.

The same results are reported by Ehrenberg (1959) for British consumer panels. Additional evidence that conditioning effects in panels are generally very small, if present at all, is given by Cordell and Rahmel (1962) of the ACNielsen Company. They give a comparison between homes that kept Nielsen diaries for several years and new random samples of households. Both groups were telephoned, and their viewing behavior at the time of the call was determined. There was a slight tendency for panel cooperators to watch more often than noncooperators because they were home more often. When adjustments are made for this tendency, there remains no indication of any conditioning effect. Table 6.4 shows these results.

To summarize the results of this section, users and operators of consumer panels need not fear short-term conditioning effects unless they do something deliberate to spotlight certain products or events. In this case, there will almost certainly be short-term effects that must be measured using the experimental procedures discussed in Chapter 5. Even these short-term effects will disappear after several months unless the stimulus is renewed.

Table 6.4
Percentage of Households at Home Using Television Among New Random Samples and Old Nielsen Panel Samples

Time	Old Nielsen Panel Households	New Random Sample Households
Total all hours	56.4%	56.2%
Total daytime hours	39.1%	38.3%
10–11 A.M.	33.4%	31.8%
2–3 P.M.	36.9%	38.4%
5–6 P.M.	45.5%	43.4%
Total nighttime hours	71.6%	71.7%
7–8 P.M.	67.1%	68.4%
8–9 P.M.	75.0%	75.5%
9–10 P.M.	72.8%	71.1%

The Long-Term Effects of Conditioning

The major concern with long-term effects is that panel households become fatigued and uninterested in the process of keeping diaries, so that the quality of reporting declines over long time periods. With online panels, an additional concern is attributed to the initial novelty that the Internet holds for some people. As the novelty decreases or when "the thrill is gone," the deliberateness and the quality of the responses might also decrease. Because of this concern with a decrease in quality, some panel operators routinely drop households after a specified time period. There is no evidence, however, to suggest that there are long-term conditioning effects. Consumer panels are continuously validated against outside data. There have been no noticeable drifts of panel data away from validation data over periods of several years.

In the long term, major changes occur at the household level and in market conditions, as follows:

1. At the household level—Household size, age of household members, income of household, geographic location, and many other demographic and nondemographic characteristics undergo major changes through time. These, of course, influence changes in purchase behavior.
2. In market conditions—Size and type of stores, sizes, brands, and prices of products, and even the kinds of products sold change.

The changing universe and panel sample make controlled experimentation difficult, but comparisons can be made between "old" and "new" people.

A classic study by Ehrenberg (1960) describes several studies of long-term conditioning in Europe. He points out that over a ten-year period, the Attwood Organization compared its reports with client shipments and, as in the United States, could discern no systematic drifts. He goes on to describe controlled experiments in the Netherlands and Great Britain.

The Attwood Consumer Panel of homemakers in the Netherlands had been running for more than three years when it was decided to increase the sample size. This operation provided an opportunity for comparing purchases recorded by "old" and "new" panel homemakers. Both the old and new panels were in other respects directly comparable, being random samples from the Dutch private household population.

At the same time, the Attwood Consumer Panel of homemakers in Great Britain, which had been running for almost ten years, was doubled in size. This provided an opportunity, similar to that in the Netherlands, of comparing purchases recorded by an old panel of homemakers, about half of whom had been panel members for more than five years, with a completely new panel.

Comparisons between the old and new panels were made in both the Netherlands and Great Britain for total purchases and brand shares. The results indicated the following:

1. There were no general systematic differences in the old panel results compared with the new ones.
2. Such differences as existed between the old and new results showed no trend of either increasing frequency of purchase of the product or increasing brand share.
3. The discrepancies between the old and new purchasing rates or brand shares were generally small. Most differences in amounts purchased were less than 5%, with some at about 10%, and only one or two still larger ones; few of the brand share differences were more than one or two percentage points.
4. The two sets of experimental results, from Holland and Great Britain, were in agreement.

Ehrenberg (1960) concluded that these findings confirm the impressions that for consumer panels of the kind described, the length of panel membership, even when stretching over many years, does not systematically affect the reported results. Any "conditioning" of the homemakers caused by having to record their purchases is likely to wear off or stabilize after a few weeks.

These results suggest that it is wasteful to drop cooperating panel households after some arbitrary time period. It is, however, necessary to add new household formations and drop dissolved households from the panel, as discussed in Chapter 3.

Summary

The results presented in this chapter are comforting to both panel operators and users of panel data. They indicate that general purpose panels covering a wide variety of products or topics are unlikely to have their trend results distorted by conditioning effects, at least after the initial period. It is possible to influence panel households by the use of special reminders, questionnaires, or diaries that concentrate on only a single item. Any such special stimuli should not be introduced into an ongoing panel without provisions for measuring the effects. Yet the impact of these special effects fade after several months, and panel reporting behavior returns to previous levels.

Chapter 7

Processing Data and Projecting Results

The big key to panels is developing a system. Once your back-end system is established (coding, file maintenance, and processing), things become efficient. You can then spend your energy digging up insights.

—Vice president of research at a Fortune *500 company with an in-house panel*

T he data are in!—4500 records and 212 variables. Processing panel data is complex and costly. Depending on the quantity of data processed, as well as the details required, the cost may substantially exceed the cost of data collection. This may be surprising to researchers whose previous experience has been with one-time surveys, for which the cost of data collection accounts for the majority of the total cost.

One advantage of panels is that whatever systems are developed can be used repeatedly over a wide range of applications. This means that efficient data-handling systems can be developed even if the start-up costs are high because these start-up costs can be amortized over time and clients. In the end, the costs of systems development charged to any single project are small.[1]

---

[1]Researchers developing a system to handle panel data for the first time should be cautioned that, inevitably, such systems require more person hours and cost more than initially anticipated. This is because initial estimates are almost always based on the volume of data expected (which can be reliably estimated), but they ignore the extensive work required to establish and maintain the records of household cooperation. Even the discussion here of what these files contain does not indicate the full range of contingencies that must be considered. Sensible budgeting must substantially allow for these unexpected contingencies.

As in other survey research applications, it is useful to separate (1) the coding and manual editing of the data from (2) the computer preparation and maintenance of files from (3) the use of these files to produce data. In this chapter, we describe procedures that are typically in current use to code and process data, and we show how the data that are received can be projected onto more general populations.

Coding Panel Data

Although it appears easy to cut costs on coding by using fast but inexperienced coders, this can often backfire because of additional verification costs. The coding of panel data is best done by experienced coders who code the same information period after period and become knowledgeable about any special data problems. A basic version of coding that simply asks panelists to identify the "last brand bought" for breakfast cereals is presented in Exhibit 7.1. It shows how even the most basic data can become increasingly complex to collect when additional variables (for example, size) are also requested.

When the data are complex, large and detailed codebooks that give all known possible answers should be prepared for the coders' use. These codebooks are generated by three methods. The first has the manufacturers that are clients of the panel companies provide information on their product types, brand names, sizes, and flavors, as well as some indication of the prices that are being charged at the retail level. A second method sends shoppers into a sample of retail stores to record the available brands, sizes, and prices. This would normally be done only when a new product category is introduced into the diary. The third method establishes codes on the basis of reports from panel households. Thus, brands, types, flavors, and prices that were reported by several households would be accepted as legitimate, and codes would be assigned.

After an initial codebook is established, it is revised and corrected by changes reported by the manufacturers and by data reported in the diaries of the panel households. Thus, when several households report the purchase of a new brand or type, it is evident that a new entry must be made in the codebook. Sometimes, all purchases will be concentrated in limited geographic areas, indicating that test marketing is underway. The appearance of these new products is in itself important marketing intelligence.

An example of the coding of coffee purchases by type, subtype, and brand is given in Table 7.1. Many of the details of the purchase may not

Exhibit 7.1
Coding the "Last Brand Bought" for Ready-to-Eat Cereals

↓

VV4XKT672-1A   ABOUT READY-TO-EAT CEREAL   1-9
                              (ANSWER THIS SIDE FIRST)

We are interested in your household's use of **cold, ready-to-eat cereal**.

A. **Write in the age and sex of EACH MEMBER of your household, including yourself.** Use a separate section for each family member. If you have more than 5 people in your household, list the oldest 5.

B. Indicate whether or not that person ate **any cold, ready-to-eat cereal in the PAST 7 DAYS**.

C. If "YES", **write in the 3-digit BRAND CODE of the cereal that person last had to eat** – that is, the brand eaten most recently by that person. *If you, the panel member, are not sure of the brand, please ask that person.*

> REFER TO THE BRAND LIST ON THE OPPOSITE SIDE; PLEASE REVIEW THE LIST CAREFULLY TO BE SURE YOU ARE RECORDING THE CORRECT BRAND CODE.

Household Member #1
A. Write in this person's age & indicate their sex: └──┴──┘ years; Male ☐ 1(16) Female ☐ 2

B. Did this person eat any cereal in the past 7 days?   Yes ☐ 1(17) →**Answer Qu. C**
                                                         No ☐ 2   →**Skip to Next Member**

C. Write in the 3-digit brand code of the cereal that person last had to eat.

   BRAND CODE (From List on Opposite Side): └──┴──┴──┘   (18-20)/ 80-2

Household Member #2
A. Write in this person's age & indicate their sex: └──┴──┘ years; Male ☐ 1(16) Female ☐ 2

B. Did this person eat any cereal in the past 7 days?   Yes ☐ 1(17) →**Answer Qu. C**
                                                         No ☐ 2   →**Skip to Next Member**

C. Write in the 3-digit brand code of the cereal that person last had to eat.

   BRAND CODE (From List on Opposite Side): └──┴──┴──┘   (18-20)/ 80-3

Household Member #3
A. Write in this person's age & indicate their sex: └──┴──┘ years; Male ☐ 1(16) Female ☐ 2

B. Did this person eat any cereal in the past 7 days?   Yes ☐ 1(17) →**Answer Qu. C**
                                                         No ☐ 2   →**Skip to Next Member**

C. Write in the 3-digit brand code of the cereal that person last had to eat.

   BRAND CODE (From List on Opposite Side): └──┴──┴──┘   (18-20)/ 80-4

Household Member #4
A. Write in this person's age & indicate their sex: └──┴──┘ years; Male ☐ 1(16) Female ☐ 2

B. Did this person eat any cereal in the past 7 days?   Yes ☐ 1(17) →**Answer Qu. C**
                                                         No ☐ 2   →**Skip to Next Member**

C. Write in the 3-digit brand code of the cereal that person last had to eat.

   BRAND CODE (From List on Opposite Side): └──┴──┴──┘   (18-20)/ 80-5

Household Member #5
A. Write in this person's age & indicate their sex: └──┴──┘ years; Male ☐ 1(16) Female ☐ 2

B. Did this person eat any cereal in the past 7 days?   Yes ☐ 1(17) →**Answer Qu. C**
                                                         No ☐ 2   →**Skip to Next Topic**

C. Write in the 3-digit brand code of the cereal that person last had to eat.

   BRAND CODE (From List on Opposite Side): └──┴──┴──┘   (18-20)/ 80-6

↓

PLEASE ANSWER BOTH SIDES

00040044 4301

00040044 430 0101 127

Exhibit 7.1
Continued

VV4XKT672-1B

ABOUT READY-TO-EAT CEREAL
(ANSWER OTHER SIDE FIRST)

BRAND CODE LIST FOR READY-TO-EAT CEREAL

GENERAL MILLS' CEREALS:
101 Apple Cinnamon Cheerios
102 Basic 4
103 Cheerios (Regular)
104 Cinnamon Toast Crunch
105 Cocoa Puffs
106 Cookie-Crisp
107 Corn Chex
108 Count Chocula

109 Fiber One
110 Frosted Cheerios
111 Golden Grahams
112 Honey Nut Cheerios
113 Honey Nut Chex
114 Honey Nut Clusters
115 Kix
116 Lucky Charms
117 Multi-Bran Chex
118 Multi-Grain Cheerios
119 Nestle Nesquik
120 Oatmeal Raisin Crisp (Raisin or Almond)

121 Raisin Nut Bran
122 Reese's Peanut Butter Puffs
123 Rice Chex
124 Team Cheerios
125 Total (Brown Sugar & Oat)
126 Total (Whole Grain)
127 Total (Raisin Bran)
128 Trix
129 Wheat Chex
130 Wheaties

KELLOGG'S CEREALS:
201 All-Bran
202 Apple Jacks
203 Cocoa Krispies
204 Complete Wheat Flakes
205 Corn Flakes (Kellogg's)
206 Corn Pops
207 Cracklin' Oat Bran
208 Crispix
209 Froot Loops
210 Frosted Flakes (Kellogg's)

211 Frosted Mini-Wheats
212 Healthy Choice
213 Honey Frosted Mini-Wheats
214 Honey Crunch Corn Flakes
215 Marshmallow Blasted Froot Loops
216 Pokemon
217 Raisin Bran (Kellogg's)
218 Raisin Bran Crunch (Kellogg's)
219 Rice Krispies (Kellogg's)
220 Smacks
221 Smart Start
222 Special K

OTHER BRANDS:
601 Kashi (any variety)
602 Sunbelt Grain
603 Your store's own brand
604 Some other brand not listed

MALT-O-MEAL CEREALS:
301 Berry Colossal Crunch
302 Cocoa Dyno-Bites
303 Coco-Roos
304 Corn Bursts
305 Frosted Mini-Spooners
306 Fruity Dyno-Bites
307 Golden Puffs
308 Honey Buzzers
309 Honey Nut Toasty O's
310 Marshmallow Mateys
311 Tootie Frooties

POST CEREALS:
401 100% Natural Bran
402 Alpha-Bits
403 Banana Nut Crunch
404 Blueberry Morning
405 Cinna-Cluster Raisin Bran
406 Cinna-Crunch Pebbles
407 Cocoa Pebbles
408 Cranberry Almond Crunch
409 Frosted Shredded Wheat (Post)
410 Fruit 'n Fibre

411 Fruity Pebbles
412 Golden Crisp
413 Grape-Nuts
414 Grape-Nuts Flakes
415 Grape-Nuts O's
416 Great Grains
417 Honey Bunches of Oats
418 Honey Nut Shredded Wheat
419 Honeycomb
420 Marshmallow Alpha-Bits

421 Oreo-O's
422 Premium Bran Flakes
423 Premium Raisin Bran (Post)
424 Shredded Wheat (large biscuit)
425 Shredded Wheat 'n Bran
426 Spoon-Size Shredded Wheat
427 Toasties
428 Waffle Crisp

QUAKER OATS CEREALS:
501 100% Natural
502 Cap'n Crunch
503 Cap'n Crunch Peanut Butter
504 Cap'n Crunch with Crunchberries
505 Cocoa Blasts
506 Frosted Shredded Wheat
507 Fruitangy Oh's
508 Honey Grahams
509 Honey Nut Oats

510 Life (Cinnamon)
511 Life (Plain)
512 Marshmallow Safari
513 Sweet Puffs
514 Toasted Oatmeal (Original)
515 Toasted Oatmeal (Honey Nut)
516 Toasted Oatmeal Squares

PLEASE ANSWER BOTH SIDES

need to be looked up because they are covered by the use of check boxes in the diary. While coding is in process, the coder will check the entry to see if the purchase details are correct (i.e., if the entry is found in the codebook). If not and the error is obvious, such as a mistake of one ounce in a size, the coder will make the correction.

Table 7.1
Category-Level Codes Used for Processing Coffee Data

DIARY CLASS 65—COFFEE

Type Codes

11	Regular coffee
12	Regular, Decaffeinated
13	—
14	Regular, Adulterated
15	Electric percolator
16	Filter rings, Electric percolator
17	Filter rings
18	Regular, Decaffeinated, Electric percolator
19	—
20	—
21	Instant coffee
22	Instant decaffeinated
23	Instant freeze dry
24	Instant, Decaffeinated, Freeze dry
25	Combination freeze dry and spray dry instant
26	Instant adulterated
27	Single serving, Freeze dry, Decaffeinated
28	Single serving, Instant, Decaffeinated
29	Single serving, Instant, Regular
46	Iced coffee, Black
47	Iced coffee, Black w/sugar
48	Iced coffee, Prelightened w/sugar
49	Iced coffee, Other flavor
60	Chocolate coffee

Subtype Codes

1	Glass jar
2	Tin
3	Bag
4	—
5	Aerosol
6	Special container–With additional cost
7	Special container–No additional cost
8	—
9	Other–box, Blister pack, Envelopes, etc.

It is not always possible to distinguish between a simple recording error and the introduction of a new product type or size. Single entries not in the codebook are almost always treated as errors unless corroborating information (such as a label) is obtained. Multiple entries by different respondents are either recorded as new products or checked with the manufacturer. This initial screening by the coder is only the start of a much more elaborate procedure during the computer processing.

As can be seen, the manual coding of data is currently a process that requires a large staff with considerable training and experience. Even so, random errors are not uncommon. The advent of UPC scanners has helped reduce some errors, and this is likely to reach another level of precision when households are given hand scanners or wands.

Preparing the Data File

The processing of panel data typically requires three major files: (1) purchase data files, (2) household cooperation files, and (3) household data files.

Purchase Data File

The purchase data file is based on the diary entries. Each entry forms a separate record in the file. These separate entries are then summarized over longer periods, such as one, three, six, and twelve months, to provide information by product class. The data record contains the following type of information:

- Household number,
- Date of purchase,
- Product class code,
- Type and subtype codes,
- Brand code,
- Units,
- Size or weight,
- Price paid,
- Deal code,
- Outlet,
- Who purchased,
- Intended user,
- Intended usage, and
- Projected purchase data (methods of projecting data are discussed later in the chapter).

Before data are summarized, a machine editing program examines each purchase for possible errors. Invalid codes are identified and corrected either manually or by a series of recoding statements. Thus, an error in the size of a brand due to either a coding or an entry error can be corrected by some machine rule that edits the entry to the nearest possible size entry or that identifies the entry for manual correction.

Prices paid can also be checked to see if the price is within the range reported by the manufacturer. If not and the price is not an obvious processing error, a decision must be made whether to accept the entry as given in the diary record or to contact the household to see if a mistake has been made. A common recording error is to give the correct price but confuse the package size. Some editing programs can electronically correct for package size in this case.

Household Cooperation File

It is necessary for many purposes to have a record of whether the household returned a diary for each time period. This record is used to determine the compensation that a household will receive for cooperating. This record is also used for panel maintenance. Households that become irregular in their diary returns must either be persuaded to resume regular reporting or be dropped from the panel and replaced. The most important use of this record is in conjunction with the data file. As an illustration, many analyses require that a family be classified as a heavy or light user of some product or service. In computing usage, it is necessary to consider the total number of diaries returned and either measure an average period usage per diary or project a total period usage by proportionately increasing the usage of households that have not returned all of their diary records.

For some analyses, such as measuring brand loyalty or switching, it is necessary to have a static sample in which all households have returned all of their diaries for the period being studied. This information is obtained from the household cooperation file. The file is updated each period by entering the records of all diaries received in that period as they arrive. This is done as a first step before the diary is coded for the purchase data file.

Household Data File

The household data file contains information about the characteristics of the household gathered from the periodic classification questionnaires. In addition to the household identification number, this file contains all the information required to sort the households into strata or cells for projection purposes. The following types of information are included:

- Geographic region,
- City size,
- Household size,
- Presence of children,
- Household income,
- Education of head and other household members,
- Age of head and other household members, and
- Employment status of household members.

Other variables, including home ownership, product ownership or usage, lifestyle characteristics, and media usage, are also available for use, along with the purchase data file. For efficiency, the most commonly used variables may be kept in a separate file so that the computer search costs are reduced. Other variables can be temporarily merged with this smaller file as needed.

Normally, characteristics such as household size and employment status are reclassified only on an annual basis for all households, though actual changes in household composition occur continuously. Changes in geographic location, however, are noted more frequently, either quarterly or monthly. This is necessary because of regional brands. Otherwise, for example, a Texan family that moved to Illinois would have its purchases of local Illinois products and store brands appearing among purchases in the South Central region.

Using Panel Data to Make Projections to General Populations

For virtually all of the uses discussed in Chapter 2, panel users want the sample results projected to the appropriate population totals. The simplest projection is merely to weight all panel households with the same weight w, where

$$w = \frac{\text{Total U.S. households}}{\text{Total panel households}}.$$

This simple weighting procedure is virtually never used in reality. Instead, more complex procedures are used for two reasons: (1) to reduce variability from period to period caused by missing diaries and (2) to reduce the effects of sample biases discussed in Chapter 3. Period-to-period variability in the fraction of diaries returned is related to seasonal factors. Thus, during the summer, the number of diaries returned drops because of households that are on vacation. During the Christmas mail rush, there are always cases of diaries mailed but lost or substantially delayed in the mail.

This variability in diary returns introduces variability into the data and can mask small but important seasonal changes. It may also be concentrated in certain geographic areas, particularly if a regional mail center gets jammed and falls behind. For these reasons, most projection systems are sorted into cells or strata, and a factor is computed on the basis of the ratio of the estimated number of U.S. households in that cell to the number of actual diaries returned in the period. This procedure eliminates variability in the data caused by variability in the diary returns.

Additional variables are used in projection systems to account for longer-term sample biases. These variables may differ from product to product depending on the correlations between product purchasing and product characteristics. Household size and income are two variables frequently included in projection systems because they are highly related to purchase behavior and because sample biases frequently occur in these variables, as seen in Chapter 3. The more detailed the projection system, the greater is its potential power to reduce sample biases. Some panel organizations use projection systems with several hundred strata, including age, sex, education, income, race/ethnicity, and geographic region.

When dealing with online data, there are methods that can be used to generalize to a larger population that includes nonusers of the Internet. The CHAID method for accomplishing this involves measuring and weighing data on the basis of people's e-mail use, frequency of Internet use, whether they have accessibility from home, their knowledge of English, their computer literacy, the year they first used the Internet, and their age and gender.

Unfortunately, there are limits to the power of projection systems to improve the accuracy of panel data. If too many cells are used, the weights for different households can have a wide range, and this can substantially increase the sampling variability of the weighted results. Stated differently, large differences in weights greatly reduce the efficiency of the sample. As an illustration, if there are a few families that are heavy buyers of a product and have large projection factors, and if a mail delay causes the diaries of these families to be received too late for one period so that they are included in the file for the subsequent period, then the data will show a period-to-period change that is merely the result of the late diaries. Thus, the requirement for a projection system to smooth out variability caused by irregular returns of diaries is to some degree in opposition to the requirement for a projection system to correct for long-term sample biases.

A simple example may help illustrate how projection systems are constructed and how variability may result. Table 7.2 considers three cells from a national panel and gives the number of households returning diaries in two successive periods. The estimated U.S. households for these cells are also given. Note that these estimates do not change during this short time interval. The projection factor w_i is found as before, except that there is a different factor for each cell:

$$w_i = \frac{\text{Total U.S. households in cell}_i}{\text{Total panel households in cell}_i} .$$

It may be that the factors change over the two periods because the number of diaries returned varies. Table 7.3 shows the raw and projected purchases of a product in the two periods. To illustrate the effects of the

Table 7.2
Example of Projection Factor Computation in Two Periods (hypothetical data)

	Period 1			Period 2		
Cell	Panel Households	U.S. Households	w_i	Panel Households	U.S. Households	w_i
1	58	700,000	12,069	63	700,000	11,111
2	55	500,000	9,091	50	500,000	10,000
3	50	1,000,000	20,000	60	1,000,000	16,667

Table 7.3
Example of Data Projection in Two Periods (hypothetical data)

	Period 1		Period 2	
Cell	Raw Units	Projected Total	Raw Units	Projected Total
1	200	2,413,800	200	2,222,200
2	240	2,181,840	240	2,400,000
3	220	4,400,000	220	3,666,740
Total	660	8,995,640	660	8,288,940

projection factor, the number of raw units is assumed to be the same in each period. Note, however, that the projected totals differ. In general, the variability in the factors and in the projected data will increase between periods as the number of cells increases and the average number of households in a cell decreases. For this reason, there is no single system used by all panels; even within the same panel, different systems are used for different products. Alternative systems are tested on long series of back data before a decision is finally made to adopt a projection system for a given product.

When a projection system is adopted, estimates of universe values for each cell must be prepared and maintained on a continuing basis. These estimates are initially obtained from either published U.S. census data or specially prepared census data.

Updating may be done at intervals, such as every three months or for each period, by interpolating estimated changes in universe totals. Except for changes in the total number of U.S. households, detailed changes in cell totals are currently limited to two consecutive decennial censuses. Some revision of universe estimates is possible based on the results of the current population surveys. If the estimates of universe totals are subject to substantial error or uncertainty in the updating of a variable, that variable will normally not be used in a projection system. In the future, the new five-year Census of Population and Housing will make these universe estimates even more timely.

When the universe estimates have been computed for each cell of a projection system, the diaries received in a given period are sorted into their appropriate cells, and the factor for a given projection system is then computed. The data in the purchase data file are multiplied by the appropriate projection factors to produce projected data. In this way, the sample data can be projected onto a universe that is familiar to whomever will be using the data. This allows direct comparisons between the panel survey results and those of independent sources such as ACNielsen, Information Resources Inc., or point-of-sale data. These data are then used in the preparation of continuing reports.

Preparing the Report

Because report formats vary so widely by panel operator and client, little can be said about this process in general. There is, however, one fact that all processors of panel data soon realize: The major need is for computers with the speed and capacity to input and output very rapidly. The actual computations within the computer are relatively simple, and the speed of these computations is less critical. Although the same thing may be said about large, one-time surveys, it is even more essential for continuing panel operations.

For many routine reports, the computer can provide instant client input or output that is camera-ready to transmit. This not only saves money but also reduces possible typing errors in report preparation and gets the report into the client's hands faster. It is worthwhile to spend a good deal of time programming the computer so that the formats will be most easily understood, because again this programming effort is spread over many products and clients.

The challenge is to provide complex findings in a clear, user-friendly manner. This is a problem for many people who have become highly familiar with data analysis. What is intuitively obvious to them may not be obvious or even understandable to people in various layers of the firms with whom they are dealing.

A vivid illustration of this can be found in the context of a company that was losing business-to-business clients because of "poor service." Surprisingly, this company led the industry in terms of accuracy, response time, analysis, and customer support, all conventional measures. A costly quality improvement program was instituted. What was found was that the dissatisfaction that clients had with the company's service was not because of the quality of its nearly impeccable work, but because of the way it reported the data and formatted the final report. Because the reports were not intuitively clear to the different people in different layers of the organization, it was assumed the data were bad, the analysts were sloppy, and the company did not care.

Summary

The need for systematized algorithms to help with data analysis has brought tremendous benefits to panel research. There have been several standardized methods for classifying, coding, analyzing, and interpreting data at impressive speeds and efficiency. There are also many useful methods to project these results onto a general population. The more important the accuracy needed for these projections, the more important it will be to use multiple methods to triangulate onto consistent estimates.

This chapter ends with a cautionary note. Although systematized algorithms have brought speed and efficiency to panel research, they have not brought a heightened sense of understanding of what the results mean or what the next, more meaningful level of questions should be. A "here you are means and cross-tabs" approach to data analysis does not leverage the tremendous value and opportunities of panel research. Although understanding the "whys" behind consumer behavior has helped push market leaders ahead of their competition, it is doubtful whether the standard means and cross-tabs package was what generated the answers to these questions.

Chapter 8

The Costs of Operating a Panel

What we are interested in knowing is how the usage of various OTCs [over-the-counter drugs] changes as different segments of people age. What would this cost us to bring it in-house?
—*Vice president of marketing (pharmaceuticals company)*

ow often do you have to use a consumer panel before it becomes more cost effective to bring it in-house? This chapter specifies the types of costs related to operating a consumer panel and, when information is available, the magnitude of these costs. This magnitude depends on the panel organization, the method, and the time period involved. Aside from information on compensation policies, actual cost data are primarily available from academic operators of panels. Nevertheless, even the limited data available are sufficient to make it obvious that consumer panels, especially offline panels, are generally far more expensive to operate than are one-time surveys with the same number of households. When the cost per unit of information over time is examined, however, the cost comparison reverses sharply in favor of the panel. The final section of this chapter presents a comparison of costs for panels versus alternative procedures.

Panel operating costs may be split among costs directly related to data collection, costs of data processing and file maintenance, and costs of report preparation and analysis. The next three sections consider each of these cost components separately. Not included in this discussion are overhead costs and profit contributions. These need to be added to the direct costs to obtain an estimate of the total cost of purchasing a panel service. As a first approximation, one might double the direct costs to estimate the total cost. The costs shown here will change with price levels but can be adjusted by the use of the Consumer Price Index.

Cost Components of Data Collection

Before data collection can begin, substantial setup costs are required to establish a panel. These are the costs of recruiting and training panel households associated with the procedures discussed in Chapter 4. There will be great differences in costs depending on whether recruiting is conducted face-to-face, online, over the telephone, or by mail. We therefore discuss these four methods separately. For this discussion, it is assumed that the organization already has or can hire a field force of experienced interviewers. If it is necessary to recruit, train, and maintain a totally new field force, substantial additional costs will be involved. Depending on location and number of interviewers hired, each new interviewer might cost hundreds of dollars.

For comparison purposes, costs in this chapter are given per thousand households. Fixed costs that do not depend on sample size are shown separately, but it should be remembered that the relative importance of these fixed costs on total cost varies as the panel size is increased or decreased. Interviewer salaries are estimated at $12.00 per hour and car expenses at the rate of $.35 per mile. Field supervisor salaries are assumed to average $65,000 per year. As wages and salaries change over time, these cost estimates will need to be adjusted accordingly.

Setup Costs for Panels Recruited Face-to-Face

To recruit 1000 households with a reasonable balance of characteristics, it is necessary to either start with a much larger number or replace households that drop out. The interviewing costs of both alternatives are identical, but other costs will vary. A key factor in computing interviewing costs is the expected cooperation rate of respondents. For estimating the costs of face-to-face recruiting, we assume an initial cooperation rate of 60% in the setup period. This rate is not independent of the methods used and the costs of other aspects of recruiting. Thus, reducing compensation costs will also reduce the cooperation rate and increase the interviewer and total recruiting costs.

It might at first appear that to obtain 1000 households, we would need to start with 1000/.6 or 1667 households. This initial sample is insufficient because the probability of refusal is not evenly distributed over all household types. To ensure, for example, that enough small, young households are recruited, it is necessary to start with an even larger over-sample. This can be shown by assuming that the general population consists of four equal sized strata with the following cooperation rates:

Stratum	Cooperation Rate	Sample Required	Initial Sample
1	90	250	277
2	70	250	357
3	50	250	500
4	30	<u>250</u>	<u>833</u>
		1000	1967

Thus, although the overall cooperation rate is 60%, it is necessary to start with an initial sample approximately double that ultimately required. If the initial cooperation is 50%, the initial sample will need to be 2.5 times the final sample size.

The costs for recruiting and training households are based on studies conducted by the Survey Research Laboratory at the University of Illinois (Sudman and Ferber 1974; Sudman, Wilson, and Ferber 1976). Because these were state and local panels, supervisor salaries and expenses may be low relative to a national panel.

Table 8.1 gives the estimated costs of recruiting and training panel households face-to-face based on data from these panels. The data

Table 8.1
Direct Interviewer Costs for Face-to-Face Recruiting and Training 1000 Panel Households

Cost	Hours/Case	Cases	Pay Rate	Total
Initial Call				
Interviewing	1	2000	$12.00	$ 24,000
Travel	1	2000	$12.00	$ 24,000
Editing and clerical	.5	2000	$12.00	$ 12,000
Mileage	30 miles	2000	$ .35	<u>$ 21,000</u>
				$ 81,000
Retraining Call				
Interviewing	1	1500	$12.00	$ 18,000
Travel	.75	1500	$12.00	$ 13,500
Editing and clerical	.25	1500	$12.00	$ 4,500
Mileage	25 miles	1500	$ .35	<u>$ 13,125</u>
				$ 49,125
Interviewer training	20	25 inter-viewers	$12.00	$ 6,000
Total direct interviewer costs				$136,125

assume that the initial contact consists of a long interview during which demographic and other information is obtained before the household is recruited and trained to keep diary records. A second, shorter interview is included, during which retraining occurs and motivation to cooperate is reinforced. If this second interview is excluded, costs are lowered but so is cooperation. Note, however, that the retraining interview is conducted only with households that have indicated some initial willingness to cooperate. For Table 8.1, reinterviews are assumed for 75% of the households contacted initially.

Direct interviewer costs for recruiting and training total $136,125, or a little more than $136 per household. Other direct costs of recruiting and training a panel are presented in Table 8.2. These include the costs of field supervisors, field office staff, materials, sampling, and initial compensation for cooperating households. These costs are more difficult to estimate precisely because they depend on administrative decisions. Nevertheless, the estimate of $212,000 for other direct expenses seems to agree with the experience of field organizations that direct interviewer costs are roughly one-third of total field costs, including field overhead.

Table 8.2
Other Direct Costs for Face-to-Face Recruiting and Training 1000 Panel Households

Cost	Number	Rate	Total
Personnel			
Supervisory salaries	1 person	$65,000/year	$ 65,000
Supervisory travel	20 trips	$ 800/trip	$ 16,000
Field office staff	2 persons	$24,000/year	$ 48,000
Panel maintenance staff	2 persons	$24,000/year	$ 48,000
			$177,000
Materials			
Printing			$ 5,000
Machines			$ 2,000
Office supplies			$ 3,000
Postage			$ 4,000
			$14,000
Sampling			$ 6,000
Initial compensation	1500 households	$10.00/household	$ 15,000
Total other costs			$212,000
Total direct interviewer costs			$136,125
Total cost			$348,125

Combining direct interviewer costs and other direct costs gives an estimate of $348,125 per thousand cases, or about $348 per case. (Adding overhead and profit contributions to this figure would probably at least double it, so the total cost to the users of setting up a national panel of 1000 households using face-to-face procedures would be about $700,000.)

Setup Costs for Panels Recruited by Telephone

It is less expensive to make contact by telephone than face-to-face, but the final cooperation rate for telephone procedures is lower than that obtained from face-to-face contacts. For Table 8.3, which estimates the costs of recruiting 1000 panel households by telephone, we estimate that the initial cooperation rate will be 45%, which is .75 the cooperation rate on face-to-face recruiting. This means that a sample of about 2700 is needed to obtain 1000 households.

Telephone procedures eliminate travel expenses but substitute telephone charges. An organization recruiting a panel would almost certainly use WATS lines in the United States. In the cost estimates of Table 8.3, a charge of $2,500 per month per WATS line has been

Table 8.3
Direct Interviewer Costs for Telephone Recruiting and Training 1000 Panel Households

Cost	Hours/Case	Cases	Pay Rate	Total
Initial Call				
Interviewing	.75	2600	$12.00	$ 23,400
Calling	.25	2600	$12.00	$ 7,800
Editing and clerical	.25	2600	$12.00	$ 7,800
Phone charges (WATS line)	150 cases/mo.		$2,500/mo.	$ 16,750
				$ 55,750
Retraining calls (2)				
Interviewing	.75	1500	$12.00	$ 13,500
Calling	.5	1500	$12.00	$ 9,000
Editing and clerical	.5	1500	$12.00	$ 9,000
Phone charges (WATS line)	150 cases/mo.		$2,500/mo.	$ 16,750
				$ 48,250
Interviewer training				$ 6,000
Total direct interviewer costs				$110,000
Total other costs				$196,000
Total cost				$306,000

assumed. This might be too high for organizations that already have WATS lines that are not being used to their full capacity. Comparing the telephone charges in Table 8.3 with travel expenses in Table 8.1, there is only a small saving obtained by using telephone procedures.

In total, the direct interviewer costs using telephone procedures are $110 per case, compared with $136.13 for the face-to-face procedures. This is a saving of 19%, which may be less than might have been expected before doing a detailed analysis. Among other direct costs, the only saving for telephone procedures is the money spent on supervisory travel. Subtracting this $16,000 from the total of $212,000 in Table 8.2 yields the estimate of $196,000 in Table 8.3. The total direct cost of telephone procedures is $306 per case compared with a total of $348 for face-to-face procedures. Thus, overall, telephone procedures are approximately 12% cheaper than face-to-face procedures.

Setup Costs for Panels Recruited Through the Mail

Ignoring the possibility of very large sample biases, the costs of establishing panels by mail are considerably lower than the costs of face-to-face or telephone methods. The cost estimates presented in Table 8.4

Table 8.4
Costs of Mail Procedure for Recruiting and Training 1000 Panel Households

Cost	Number	Rate	Total
Postage (1st class)			
Initial mailing out	25,000	$.34	$ 8,500
Initial return	2500	$.21	$ 525
Follow-up mailing out	2 × 1500	$.34	$ 1,020
Follow-up mailing return	2 × 1500	$.21	$ 630
			$ 10,675
Personnel			$ 72,000
Materials			
Printing			$ 10,000
Machines			$ 2,000
Office supplies			$ 6,000
			$ 18,000
Sampling			$ 8,000
Initial Compensation	1500	$10.00	$ 15,000
Total Cost			$123,675

assume that to achieve a balanced sample of 1000 households, an initial mailing of 25,000 will be required. Although interviewer costs, travel expenses, and supervision are eliminated, there is a major increase in the cost of postage.

It is assumed that all mail is sent first class to ensure prompt delivery. Bulk mailing costs would be lower but require more time. It is also assumed that there will be two follow-up mailings to those households that respond and are retained in the balanced sample. It is also assumed that postage rates are as given.

Based on these assumptions, the postage charges are approximately $10,675 per 1000 households. The other cost figures are obtained by eliminating the cost of interviewers and supervisors from Table 8.2. The panel maintenance costs are still required, as is an additional person to handle the large volume of mailings. Printing and office supply costs are also double to reflect the larger mailings and the need for better designed and better printed mailing material. Sampling costs are increased slightly because a much larger sample is used; it is assumed that the names will be purchased from a mailing list provider.

Total direct costs for mail procedures are estimated at about $123 per case, slightly more than 35% of the cost per case of face-to-face recruiting and slightly more than 40% of the cost of telephone recruiting. Even lower costs are possible if the initial compensation cost of $15,000 is omitted and if the mailing is contracted to a firm that specializes in large-scale mailings. The latter could reduce personnel costs by $15,000 or more. The total direct costs for mail procedures would then be about $93 per case.

Setup Costs for Panels Recruited Online

The cost to design a good panel survey is the same regardless of the method of transmission, but Internet surveys have been found to be less expensive to execute. The most expensive part of any study is data collection, because it includes the cost to screen the target customer and to ask carefully crafted questions (either on the phone or in person).

The specific setup costs for online panels vary dramatically and are difficult to assess. If, however, we examine the costs compared with the size of the panel, one generalization is that they follow an S-shaped curve. That is, for small panels, the operation costs are typically low. This is because the largest costs are variable costs and labor. However, as the size of the panel grows, so too do hardware and programming needs. At some point, larger scale investments must occur, and this dramatically raises the costs for medium-sized panel operations. After these investments are made, however, the incremental cost of increasing the size of a panel is relatively small, and the per-panelist costs begin to decline.

At that point, it becomes economical for an online panel to quickly reach 2000–10,000 panelists. As a result, some of the newer online panel companies claim they can provide an online panel for 20% to 80% of the cost of an offline mail panel. This cost effectiveness is the result of several things. Travel, lodging, and facility costs are all eliminated. There is no huge difference between a survey of 10 and a survey of 10,000 when it takes place on the Web. Internet-based surveys are particularly cost effective for large samples and may also be so for discontinuous panels.

One perhaps surprising source of cost savings for online panels is labor costs associated with interviewing and coding. Whereas the time savings is not surprising, the real savings might be in accuracy. Interviewers can make errors due to a lack of interest, familiarity, or concern. Enough of these errors could invalidate a survey. Furthermore, interviewers can also inadvertently express their personal bias and affect results because of mood swings, a dislike of the subject matter, or dislike of the panelist. The interviewer for Web-based surveys is always the same. The interviewer never gets tired, moody, impatient, or opinionated, nor does it ever express any prejudice. Under these circumstances, the resulting data are therefore "cleaner" and require less editing. This also results in cost savings.

Although there are various cost savings associated with online panels, there are three major costs: (1) the cost of the technology, (2) the cost of securing the site, and (3) the cost of hosting the Web. The cost of the technology includes not only the hardware, but also the application agency that is used. These application agencies perform many different business processes and are essentially the business consultants of the Internet industry.

Securing the site becomes costly because of the issues related to the security of the data. Some companies are using the same technology used by financial sites, called a secure socket layer, to secure their survey Web sites. Others are erecting fire walls to prevent hackers from illegally obtaining demographic or survey information or e-mail addresses. Another issue that is arising is the potential costs that may soon come with "malpractice" insurance to protect companies from litigation from consumers who believe their data have been mishandled (i.e., sold to another) or their privacy has been somehow breached. Although this insurance is available, it has not yet become commonly purchased.

Finally, the cost of hosting the Web site can be considerable. Aside from the hardware, the software and programming required to host the site can be prohibitive for anyone other than very large panel organizations. Many marketing research companies outsource the hosting of the survey site and, when applicable, the panel population site.

Continuing Costs of Panel Data Collection

The need to maintain the infrastructure of the panel community is critical. Even with online panels, it is estimated that 30% of staffing costs relate to panel management issues. These issues include making sure that panelists are happy, deciding which panelists will be solicited and when, and ensuring that e-mail addresses are up to date.

To illustrate the continuing costs of panel data collection, we use mail surveys because there is more accurate data available for them and because of their prevalence. In addition, the principles here can be easily appropriated to the other contexts, including specialized panels and panels of professionals such as physicians.[1] Table 8.5 gives the cost components and estimated costs of data collection for an established panel of 1000 households. It is assumed that diaries are printed quarterly, mailed to the panel households monthly, and returned weekly. It is also assumed that approximately 90% of all diaries will be returned, so that return postage will be paid on (1000) (.9) (52), or 46,800 diaries. An average compensation of $100 per year is also assumed, based on the results of Chapter 4.

Even in an established panel, approximately 20% of all households may need to be replaced every year because of dropouts and household dissolutions. The costs of replacing these households will vary depending on the replacement procedure used. For estimating costs, it is assumed that about a 10% reduction in the unit costs seen in Tables 8.1–8.3 of face-to-face and telephone procedures would be obtained because of the elimination of setup and interviewer training costs. Unit mail costs, however, would remain as in Table 8.4.

---

[1]Creating and maintaining physician panels or other professional panels is more costly than consumer panels. People in these panels are more sensitive to the length of the survey. To maintain high cooperation rates, it is important to ensure that these surveys are not complicated and that they can be completed within 20 minutes. Recruitment tends to occur through partnerships with affiliated Web sites. When recruited on the Web, these panels tend to be opt-in panels. Because it is so costly to create professional panels, care is taken to keep attrition rates low. All names and addresses are verified. Any bouncebacks are immediately followed up on. Response rates range from 25% to 33% but tend to be very fast. Thirty-three percent of the total responses needed often are filled within four to five hours of the survey being sent out. Most surveys are closed within two to three days because the required number of responses have been sent in.

Depending on the replacement procedure used, the cost of data collection activities per panel household ranges from about $100 to $88 per year. This is slightly lower than the initial setup costs. Note, however, that the differences between procedures have only a relatively small effect on continuing costs, though they have a much larger effect on setup costs.

Costs of Data Processing and File Maintenance

The costs of coding, editing, and cleaning the data and preparing data files are a function of the amount of data processed. For the estimates given here, we assume weekly diaries for about 50 different product groups with an average of about 20 entries per diary. The costs of coding and processing are based on recent studies on food-related behaviors by the Food and Brand Lab at the University of Illinois. Long-term costs

Table 8.5
Continuing Annual Costs of Panel Data Collection for Panels of 1000 Households

Item	Number	Rate	Total
Diaries and mailings			
Printing	4 quarters	$2,500/quarter	$ 10,000
Postage mailing out	12,000	$.34	$ 4,080
Postage return	46,800	$.21	$ 9,828
Office supplies			$ 6,000
Mailing staff	2	$24,000	$ 48,000
			$ 77,908
Panel maintenance			
Office staff	2	$24,000	$ 48,000
Compensation	1000	$100/year	$100,000
			$148,000
Total cost (excluding replacements)			$225,320
Field replacement	200		
Personal	115/case		$ 23,000
Phone	95/case		$ 19,000
Mail	54/case		$ 10,800
Total Cost (with replacements)			
Personal			$248,320
Phone			$244,320
Mail			$236,120

of panel operators may be lower than these costs because more efficient procedures can be developed over a longer time period.

It may be seen that the costs of data processing and file maintenance given in Table 8.6 substantially exceed the continuing costs of data collection. The total cost of more than $980,000 is nearly four times the cost of data collection. The cost per individual product group spread over 50 groups is much smaller, but similarly, the costs of setting up a panel and the costs of data collection are much smaller when spread over all products.

The single largest cost of processing is the coding of the diary. We estimate that one diary can be coded per hour. The food-related diary mentioned previously contained about 226 entries and took about 12 minutes to code. This time could probably be reduced as coders became more experienced. Coding costs are, of course, directly related to the number of items processed. A diary with fewer entries would take proportionately less time.

Table 8.6
Annual Costs of Data Processing and File Maintenance for Panels of 1000 Households and 20 Entries Per Diary

Item	Number	Rate	Total
Coding			
Supervisor	1	$60,000/yr.	$ 60,000
Coders	1 diary/hr.	$12.00/hr.	$561,160
			$621,160
Data entry (keypunch)			
Staff	5 diaries/hr.	$12.00	$112,200
Machines			$ 10,000
Material			$ 3,000
			$125,200
Cleaning and editing			
Staff and machines	52 weeks	$1,150/wk.	$ 59,800
Control			
Staff and machines	52 weeks	$1,250/wk.	$ 65,000
File maintenance			
Supervisor			$ 65,000
Staff			$ 45,000
			$110,000
Total Cost			$981,160

Costs of keypunch or data entry are based on a processing rate of five diaries per hour. Cleaning and editing and control costs are estimated on the basis of weekly costs. Note that data entry, cleaning, and control all cost approximately the same amount. Not all computer expenses are included here. Additional computer costs related to report preparation are given in the next section.

The magnitude of the costs of data processing and file maintenance highlights the value of developing efficient processing systems. The repetitive nature of the tasks makes it possible to improve procedures, and the results here suggest that large cost savings are possible.

Costs of Report Preparation and Analysis

The major costs of report preparation and analysis are the salaries of the analysis staff. In most panel organizations, the senior analysts are also involved in the selling of panel services. In Table 8.7, which gives estimates of the costs of report preparation and analysis, it is assumed that the analysis staff consists of two senior and two junior analysts. This is a fairly arbitrary assumption, because the actual number of analysts will depend on the number of products and clients and on the kinds of analysis required by the client.

Computer staff requirements are assumed to be about the same as those for file maintenance. Report production and chart preparation are assumed to cost about $1,000 each per month.

Table 8.7
Annual Costs of Report Preparation and Analysis

Item	Cost
Analysis staff	
2 senior analysts	$140,000
2 junior analysts	$ 80,000
2 administrative assistants	$ 60,000
	$280,000
Computer staff	$ 80,000
Reports and charts	
Report reproduction	$ 12,000
Chart preparation	$ 12,000
	$ 24,000
Total cost	$384,000

Comparisons of these report preparation and analysis costs with the other panel costs must take into account that these costs do not depend on the sample size of the panel, whereas the costs in the previous tables do. Thus, although the costs of analysis are greater than the costs of data collection for a panel of 1000 households, the costs of data collection would be greater than the costs of analysis for panels of more than 2000 households.

The Cost of Consumer Panels Relative to Alternatives

Table 8.8 summarizes the continuing costs of panel operation for panels with sample sizes of 1000 and 5000. Analysis costs are assumed not to change. Data collection costs are proportional to sample size. Data processing costs are also assumed to be proportional except for file maintenance costs, which are assumed to be fixed. Here, data processing costs continue to account for the largest fraction of the total cost. Therefore, a large national panel is a multimillion dollar operation, and the cost per panel household is hundreds of dollars per year.

In many cases, the cost estimates given in this chapter are based on some fairly broad assumptions; the actual costs of individual panel operators may vary significantly from the detailed figures given here. In total, however, these results appear to reflect real-world costs. It should be evident that large national panels are economical only when the costs can be spread over many different products.

We turn now to a comparison of panel costs with those of one-time surveys that collect the same amount of information. For the purposes of this comparison, we shall assume a face-to-face interview of 1000 house-

Table 8.8
Summary of Annual Panel Costs for Panels of 1000 and 5000 Households

Cost	Panel Size	
	1000	**5000**
Data collection	$ 250,000	$1,250,000
Data processing	$ 981,160	$4,905,800
Analysis	$ 384,000	$ 384,000
Total cost	$1,615,160	$6,539,800
Cost per case	$ 1,615	$ 1,308

holds lasting about an hour and costing about $136,000 per study. In this interview, households are asked about their purchases in the past week or month or their most recent purchase. We ignore the very large problems of error in recall surveys, which are discussed in Chapter 5. For this comparison, we also ignore the relative sampling error advantages between panel and one-time surveys that depend on whether the researcher is interested in measuring levels or trends.

We cannot ignore, however, differences in the amount of information that can be obtained from the two procedures. Conservatively, an average diary contains about as much detailed information as could be obtained in an interview. Thus, four weekly diaries contain up to four times the amount of information that could be obtained in a single interview, though some of the information may be repetitive. (The single interview could cover only a limited number of products in any detail, or it could cover more products if only limited purchase data were required.)

Summary

To summarize, on an annual basis, we would need to conduct 52 weekly surveys to obtain the same information that could be obtained from a continuing panel. These 52 independent samples would cost $7.1 million, or more than four times the cost shown in Table 8.8 for panels. Of course, no panel user would be interested in all products covered in a panel diary. This is the reason that panels provide syndicated services.

There are important uses of one-time surveys to obtain information that cannot be obtained from a continuing purchase panel. If the researcher is interested in continuing consumer expenditures, however, panels are by far the most cost efficient procedure yet developed.

Chapter 9

Choosing a Consumer Panel Service

Any recommendations?
—Various brand managers and marketing research directors

G iven the widespread use of consumer panel techniques in marketing, nearly every marketing executive or researcher concerned
with consumer goods will need to consider at one time or another
how to use this technique in his or her work. Choosing a consumer panel
service then becomes of considerable importance, because it is far
cheaper to "buy into" an ongoing consumer panel than to set up a separate panel for one's own use. Although the latter procedure guarantees
confidentiality and exclusive control, it also entails large expenditures, as
well as the necessity of recruiting a special staff, which very few manufacturers or retailers care to incur.

It therefore seems appropriate to outline the principal factors that
should be kept in mind in selecting a consumer panel service. Moreover,
considering such questions as how to determine the most suitable consumer panel for a particular purpose and how to evaluate the relative
merits of panels also helps integrate much of the material covered in the
preceding chapters.

Twelve Points in Choosing a Panel Service

Although the principal points to consider in selecting a consumer panel
service vary to some extent with the type of product and the problems to
be solved, certain basic factors are applicable to all types of panels,

including continuous purchase panels, product-testing panels, copy-testing panels, and others. These factors are brought out in this chapter in the form of a series of 12 points that should be followed in considering a consumer panel service. It should be noted that all of these points relate to the objectives and the technical aspects of the panels, not to the cost. This is because trying to save some out-of-pocket costs, and thus running the risk of getting highly unreliable information, is a case of being penny-wise and pound-foolish. In using consumer panel information—regardless of whether it is collected online or offline—the objective should be either to obtain appropriately reliable information for the problem or not to spend any money at all.

1. Ask "How Could These Results Possibly Change What I Would Do?"

Our training as researchers and as businesspeople has always led us to believe that when it comes to data, more is better. Although it is not surprising that data come at a cost, data are most valuable when they inform a decision. Suppose we are trying to find out how people shop. If the range of possible outcomes of this research will not alter any decision we will make, the research should not be done. Unfortunately, much nondiagnostic research is conducted every day. It usually begins with someone saying, "Wouldn't it be interesting to know…." The problem is that when the resulting cross tabs, bar chart, or pie chart is presented, part of that year's research budget is gone, and managers are not any wiser than they were before the research.

One way to avoid this is to proactively specify a wide, discrete set of findings or outcomes that could occur if the research was done. For each of these outcomes, write down what the resulting managerial action would be. If the managerial actions (or responses) are the same for each of the outcomes, there is no need to do the research. If there is a wide variation of what your managerial response would be, this exercise will probably also suggest additional questions you will want to ask.

2. Choose Either Static or Dynamic Panels

Having a panel composed of the same consumer units or individuals throughout a given period makes a static panel especially useful for evaluating the effects of advertising or other stimuli. By providing before-and-after purchase records for the identical panel members, a static panel helps keep extraneous factors constant and brings out more clearly the effects of any experimental treatments used.

If, however, panel data will serve as a basis for making generalizations about the market, a dynamic sample is necessary. Such a panel will provide for rotation of the consumer units so that the distribution of its members is kept in line with current shifts in population characteristics. Such a rotation pattern should occur on a staggered basis and should allow for estimates to be made of the population based on the composite results of both the old and the new segments of the panel. In choosing between these two types of panels, it is useful to keep in mind that it is always possible to incorporate a static panel within a dynamic panel, but the reverse is not possible.

3. Does this Panel Really Sample the Population I Want?

Each method of obtaining panel research information has its benefits, and each has its self-selection biases. The crucial concern with online panels is that it is presently the least favorable choice for research in terms of accuracy, according to a president of a large online research firm. There is a concern that online panels tend to be psychographically biased toward progressive technology innovators and demographically biased toward younger, male professionals. For many situations, this population does not represent the ideal sample. For example, many consumer packaged goods and other grocery store purchases are not likely to be fairly represented by a sample of online panelists.

Yet the representativeness of online panels to the general population of consumers is only important if we are actually interested in the general population of consumers. There are situations in which the population of interest—for example, people who purchase on the Internet—may be best captured by an online panel. Whereas packaged goods and grocery purchases may not be accurately represented by a sample from an online panel, items that can easily be bought using the Internet—books, compact discs, airline tickets, magazine subscriptions, home banking, investment services, and software—are probably good candidates for online consumer panels.

Despite biases related to the general population, there are subgroups within the population that may be better represented through the Internet than through other methods. Teenagers, for example, have been an elusive group with respect to consumer panels prior to online consumer panels. In addition, these panels can represent subsets of consumers who are single, affluent, and well-educated audiences, such as doctors, lawyers, professionals, and working mothers.

In general, online consumer panels may be successful as long as adequate representation of the target buying population can be assured. In the United States, more than 50% of households have Internet access, and 25% go online daily. This suggests that previous biases toward young, male professionals being the main Internet users are changing every day. As Internet use increases, biases will decrease, and online panels will be better able to access a more general population.

4. Do Not Confuse Panel Data with One-Time Survey Data

When it comes to one-shot surveys, online versions save time, eliminate interviewer bias, offer better international coordination, provide multimedia capabilities, and can help improve data quality. Pop-up definition boxes and relational navigation links make the survey more understandable for respondents and more simple to complete; versing, skips, rotations, and piping allow for more complex questionnaire design and enable conjoint and pricing studies to be completed more efficiently.

Although these advantages are attractive for one-time surveys, they may not be worth the costs for continuous panels. For certain panels, time savings is not necessarily an issue because reports occur at a regular interval, and the results are seldom urgent but are more long term in nature. For panels, many of these features may not necessarily be worth the trade-offs that might need to be made relative to sample representativeness or data accuracy. Representativeness was covered previously; let us address data accuracy.

The primary objective in panel research is to find consumers who will consistently and accurately complete the entries in their panel diary. Hard-copy diaries are always available (perhaps it is sitting on a desk) when entries need to be made. If online use is irregular, or if computer and Internet access in the household is a competitive resource, a more convenient form (such as hard-copy panel booklets) might provide more accurate and consistent responses.

For continuous panels, panel members become efficient because the format of the instrument is static and the directions are familiar. The features that make the Internet effective for some types of surveys are less beneficial here and may even detract from a panel's effectiveness. When assessing the necessity of features, it is important to make certain that they will be worth the costs or trade-offs associated with them.

5. Double-Check Panel Representativeness

Be sure that the panel is representative of the particular population to be studied and with regard to the population characteristics that need to be analyzed. To say that a sample is representative of a population without specifying in what respect it is representative is meaningless. What you invariably want is a panel that will yield accurate purchase estimates for each of the consumer characteristics that may affect the sale of the product. Representativeness for one characteristic does not ensure a panel's representativeness for other characteristics. It is therefore important to make sure that the panel is representative with respect to all of the characteristics to be studied.

It is especially important to make sure that the panel is concentrated in those areas among the population groups that are the principal purchasers of the product. Thus, a broadly representative national consumer panel may be wasted for a manufacturer of products that are sold primarily in rural areas. A concentrated panel is likely to be cheaper per dollar expended, and it also permits a more intensive analysis of purchaser characteristics.

It is important to check the representativeness of the reporting sample rather than that of the mailing sample. Consider mail diaries. Because response rates vary by population groups, a perfectly representative, stratified distribution of families on the mailing list will not yield a perfectly representative distribution of reporting families. A competently run consumer panel should contain a disproportionately high number of lower-income, poorly educated families with a low response rate. Remember that the purchase data received will be based on the reporting panel, not on the original mailing list.

Request each panel operator bidding for your patronage to provide the number and type of sample controls used to keep the sample representative and the date of the population estimates on which these controls are based. A progressive panel service will try to keep the sample representative in a great many different ways (if it is a stratified sample), and it will be continually revising its controls to keep them up to date with the changing characteristics of the population. The latter is especially important when large population shifts are taking place. Indeed, this is the only way of maintaining the representativeness of a dynamic panel.

6. Double-Check Data Reliability

Inquire into what the panel service is doing to determine the reasons for not reporting and ensure the accuracy of the purchase reports of its members. Both of these points are important potential sources of bias, and they require continual checks. No panel is perfect in these respects, and none ever will be. But a progressive organization will perform continuous studies and check-ups on these points and should be able to show concrete evidence of this work.

A progressive panel operation will also be conducting research and testing methods of increasing the accuracy of the purchase reports. Low accuracy of reports is perhaps the major problem of continuous purchase panels, and it is a problem that characterizes even families that are initially fully cooperative. Therefore, continual checks need to be made on the accuracy of the reports and on what biases are occurring as a result.

If possible, have the panel services submit per-family or per-capita sample purchase figures of products that are related to your own and whose sales can be checked independently. Without divulging these figures, ask your researchers to prepare comparable purchase estimates from the production and/or sales records of these products. Then compare the two sets of estimates. The more reliable your estimates and the closer these related products resemble your own, the more accurate this procedure is in indicating the relative accuracy of the competing panel services in your case. Needless to say, a similar comparison may be made if any of the panel services have past records on the consumer purchases of your own product.

Keep in mind also that if the primary interest is measuring the flow of a product from the warehouse to the consumer, a store or warehouse inventory panel may be preferable to a consumer purchase panel. For food and drug products, for example, a statistically valid panel of food and drug stores is likely to yield a more accurate picture of purchase flows than a consumer panel. However, if the primary interest is correlating changes in purchases with the characteristics of the purchasers of the product, a consumer purchase panel is clearly indicated.

7. Pay Only for the Precision You Need

Precision can come in two forms. The first is in the form of multiple questions asked in multiple ways that triangulate on the same construct (i.e., using a Likert scale, a semantic differential scale, and a estimated purchase frequency question to measure purchase intentions). The second form of precision is obtained by getting a larger and larger sample, thereby reducing sampling error. The entire concept of sampling is based on the notion that it is infeasible and unnecessary to survey an entire population. So too is there a point at which a sample size is large enough to effectively answer the questions for which it is intended.

Although precision is good, after some point there is less and less value to being more and more precise. The cost of asking multiple questions for every construct of interest can be measured in a lower response rate and higher error due to fatigue. On the back end, this cost can be measured in increased data handling and increased analysis and reporting.

To ask something because it "might be interesting" is expensive. The more diagnostic the questions, the better and the greater the need for precision is. One rule-of-thumb is to ask how much the outcome in a measure would need to change before it would change a decision. If a change from 4.0 to 3.9 would result in a product being launched or a old product being dropped, there is a high need for precision. That is, a large sample size and multiple questions are necessary. If, however, the change from an estimate of 4.0 to 2.5 would still not change a decision, the sample need not be as large, and multiple questions might be trimmed.

8. If Accuracy Is Critical, Measure Sample Error

Determine whether you want sample data that will permit you to measure the sampling error. In most cases, estimates of the sampling errors in the purchase data are extremely desirable. Without such estimates, there is no way of knowing to what extent sampling variations may have introduced errors in the purchase figures. Unfortunately, such error estimates are not possible with some continuing consumer panels because their members are not selected in the true random fashion that is the basic prerequisite for the applicability of sampling error formulas.

A knowledge of the sampling error is not so important for some purposes as for others. Thus, in general, knowledge of the sampling errors is not as necessary in studying trends as in "blowing up" the sample data to population estimates. However, even in the former case, much greater reliability can be placed on a panel whose sampling error is measurable.

Furthermore, if a panel is selected whose sampling error can be measured, be sure that the panel will yield results within the required sampling error limits for strata and substrata, as well as for the total sample. As a rule, a major requirement is to have a sample that yields acceptable error limits at the smallest levels of aggregation. The specifications of strata and substrata, as well as acceptable sampling error limits for these entities, are frequently the critical considerations for sample size. It makes a huge difference, for example, whether a sampling error of five percentage points at the 95% confidence level is desired separately for each of four different income levels and three different age groups or whether the same sampling error is desired for the combinations of income level by age. In the latter case, minimum adequate sample sizes must be considered for each of 12 income-by-age strata, which would require a sample many times larger than that needed for minimum sampling errors for income and age strata separately. This also means that we should not ask for a lower sampling error than is absolutely needed, because generally, the lower the sampling error, the higher is the sample size and the higher is the cost of the service.

9. Think Sample Reliability, Not Sample Size

Do not rely on sample size alone as a criterion of the reliability of the results. Other important considerations are the sampling method used to set up the panel, how the individual panel members are selected, and how the data are collected. The sampling method is particularly important. A small, randomly selected sample is likely to be far more reliable than a much larger, arbitrarily selected sample.

The principal determinant of the reliability of the sample data is not the sampling variance but the mean square error. As a rule, the bias component of the mean square error tends to be many times that of the sampling variance in consumer purchase studies, so that primary attention must be given to the nature and magnitude of the nonsampling errors inherent in the panel operation. Therefore, it is important for a panel operation to make constant checks on the accuracy of the purchase reports and other sources of nonsampling error.

10. Stratum Sample Size Is More Important than General Sample Sizes

Be sure that the panel is large enough to supply reliable purchase figures for each of the breakdowns required. Not only must the panel service be able and willing to supply the necessary breakdowns, but there must also be a sufficiently large number of members in each stratum and substratum for which figures are desired. Exactly what constitutes a sufficient number depends primarily on the popularity of the product; the less widely purchased it is, the larger the number of sample members is required in a particular substratum to yield a cross-section of the characteristics of its purchasers.

In general, it would be wise to insist on at least 25 panel members in each stratum for which purchase data are requested, though at times this figure may be much too low. For example, if only 3% of the families in a certain city purchase Product X, a panel substratum of 25 to 30 members in that city may easily contain not a single purchaser of the product.

11. Sort Out the Offline Versus Online Decision

For some situations and some questions, offline panels are the obvious choice. For other types of questions, online panels are obvious. The difficulty lies in the gray areas. Online panels can have some tremendous benefits when the population is accurately sampled. Online panels are fast, can generate tremendously large samples, can be inexpensive (no mailing or printing costs and lower labor costs), can show graphics and video, and can provide seamless international coordination. Furthermore, they can reduce in-house errors associated with interviewer bias or coding and data entry errors.

Despite these benefits, there are concerns that Internet-savvy consumers are not representative of the general population. Although no method, offline or online, is perfectly representative of the population being studied, there is a sizable concern that online panels are psychographically biased toward progressive technology innovators and demographically biased toward young, male professionals. If this is true, then the typical grocery shopper is probably represented more accurately by offline panels than by online panels. In this case, the decision of which type of panel to use to study grocery shopping would involve a trade-off: the speed and savings of an online or the increased accuracy of an offline panel. For certain questions, accuracy is less important than other issues.

As detailed under point three in this chapter ("Does this Panel Really Sample the Population I Want?"), the representativeness of online panels to the general population is only important if we are actually interested in the general population. For example, online panels can be used to accurately investigate products that are frequently purchased on the Internet (see Chapter 3).

Furthermore, there are elusive subgroups within the population (such as teenagers) that may be better represented through the Internet than through other methods. This may also be true of well-educated audiences, such as managers, doctors, and lawyers.

In summary, the online versus offline decision depends on the products and the populations being studied and the level of accuracy needed. Over time, as Internet services become as commonplace as telephone and television services, the self-selection biases that occur for online surveys will become less pronounced and the benefits more pronounced.

12. Do Not Ask for More Data and Printouts than Needed

The more data you request, the more you pay—not only for the panel data, but also for the time your researchers spend in analyzing and cross-analyzing the figures. In the long run, it pays to concentrate on those consumer characteristics that affect the sales of your product most strongly. To accomplish this, try to obtain purchase reports for your product according to as many different characteristics as possible the first few times. By analyzing these reports, you can determine which characteristics have the least influence on the purchases of the product and so can be dropped from future reports—except, perhaps, for occasional checks. If desired, the savings resulting from this procedure could be spent on obtaining more intensive breakdowns of relevant characteristics. For example, if the purchases of Product X vary greatly by region and by city size but not by income or occupation, the two latter classifications might be dropped, and a larger number of region and city size breakdowns could be requested, such as a finer breakdown of regions and city sizes or of purchases by city sizes within regions.

It is especially desirable to keep the number of printouts requested to a minimum, because they can multiply astronomically when comparisons are being made not only by population characteristics but also over time. Unless the office is in danger of being blown away by a tornado, it is wise initially to ask for printouts on a very selective basis, because the sheer volume that can be turned out by a computer in batch mode is enough to discourage even the hardiest of researchers from plowing through them. For exploratory purposes, a highly efficient (though not the cheapest) means of selecting relevant characteristics and key tabulations is to keep the computer tape of the panel data online and produce alternative frequency counts and tabulations interactively on a cathode ray terminal. Many forms of multivariate and more sophisticated analyses can also be carried out in this manner, and many alternatives can thereby be sifted out without having the office take on the semblance of a paper warehouse.

Summary

It should be clear from the foregoing points that the best panel service is not necessarily the cheapest. To save a few dollars at the expense of reliability may jeopardize the value of the entire operation. Most important is obtaining the greatest reliability for your dollar. If you subscribe to the panel service that can give this to you, any additional expenditure for that service will be well worth the cost.

Chapter 10

Building a Successful Convenience Panel

How do you set up a panel for "quick and dirty" tests
or to prescreen people to come in for focus groups or
lab experiments?

—Professor at Stanford University

arge panels offer size, representativeness, and anonymity. Yet there
are times when generalizability and projectability are not the goals
of the study. In these cases, convenience panels can be very useful.
They can be "cheap, quick, and good" by offering ease and speed of
access. Locally focused panels offer the additional opportunity to prescreen people for focus groups, in-depth interviews, and face-to-face
experimental tasks.

Convenience panels are called by different names depending on who
is using them and how they are used. Companies often call them "pilot
panels" because they are used for pilot studies or measurement development. Academics call them "research panels," but can formally name
them on the basis of the focus of their research (e.g., the Food
Psychology Panel, the Brand Revitalization Panel). Despite the differences in names, all convenience panels tend to have similar purposes: to
easily and quickly generate data (albeit not generalizable) that will be
helpful in questionnaire design, idea generation, or theory testing.

The objective of this chapter is to show how to build a successful convenience panel. As noted in the left-hand box of Figure 10.1, the chapter
begins by outlining three ideas for using convenience panels: (1) to preselect people for interviews, (2) to generate ideas and conduct experi-

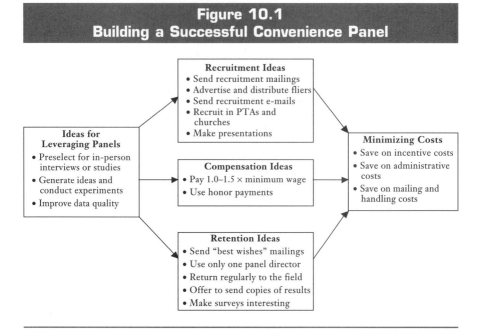

Figure 10.1
Building a Successful Convenience Panel

Ideas for Leveraging Panels
- Preselect for in-person interviews or studies
- Generate ideas and conduct experiments
- Improve data quality

Recruitment Ideas
- Send recruitment mailings
- Advertise and distribute fliers
- Send recruitment e-mails
- Recruit in PTAs and churches
- Make presentations

Compensation Ideas
- Pay 1.0–1.5 × minimum wage
- Use honor payments

Retention Ideas
- Send "best wishes" mailings
- Use only one panel director
- Return regularly to the field
- Offer to send copies of results
- Make surveys interesting

Minimizing Costs
- Save on incentive costs
- Save on administrative costs
- Save on mailing and handling costs

ments, and (3) to improve data quality. Next, five techniques are described that can be used to successfully recruit panelists. Following this, the issue of compensation is addressed. Specific guidelines for how much to pay and suggestions for using "honor payments" are next described. Because attrition is an important issue for convenience panels, five methods for retaining panelists are presented. The chapter ends with suggestions that panel directors on tight budgets can use to reduce administrative, mailing, and incentive costs.

Ideas for Leveraging Convenience Panels

Convenience panels are useful when there is no intention to try and project from the panel to a general population. This is common with pretests, questionnaire design, measurement development, and crossed (e.g., 2 × 3 between-subjects) experimental designs. A convenience panel can provide quick turnaround and follow-up feedback on the telephone (or face-to-face) regarding what questions seemed cumbersome or difficult to answer. In addition, people in these panels tend to be experienced and "well behaved," and a higher percentage of returned responses are usable. This enables easy trouble-shooting of problem areas, more effective idea generation, and less noisy experimental results.

Use Panels to Preselect for Interviews or Recruit for Experiments

Sometimes it is important that there be face-to-face meetings with panelists. This is the case when there are follow-up questions that need to be answered in a focus group or when in-depth interviews are needed. The closer panelists live to a central, convenient facility, the easier this can happen. Previous records from panelists can be used to electronically prescreen them before interviews. Suppose one is interested in interviewing consumers who have swimming pools. Previous information on panelists can indicate which of them have swimming pools, and they can quickly be prescreened on this basis.

Panelists can also be prescreened on the basis of the type of person they are. Suppose it is believed that consumers who have a high need for cognition will make different types of product comparisons and decisions than will those who have a low need for cognition. On the basis of questions asked of them upon first joining a panel, these panelists can be prescreened according to these answers. That is, one group of consumers can be invited in because they scored high on the need for cognition scale, and another group can be invited in because they scored low on the same scale.

The real value of convenience panels lies in their ability to be involved in face-to-face studies in which interaction is important or consumers' behaviors (such as the pouring of a product or the way in which they search for information on a label) are being observed in real time. One study used a convenience panel to determine how different types of ads influenced the subsequent consumption frequency of selected products over a three-month period (Wansink and Ray 1996). In this case, panelists were prescreened on the basis of their preference for three products (canned soup, gelatin, and cranberry sauce) and were invited to a central test facility where they were shown different types of commercials for these products. Following this, their consumption frequency of these target products was tracked through a consumption diary. Whereas the different test commercials could have been downloaded onto the Web, this would have entailed time, technological sophistication, and hardware capabilities. Furthermore, it would not enable the researcher to control the level of attention the people allocated to watching these test commercials.

In a second case, it was of interest to determine how pantry stockpiling influenced the consumption rate of products (Chandon and Wansink 2002). Concerns of causality necessitated that this be studied in an experimental context. To do this, panelists were asked to meet at a central facility. In exchange for a shopping basket of target products, they were asked to track their consumption of these products using panel diaries. Panelists could have been mailed their basket of products, but the two factors of cost and control came into play. Not only would the packing, handling, and mailing costs have been unnecessary, but the reasonably complex rules and motivation to behave cannot be reinforced and controlled without face-to-face meetings and the opportunity to ask questions.

Use Panels to Generate Ideas and Conduct Experimental Tests

Suppose that we are trying to determine who the gatekeeper of food purchases is in a household. That is, when is it the meal planner and when is it the meal eaters? Using a convenience panel can either help us confirm suspicions or be used in brainstorming further thoughts. If the answers are thought to be different with different populations, or if they are important enough to generalize, a full panel study can be more parsimoniously conducted at a later time.

A well-trained panel can be given a wide range of open-ended questions along with scaled and frequency questions. A general method in exploring a new context or research area is to ask dyadic questions, such as "When do you _____," and then asking "When do you not _____." In both cases, a series of scaled questions can be asked about each of the events. Similarly, asking people in convenience panels to describe recent scenarios (the last time they bought something on impulse or the most recent comfort food they ate) and answer scaled questions related to it can provide great insights for exploratory analysis and thinking (Wansink 1994).

In Chapter 2, it is shown that panels can be used to conduct actual experiments in which different groups of people are given different stimuli to see how they respond. For example, four different executions of an ad could be given to four different groups of 500 consumers to determine which was most appealing. Or, two different price levels could be crossed with three different bundles of features to see which of the six combinations was most attractive to consumers.

There are other times when the speed, cost savings, or follow-up ability of a convenience panel will overshadow the importance of its representativeness. Convenience panels can be used when there is little or no need to generalize to a larger population. For example, in many academic experiments, the goal is simply to determine if a general prediction or hypothesis works with a reasonable segment of the population. Suppose a researcher is examining the memorability of different types of business names under conditions of interference. What is being studied is whether the predicted results occur with a reasonable population segment. If these results are found, additional work—perhaps a full-scale study—can be conducted to determine the generalizability of these results.

Use Panels to Improve Data Quality

There is always a trade-off between accuracy and cost. In some work, such as academic methodology studies, there is a premium placed on the precision and accuracy of a panelist. Some consumers are simply more careful, precise, accurate, and diligent than others. By using panels, consumers can be screened or preselected on the basis of how careful and accurate they are. They can then be useful whenever a situation places a premium on low error variance. This can be easily and statistically accomplished. Consistency in answering questions can be checked across times. Responses to reverse-scaled items of a similar nature can provide an indication of how careful subjects are, and an analysis of missing data can give some indication of diligence.

In general, convenience panels, when managed well, help provide a certain guarantee about the quality of the data. Panelists with whom a researcher has regular contact can be more useful, more patient, and more precise than those who are merely "doing it for the money."

In addition to increasing the quality of data, people in convenience panels can be used more frequently than can typical panelists. This is because the two big concerns with typical panels—burnout and contamination—are less prevalent with convenience panels. Because the nature of the questions these people are asked is not intended to be representative of a general population, there is less concern about the contamination that comes with fears of overusing a panel. In addition, because of the additional attention and appreciation these people receive, it is often not a concern that they will burn out. They self-selected themselves to be reasonably involved with the panel. This interest, along with efforts to keep their morale high, will make them loyal panelists who can be called on more frequently than would be the case with larger, more general panels.

How Can Convenience Panelists Be Recruited?

For the most part, convenience panels are local panels. The panelists live close to a research facility, and they are quickly and inexpensively accessible by telephone and in person. For pilot panels, a larger percentage can be from outside the area if coming into a central facility does not place too great a burden on them.

Send Recruitment Mailings

Within a specified area, mailing lists can be purchased, and people can be recruited through mail solicitations. The solicitation letter must explain the general purpose of the panel, how the data will be used, what they will receive for compensation, and an assurance that their privacy will not be compromised. In these circumstances, the solicitation mailing will include a business reply envelope and a brief questionnaire that will help with prescreening for future studies.

It is critical to assure people that their names and addresses will not be sold to companies. If a small amount of money is included, it is not uncommon for a solicited response rate to be as high as 15% to 20%. Exhibit 10.1 shows an example of a recruitment letter that generated a 42% response (Wansink 2002).

This qualification questionnaire should be reasonably brief (two to four pages) and should contain a wide enough range of questions to determine the types of tasks for which respondents would be well suited. Instead of sending a short qualification questionnaire, another approach is to send a more involved questionnaire and include compensation in the packet (see the upcoming section "Honor Payments"). This works well for large-scale recruitment efforts when one is first building a panel but is less cost effective for the small, ongoing recruitment efforts that must be done to maintain panels.

Advertise and Distribute Fliers

Display ads and help-wanted ads are commonly used to recruit local panels. Although this successfully locates eager panelists, they are not always ideal. Many people reading these ads are looking for extra money and will treat the panel as a means to an end. Panelists who are recruited through advertisements have a higher burnout rate and a slightly lower percentage of usable questionnaires than those recruited randomly through the mail.

Types of advertisements that work reasonably well at recruiting panelists are targeted advertisements. One target population of panelists that is very useful for certain research is the segment of stay-at-home mothers. These women have some time and flexibility and are not employed full-time at the level their experience and education would merit. Many are looking for something "interesting" to break up their day. Whereas

Exhibit 10.1
Recruitment Letter Sent to Prospective Panelists

August 5, 2000

Dear Member of America's Greatest Generation,

Your generation represents what Tom Brokaw call's America's Greatest Generation. It is the generation of Americans who grew up during the depression and who lived through WWII, helping as either a civilian or as a soldier. I am a Professor at the University of Illinois and with the cooperation of the U.S. Government, we are conducting one of the last and one of the most comprehensive large scale panel surveys of your generation.

There is a tremendous amount that future generations can learn from you. They can learn about your character, your sacrifices, and how your experiences in the depression and during WWII shaped your habits and behaviors over the years. The results of this panel survey will be used to write academic articles and books that will help preserve an understanding of your generation.

Your name was given to us from a random list of individuals (born 1920-35) from all 50 states. The survey is comprehensive, and it covers many aspects of you and your life. If there are parts of it you would rather not fill out, that is fine. Yet the more complete you are, the more complete of a picture we will be able to have of you and your generation. Your responses to the survey will be anonymous and no companies will be given any information.

While this survey not short, the time you spend with it will help preserve and document the character of your great generation. When you complete this first survey and return it in the enclosed postage-paid envelope, a small donation will be given in your name to the WWII Memorial that is being built in Washington DC. In addition, if you would like a summary of some of the results of this study, please enclose a self-addressed envelope.

Thank you for your time and for all that you've done.

Sincerely,

it is unlikely these women would be reading the classified ads for part-time jobs, they may read the ads in the back of their son's school band program or the display ad in the program for their daughter's school play. Both of these methods are successful in recruiting long-term cooperation from those who have responded.

Fliers are less expensive than ads, but their success is wholly dependent on where they are placed. The most successful fliers are those placed on bulletin boards at churches and community centers. The people recruited through these fliers are sincere and often end up being long-term panelists. Fliers placed on bulletin boards in grocery stores tend to generate a reasonably large response, but the response quality is lower. Fliers placed in laundromats generate a high level of response, but the panelists have a high level of attrition from the panel. In general, there have been uneven responses from people recruited through Internet bulletin boards, and it appears to be the least successful recruitment method at this time. More targeted e-mail recruitment is a more preferred electronic recruiter, as is noted next.

Send Recruitment E-Mails

When the researcher is dealing with a large central community, such as a university or a large company, an easy method of recruitment is through e-mail. Communications directed toward staff (secretaries and administrative assistants) receive the greatest response. But because of increased sensitivity toward "junk" e-mail and because of a perceived issue of hierarchical power, these e-mails need to be very delicately written. A message that is too persuasive might be regarded as inappropriate or even coercive if it is sent by a perceived "superior."

It might seem that the best message strategy is to emphasize that the purpose of the panel is consistent with the purpose of the organization. This strategy, however, is not as effective as one that decouples the panel from the institution and from any confusion as to whether the person must be involved. The best approach is one that emphasizes that being a panelist is a reasonably amusing way to spend some time that is appreciated, convenient, and compensated. Before sending this message, it is important to personally show it to various people in the target population to make sure it communicates effectively, persuasively, and inoffensively.

Recruiting in PTAs and Church Groups

One of the most successful methods of recruiting panelists is face-to-face, and few other face-to-face techniques work as well as meeting them in groups. Two groups that have been most successfully used across the

United States and in the Netherlands have been elementary school parent–teacher associations (PTAs) and church groups.

These organizations are frequently involved in fundraisers to buy school supplies or send kids to church camp, and they are often searching for painless fundraising ideas. One solution for this dilemma is the Fundraising Survey. Simply put, for each person the PTA or church can get to complete a qualifying survey, the organization is given $8–$12 (50 people results in a $400–$600 fundraiser). In effect, they do the basic prescreening, and when all these subjects are met, long-term panelists will be recruited.

The best way to approach PTAs and church groups is to call the school or church to learn the name of the president and contact him or her by telephone or through the mail. If contacting over the telephone, it is most effective to call this a "Survey Fundraiser," to explain that other schools or churches in the area are cooperating, and to ensure that it will be an easy, fun, profitable experience for members. Typically, the president needs to "pitch" the idea to a board or committee, so instead of asking for a date or commitment, offer to meet with her or him or to mail a packet of information and follow up in a week or two. The information packet you send should contain the following:

1. A letter emphasizing the benefits of participation, noting the participation of other groups, and addressing possible reservations (see Exhibit 10.2);
2. A sample of the questionnaire you will be handing out;
3. Your biography and institutional information;
4. Sample articles or newsletters that show the benign ways the data will be used; and
5. Thank you notes or letters of testimonial from other groups.

If in agreement, two or three dates are set. The PTA or church group will contact its own members, but it will be important to follow up as a reminder and obtain an estimate of how many members will be in attendance on those dates. Typically, church groups are met right after a Sunday morning service, and PTA groups are met at 6:30 P.M. or 7:00 P.M. on a weekend. For every person who attends and completes a 45-minute qualifying question, $8–$12 is donated to the organization. Coffee and cookies are served, and members are able to discharge their fund-raising obligation in about one hour.

Arrive 45 to 60 minutes ahead of schedule to visit with the president of the organization and mingle with any members who arrive early. If possible, bring one or two assistants who fit a similar demographic profile (30–45 years of age with children) and who can informally talk about

Exhibit 10.2
Fundraising Letter Sent to Organization Presidents

Professor Brian Wansink, PhD
Director
350 ComWest
University of Illinois
Champaign, IL 61820-6980

September 3, 2001

PTA President – Ms. Bethany Carson
Carrie Busey School
1605 W. Kirby
Champaign, IL 61821

Dear Bethany,

It was good to visit with you the other day about having your PTA group be involved with the **University of Illinois Survey Fundraiser**. The Fundraiser is simple -- for each parent who fills out a 45 minute survey (typically 50-200 per PTA), we donate $6.00 to their PTA group. In the last 14 years we have helped 73 different PTAs in California, New Hampshire, Pennsylvania, and Illinois raise over $44,000 with Survey Fundraisers. We use these surveys to study why people buy what they buy and why they eat what they eat. We then publish the results in academic journals (we don't give it to companies).

We typically do this in November. We will pick one or two dates (say, Monday or Tuesday night from 7:00 to 7:45), and any parents who wanted to fill out the survey would show up at your school on that evening. One of my Ph.D. students and myself will hand out the surveys (along with cookies and soft drinks), and collect them an hour later. If 100 parents show up, my research lab at the University of Illinois would give your PTA a check for $600.

This is quick, easy, and some people even think its fun. Most PTAs we have worked with have used this as their primary fundraiser for multiple years. I've enclosed a couple of thank you notes from these PTAs, a sample of one of the surveys used last year, a biography of myself, and some news stories about some of the research we've done in the Lab.

Even though we won't be doing this until November, I wanted to let you know about this ahead of time. If you have any questions, please give me a call. If you think it is necessary for me to attend one of your meetings and present this in person, I would be happy to do so.

Sincerely,

Bri Vak

Email Wansink@uiuc.edu • Phone 217-244-0208 • Fax 217-244-7969 • www.ConsumerPsychology.com

the panel and your institution before and after the session. Bring cookies and candy for snacks and offer to help make coffee if the facilities are available. Not only does it make the potential panelists feel more at ease, but the snacks provide energy and enthusiasm and helps their focus and concentration.

On the last page of the survey, people are given the opportunity to join the panel. They are told that subsequent research will be conducted in this area and that they will receive compensation if they want to be involved in future surveys. The wording in Exhibit 10.3. has been effective. Note that it refers to the valued nature of the group and the willingness to disclose what is learned (through the Web site). In addition, it asks for participants' name, address, and signature.

Potential panelists need to be assured that the panel is legitimate and that it is something they would be proud or interested to be involved with. A big part of the impression they will have of whether they want to be involved in the panel is based on what they think of you during the session itself. Although it may be tempting for a researcher to view this as a "tedious site visit" and outsource it to associates, doing so under-

---

Exhibit 10.3
Convenience Panelist Recruitment Form

Would You Like to Become a Member of the Food Psychology Panel?

Once or twice each year, a survey such as this is mailed out to the University of Illinois' Food Psychology Panel. This is a confidential and valued group of consumers that helps us better understand what consumers like and what they want. The information will not be given to companies but is used for educational purposes in the University (see www.consumerpsychology.net).

As thanks for helping fill out the surveys, each panel member receives a small check (from $3–$8). If you would like to be a part of the Illinois Food Psychology Panel, please check the following box and return this in the return envelope you'll find in your packet.

❏ Yes, I would like to be a member of the Food Psychology Panel.

❏ No thank you, I would not care to be a part of the Food Psychology Panel.

Name _____

Address _____

City _____

Phone _____

E-mail _____

Signature _____

mines the purpose of recruiting panelists. Potential panelists should think of this first experience as interesting, relaxing, and personalized.

Recruiting Through Community Presentations and Executive Education

Another useful place to find potential panelists is through civic presentations or lectures. From time to time, researchers are asked to give talks to civic groups or associations. When the individuals in the audience fit the profile of those wanted in the panel, they can be easily recruited as panelists. In these cases, a general sign-up form can be passed around after the talk (during the question-and-answer period), and the names can be collected in a database. When the time is appropriate, they can be mailed an initial participant panel survey.

Although our discussion of panels has been confined to consumer panels, many of these techniques can be modified to use with panels composed of professionals, such as businesspeople. One way such panels can be developed quickly and easily is by holding full-day seminars in major cities. The seminars can be directed toward topics in which the researcher specializes, and a nominal fee can be charged. For researchers in universities, the mailing lists can primarily be to alumni in that city. For those related to companies, the mailing lists can be Standard Industrial Classification code companies that are potential clients.

Business executives who are interested in the seminar can then be sent a schedule that has two time slots during the day that are allocated to panel-related surveys. During these sessions, the panel survey should be positioned as a precursor to the follow-up sessions that day. At the end of the second survey, the executives should be asked whether they would like to be involved with the panel on a more regular basis. The sign-on rate varies depending on the quality of the seminar and the audience. Generally about 45% will show an interest in being on the panel, and 30% will become regularly contributing members. If part of their compensation for being on the panel is that they receive summaries of the research findings, initial participation can be increased to as high as 70%.

How Should Panelists Be Compensated?

As noted in Chapter 4, large panel companies compensate consumers using tangible rewards such as gifts, cash, lotteries, or redemption points. Although some institutions employing convenience panels have tried to use only intangible rewards such as "membership prestige," copies of results, and pats on the back, the more successful convenience panels use a combination of tangible and intangible rewards. Company panels should provide a slightly higher tangible-to-intangible mix of rewards than universities (especially compared with state universities). Yet even university panels need to offer some tangible reward to keep panelists happy and involved.

How Much Should Panelists Be Paid?

A reasonably good payment rule of thumb is to pay 1.0–1.5 times minimum wage. To use this benchmark, it should be determined how long it will take a reasonable person to complete the questionnaire. It is important not to use the "mean" completion time but instead to use an estimate of the "reasonable completion time."

The reasonable completion time is the time it takes for 70% of the test respondents (the 70th percentile) to complete the particular panel survey instrument. Using this number of minutes, 1.0–1.5 times the minimum wage will give a range of what is a reasonable incentive for consumers. For most convenience panel studies, it is unreasonable to have them last for more than 40 minutes. Past that point, fatigue compromises the quality of the responses, as well as future cooperation. In such a case, assuming it is January and the minimum wage is $5.00 per hour, a questionnaire that takes 40 minutes to complete would be paid between $3.66 (40/60 × $5.00 × 1.0) and $5.00 (40/60 × $5.00 × 1.5). In most cases, it is best to round to the nearest $.50 level, so a panelist would receive a check for either $3.50 or $5.00.

This 1.0–1.5 rule of thumb is a valid one to use during September through May. In the summer, the ratio changes to 1.5–2.0 times the minimum wage. To keep a consistent response rate across the year, the reasonable range for each month of the year is as follows:

- January   1.0–1.5 times the minimum wage
- February   1.0–1.5 times the minimum wage
- March   1.0–1.5 times the minimum wage
- April   1.0–1.5 times the minimum wage
- May   1.3–1.8 times the minimum wage
- June   1.5–2.0 times the minimum wage
- July   1.5–2.0 times the minimum wage
- August   1.5–2.0 times the minimum wage
- September   1.3–1.8 times the minimum wage
- October   1.0–1.5 times the minimum wage
- November   1.0–1.5 times the minimum wage
- December   Wait until January

What determines what end of the pay scale to use? This depends on who the sample panelists are, what their time is worth, where they are located, what the institution is (company versus university), and what the topic and interest level is in the panel's survey. The Food Psychology Panel at the University of Illinois, for example, generates a 60%–80% winter response rate at a 1.0 incentive rate. An increase to 1.5 times the minimum wage has no appreciable difference on the response rate. For some panelists, it appears that "the thought is the count."

For institutions such as universities, there is a different level of benevolence that some consumers have than they have for companies. In addition, this benevolence is much higher for a state institution than for a private one. Indeed, panels associated with state universities receive a higher response rate than those associated with private universities, but both have higher response rates than companies. Interestingly, the response level for universities is high, even at low levels of payment. In one case, 41% of the panel responded to an 8-page (25-minute) questionnaire when only $1.00 was included. In another, 42% responded to a 16-page (120-minute) questionnaire that included no money but offered to send the results.

When panelists must come in for face-to-face studies or interviews, the compensation must be much higher. They incur costs of transportation, parking, and possibly child care. When these people are on site, they can be effectively used for about 90 minutes if the tasks they are involved in are broken up with variety. For such a situation, it is difficult to recruit them for less than minimum wage. Typically, the payment rate will be 2.0–2.5 times the minimum wage. If it is an inconvenient time of the year—say, during the holiday season or summer—the required amount of payment can become prohibitively high for people with children.

Whenever recruiting for an on-site study, there are two important rules of thumb. First, overbook the number of respondents needed by 20%. If 100 people are needed, recruit 120. Second, "maybe" means "no." Typically a person who says they will "try to be there" or they "need to check on child care" will not show up.

After panelists are booked, it is also important to call them the day before the event and remind them about the time and place of their session. It is important to overestimate the time you think they will be needed by 30 minutes. This provides a margin of error, and it keeps them focused for a longer time period. If they believe they will be needed for only 60 minutes, they will have mentally "checked out" at the 40-minute point. If they believe they will be there for 90 minutes, they will still be focused at the end of 60 minutes.

Honor Payments: A New Method for Paying Panelists

There are two ways to pay panelists. The most common method is by sending them personally addressed checks upon return receipt of their panel booklet. In doing so, there is control over the checks, accountability, and accuracy in reporting. Unfortunately, there are extra administrative steps, and the response rate is reduced because the reward is so delayed.

An alternative is to include unaddressed checks when the panel booklets are sent. These are called "honor payments" (Wansink and Park 2000). After the appropriate amount that will be paid panelists is determined, checks can be preprinted with that amount and signed with a stamped signature. Exhibit 10.4 gives an example of an honor payment check.

It is important to indicate to consumers that the check should be cashed only if the survey is completed. Similarly, the cover letter should emphasize that the check is being sent in a good faith effort, and if the consumer does not wish to complete the panel survey, he or she should simply tear up the check and throw it out with the survey.

The fear of cynical researchers (particularly economists) is that the response rate for the survey will be 35%, but the response rate for cashed checks will be 100%. This is not the case. Tracking studies have shown that there is a strong correspondence between those who fill out the survey and those who deposit the checks. When a convenience panel study

Exhibit 10.4
Example of an Honor Payment Check

http://www.unionplanters.com

PROFESSOR BRIAN WANSINK
350 COMMERCE WEST
UNIVERSITY OF ILLINOIS
CHAMPAIGN, IL. 61820

4620
70-7169/2711

*Date*____AUGUST 1, 1999____

*Pay to the Order of*____LCHS____ $ 3.00

333147895 00 042500

THREE AND 00/100--------   *Dollars* Security feature included. Details on back.

△UNION PLANTERS BANK

FOR COMPLETING SURVEY

*For*____

©HARLAND 1997

sends checks for under $5.00, approximately 95% of those who return their surveys will cash their checks, and 2% to 3% of those who do not return surveys will deposit their check. For checks over $5.00, nearly 100% of those who complete the survey will deposit their check, and approximately 5% to 8% of those who do not complete the questionnaire will deposit the check. Some people lose or misplace the checks. Others mistakenly cash it, intending to fill out the survey. It appears few people behave in the greedy manner anticipated by the cynic. Along with a basic level of integrity, signing the check is a barrier to illicit depositing of checks. Follow-up interviews indicate that there is a concern that the checks will be tracked and corresponded to returned surveys.

One wise measure to take when sending honor payments is to do so from a protected, capped checking account. This account can be opened in the name of the project or the primary investigator. Personal accounts have slightly lower illicit check cashing rates than do more institutional-sounding account titles. Banks can preprint enough checks for the study, and they should be informed not to accept payment for any checks from that account that are greater than the preprinted amount.

The amount of money that needs to be seeded into the account can be calculated by estimating the response rate and adding a 20% cushion margin. As a way of managing the outflow of money, it is useful to realize that the incoming checks return at the basic rate illustrated in Figure 10.2. This can be helpful in monitoring the account. Empirically, most panelists cash their check two to three days after they mail the questionnaire back to the researcher. Others forget or misplace the check and will not cash it until months later. It is a good faith effort to keep these accounts open for at least six months after mailing the surveys.

Sending a small honor payment with the initial survey increases response rates. Follow-up interviews show that this occurs partly because of increased trust that is generated and partly because of the immediate gratification it represents. On the basis of previous experience, here are some basic generalizations about using honor payments:

- 20% of the checks will be deposited before the survey is returned.
- Most checks will be deposited on Monday. This becomes even more exaggerated three weeks after the study.
- If the face value of the check is less than $5.00, 5% of those responding will not deposit the check.
- There is only 3% to 8% "fraud" (deposited checks with no completed survey), but it typically does not occur with small face value checks.

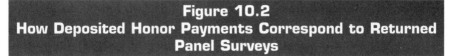

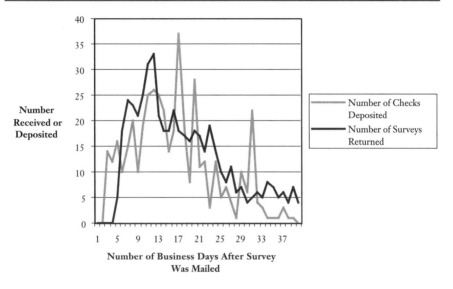

Number Received or Deposited

Number of Business Days After Survey Was Mailed

- Number of Checks Deposited
- Number of Surveys Returned

How Can Panelists Be Retained?

Panelists have some need for tangible compensation, but some part of panelists' involvement in a convenience panel is because they believe their opinion is valued and can make a difference. Reinforcing this feeling is important in helping retain panelists, and the following five guidelines will help.

Send "Best Wishes" Mailings

One approach to keep panelists involved and favorably predisposed toward the panel is to send periodic "best wishes" mailings that thank them for their participation. Two mailings per year is generally sufficient. These best wishes mailings should be sent during the holiday season and summer. Because sending holiday cards can be expensive, an option is to send a brief newsletter with a holiday greeting on the front and a recap of some of the past year's highlights, along with thanks for their help over the past year. This recap is best done in the context of a montage of press clippings related to projects from recent years, interspersed with photos of people from the lab or research organization. The card itself can be signed (a copied signature) by the primary contact person or can include signatures of other relevant people in the lab.

A similar mailing can be sent in the summer. Many people on convenience panels are stay-at-home or working mothers with children, and follow-up interviews have shown that the type of mailing that is most appreciated is a two-piece mailing. One piece is a "thank you" with warm thoughts related to appreciating what it means to be blessed with children. On the back of this, some helpful tips are provided. For example, three mailings that received positive comments are "25 Summer Day Trips," "30 Tips for a Happy Summer," and "Five Cool Snacks." The second enclosure they liked receiving was a newsletter (for a sample, see www.consumerpsychology.net) that mentions interesting results of past studies. Photos that make the researchers look human (but still professional) are well received.

Use Only One Panel Director

When a panel is developed and successfully operating, there can be a tendency to use associates, graduate students, or rookies to maintain the panel and coordinate activities when panelists come to the central location. This is often foolish. The glue that holds good panels together is a sense of commitment to an institution or individual. Many years of goodwill can be eroded by an arrogant or discontent associate or by a careless or disorganized graduate student. It is too easy for a person to treat the panel like a transaction rather than as an asset. Like other relationships, panel relationships need to be nurtured and not taken for granted.

At most institutions, there are many people who will benefit from the establishment of a consumer panel. Who should be the panel director? In the same way that large panels have figureheads and contact points (such as Janet Hall, Carol Adams, or Liz James), so too must a convenience panel have only one person as the figurehead and contact person. This makes the identity of the panel clear to panelists. Furthermore, it lessens the likelihood that easy-to-forget efforts such as the best wishes mailings fall between the cracks.

The ideal panel director is one who is vested in seeing the panel succeed and survive, a good people person, and thoughtful and patient. If the person works with assistants, the best assistants are friendly people who are demographically similar to the target population. It would probably be a mistake to put the best researcher in charge of a panel, just as it would be to put a rookie in charge of it. The researcher may not be the best people person, and the rookie is not going to be as vested in seeing the long-term potential of the panel.

Return Regularly to the Field

Even after a panel has reached the intended size, without replenishment of new panelists, the size of a panel will dwindle each year at a 5%–10% rate of attrition. An important source for some convenience panels is PTAs and church groups. One way to replenish panel membership and keep morale high is to annually (or biannually) conduct fundraisers with the original groups in which members were initially found. For some panels, this will be PTAs and church groups. These visits help replenish members, and it is a useful morale booster for those members of the organization who are already members of the panel. Furthermore, their membership in the panel is useful in recruiting others from that organization, particularly if they are publicly thanked for their help.

Offer to Send Copies of Results

It is always advisable to offer to send panelists copies of the results. As noted in Chapter 4, offering to send the results provides an important signal that there is nothing illicit happening with the data they provide, and it shows that the panel director is honest and worthy of the panelists' involvement.

The importance of offering panelists the results of the survey is in its signal value. In most cases, the panelists do not want the results, but they like knowing they could have them if they wanted. Let us consider a typical panel survey. If a researcher includes a check box (❑) on the survey that says "Please send me the results of the study," it is easy for the consumer to check the box, and approximately 40% will. But how much do they really want the results? If they are told to include a self-addressed envelope, the response rate drops to 3%–4%. If they need to include a stamp on the envelope, response drops to 1%–2%.

This depends heavily on the topic of the survey, however. Recall the panel of World War II veterans. Although the survey was 16 pages with 442 questions and took 120 minutes to complete, 42% of panelists completed the initial panel survey, and 23% of these included self-addressed, stamped envelopes to receive the results of the studies.

Clearly, a panelist's interest in receiving summary results depends on his or her interest in the topic. Whereas many shopping and consumer-related behaviors do not arouse passion and curiosity, other behaviors that are of personal or professional interest do. When panels focus on people of a specific profession, these people frequently wish to receive copies of summary findings. If a high percentage want summaries, spending the money sending findings can offset some (but not all) of the money otherwise spent on premiums and other incentives. As noted previously, any type of contact that keeps panelists feeling informed, valued, and connected is important. If sending panelists some brief summaries of this information accomplishes this at a minimal cost, it is worth doing.

Make the Panel Surveys Interesting and Fun

The quality of the responses is less dependent on the number of pages in the panel survey than on the number of minutes it takes to reasonably complete it. Panel surveys that are only 4 pages long can be excessively more complex and less worthwhile to complete than others that are 16 pages. If a panel survey looks long, boring, and complex to complete, a higher percentage of panelists will elect not to complete it and may eventually drop out of the panel altogether.

Layout and ease of readability is important for keeping panel members interested and for helping them make the decision to complete it as they initially flip through the pages. The standard view of experimental design and surveys is that nothing should be on the panel other than the minimal amount of text that is needed to attain the objectives. The contrary is true for convenience panels. For these panels, part of members' participation rate depends on how much satisfaction and enjoyment they receive from the experience. To help this, icons, graphics, and even photos can help break up the visual monotony of the page and increase the overall affect toward completing the survey and being on the panel. Do these distractions bias the results? For the same reasons that we would use a convenience panel instead of a representative panel, small additions like this will not bias what we are looking for, as long as they are consistent across conditions.

Regardless of what a researcher does to retain panelists, there will be attrition. This tends to be 8%–10% for panelists who have been in the panel for less than three years and lower (about 5%) for those who have been in the panel for longer than three years. A reasonable proportion of this attrition can be attributed to relocation. Instead of dropping these participants from the panel, they can be used for "mail-only" studies that need a focused, sincere, diligent group but that do not necessitate that the panelists visit a central facility. This can keep the panelists eligible for many other panel activities.

How Can the Costs of Convenience Panels be Minimized?

One of the advantages of convenience panels is that their responses are higher and their costs are lower. Nevertheless, they are still expensive.

For companies, the pilot and pretest is an expense that would be tempting, for a short-sighted controller, to eliminate. For academics, the shoestring nature of most social science research leaves the most productive and thoughtful academics economizing on resources. The less that is spent, the fewer distracting grants must be written, executed, and accounted for. The three biggest costs for convenience panels are panelist incentives, administrative costs, and postage.

Save on Incentive Costs

One way to save on incentives for panelists is to provide a reduced monetary incentive and supplement this with a lottery. Some mention of this was made in Chapter 4. If the mailing is large, the incentive of winning a $1,000 lottery can be effective. Sometimes, however, the per-person savings are not as great as one might think. That is, if the mailing is going to a convenience panel of 1000, a $5.00 incentive might generate 600 people at a total incentive cost of $3,000. If a $1.00 incentive is sent with two chances to win $1,000, the response is more likely to be 400 at a cost of $2,400. Although using the lottery is a little less expensive in total, the per-person cost of using a lottery is $6.00 versus $5.00 per person without one. There are four key questions when making the lottery versus cash decision.

1. Will the per-person cost be less for this lottery?
2. Will this lottery decrease long-term commitment to the panel?
3. Will this lottery bias the types of people who respond?
4. Will this lottery cause people to be less careful than payment will?

There are different perspectives on the answers to these questions. However, if more than one of the answers is yes, it might be better to not use the lottery. Alternatively, one compromise may be to increase the amount paid and decrease the amount of the lottery. That is, instead of $5.00 versus $1.00 plus two chances to win $1,000, a compromised package of $2.50 and one chance to win $1,000 may eliminate some unintended effects of the lottery.

Save on Administrative Costs

One important way to save on both administrative and mailing costs is to use the honor payment system outlined previously. This is the prepayment system in which panelists receive the check for completing the survey in the mail. If they choose not to complete the survey, they are instructed to tear up the check and throw it away. This method saves money on check handling and postage because there is no need to mail checks separately.

It is easy to believe that envelope labeling and stuffing can be done for less cost in-house. This can be a poor assumption. Mailing centers can often stuff envelopes for $.03 an item and can quickly address the envelopes. For mailings of under 200, the speed and convenience of doing this in-house (6:00–9:30 P.M. along with pizza and soft drinks) can overcompensate for what the mailing center would charge. However, when the mailing gets any larger, the opportunity costs for the postage and handling can become excessive.

Save on Mailing and Handling Costs

Mailing and handling costs can be minimized by using a nonprofit status when possible and bulk mail when not. For a 16-page survey, the non-profit status mailing can save 70% over that of a first-class mailing. For bulk mailing status, the savings can be around 40%.

One issue with bulk mailing is whether the mailings are similar or different. If the surveys are exactly the same, it will be fine to send them bulk mail as long as more than 300 are being mailed. Say, however, that four different versions of the survey (perhaps a 2 × 2 between-subjects design) will be mailed. Assuming that the surveys look similar, have the same number of pages, and are indistinguishable from their covers, many bulk mailing centers will consider them identical and allow bulk mailing privileges. Other mailing centers instead will require them to be mailed out at a first-class rate. In this case, it can be less costly to send the survey to more panelists to receive the reduction in postage that comes with the bulk mailing status.

Another issue is whether to use business reply return envelopes or pre-stamp return envelopes. The answer depends largely on the expected response rate. With business reply envelopes, if the survey is not returned, there is no charge for incoming postage. If it is returned, they are 30%–40% more expensive than the first-class rate. The alternative is to prestamp every return envelope. In this situation, no premium is paid for returned envelopes, but the stamps that are put on any nonreturned envelopes are wasted. Unless the mailing is small in number or very urgent or unless a high response rate (70%+) is expected, it is generally more cost effective to use business reply envelopes.

Summary

Convenience panels can be cheap, quick, and good when there is no intention to project to a general population. They are particularly well suited for measurement tests, experimental designs, and prescreening people for focus groups and central facility experiments. Whereas developing and managing these panels is similar to that of larger panels, there is a much greater need for personalization and "hand-holding" in both the recruitment and retention of the panels. Yet well-screened, well-trained panels can be of tremendous use in providing high-quality data, feedback, and insights, and they facilitate the trouble-shooting of problem areas, more effective idea generation, and less noisy experimental results. When generalizability is not an objective, the speed, cost savings, and follow-up ability of a convenience panel can overshadow the importance of its representativeness. For academics, it provides an easy solution for generalizing beyond an overused, 19-year-old sophomore subject pool.

Chapter 11

Predicting the Future

I think there is a world market for maybe five
computers.
—*Thomas Watson, Chairman of IBM, 1943*

T here is a danger of embarrassment in trying to predict the future. Yet the upside is often worth the embarrassment of inaccuracy. When we try to imagine what the future will bring, we bring possibilities into focus that could otherwise be lost.

The future for consumer panels is rich. The data collection experience will be richer for consumers, and the data will be richer for researchers. The challenge will be in determining how to use these data to improve a manager's understanding of his or her consumers. A mountain of data will not be difficult to collect. The difficulty lies in effectively mining that mountain for the gold it contains.

Technology will influence not only the way in which data are collected, but also the sociology of how panelists, researchers, and managers respond to these data. After offering predictions of how the future will make the data collection experience richer for consumers and researchers, we discuss future fears. These fears—or challenges—revolve around the unexpected consequences this technology has for the researchers, for brand managers, and for the privacy of panelists. Following this, specific recommendations for consumer panel users and researchers are outlined. These recommendations are intended not so much to help us control the future as much as to help us best prepare for the changes that might occur.

Predicting the Future: Richer Experiences and Richer Data

To believe that consumer panels of the future will only be in the form of Web panels is probably no more accurate than someone in 1978 believing that music of the future would be in the form of eight-track tapes. Consumer panels are now conducted in person, on the telephone, through the mail, and on the Web. The future of consumer panels may be shared with panel data that are collected on rewriteable compact disks, refrigerator panel displays, smart voice-activated appliances, video conference calls, personal displays, or high-resolution WebTV. Figure 11.1 illustrates the future of consumer panels and the organization of this chapter.

A Richer Experience for Panelists

What does the future hold for panelists? How will it be different than what they experience today? It will be more personalized, more personable, more convenient, more flexible, and more fun. For some panels, comparing the current panel experience with the future experience can

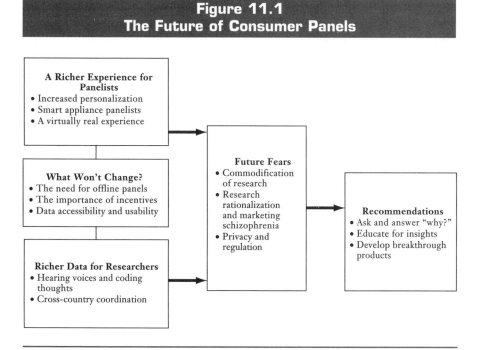

Figure 11.1
The Future of Consumer Panels

be characterized as the difference between doing homework and talking to a virtual friend and explaining what you bought and why. The new experience will be made possible by the edification of increased personalization, the convenience of smart appliances, and the vividness of virtual reality.

Increased Personalization

Forthcoming waves of increased interactivity carry the potential for increased personalization. Just as panels have often used fictitious representatives—such as Janet Hall, Carol Adams, or Liz James—to give personality and a contact point to their company, so too can they use the pleasurable voice of the virtual hostess to welcome consumers and talk them through their panel experience. Not only can this virtual hostess provide explanations and clarifications, she can also reinforce a perceived degree of personalization ("Thank you for helping us Naomi.").

A virtual reality version of Janet, Carol, or Liz could also be present on the corner of the screen of the flat panel display or on the WebTV. For panels in which most of the questions are asked and recorded verbally, the interaction between the virtual hostess and the panel member could begin to mimic a shopping-related conversation between two friends. That is, just as branching options are currently used with online panels, so too will the virtual hostess be able to refer back to previous references and modify questions in real-time on the basis of the previous answer given.

Because of cross-referenced databases, fewer questions will need to be asked and others can be more confirmatory ("Do you still drive your white Jeep Cherokee?"). For some panelists, attrition occurs because they feel anonymous or unimportant. In a small way, this ability to reference and reinforce will make the panel experience more personalized and more efficient. The objective is to reference those details that show familiarity with the panelist and reinforce the notion that a panelist's answers are important and remembered. It may be a fine line, however, between a panelist believing that "it's nice you remembered that about me" versus "it's unnerving you remembered that."

Smart Appliance Panelists

The command center of a household is the kitchen, and it is likely to be one of the most promising frontiers for panel research. It is where people start the day, gather, take breaks, regroup, and finish off with a midnight snack. With smart appliances, such as refrigerators with touch screens and stovetops with microchips, there is an opportunity to use bar coding scanners to move beyond purchase behavior and to collect more precise data on consumption and meal planning. Flat panel LCD touch screens on refrigerators (which are also voice activated) allow consumers to keep track of their inventory by scanning products, as well as make lists, order groceries online, send e-mail, check recipes, get cooking advice, and program and watch television. Just as in-store scanners enhanced our understanding of shopping behavior, smart appliances will enhance our understanding of consumption behavior.

The initial benefits of smart appliances are in how they enable consumers to maintain better inventory control and how they help with meal preparation. Using the scanner, a wired refrigerator can provide researchers with unobtrusive measures of what is being consumed and when it is being consumed. Furthermore, because smart appliances can provide advice to consumers on their screens, they provide some idea of what recipes people consider and when they make a meal choice based on a theme (Italian) versus when they make it by building a meal around a key ingredient (thawed ground beef). As inventory is depleted, automatic shopping lists will suggest repurchases that need to be made. When combined with purchase data that are collected from either the store or inventory check-ins after returning from the store, questions can be answered about why and when purchase rates lag so far behind consumption or "use up" rates for many products.

In networking smart appliances together, there is a tremendous potential for observing cooperating panelists. For example, the same surveillance camera system that allows a mother in a kitchen to monitor her sleeping baby in an upstairs bedroom can also record how she is preparing food and the order in which meal preparation decisions are made. With the refrigerator serving as a cortex, it will not be long before it becomes networked with smart telephones, ovens, toasters, televisions, garbage cans, and heating and air conditioning units.

A Virtually Real Experience

The panel experience will move from pictures and sound to slides, full-screen video, and product dimensionality. Furthermore, whereas WebTV and computer monitors are limited to two dimensions, the advances in holography and a variety of innovative peripherals could alleviate even this constraint. Consider an experiential walk-around that involves interacting with a product, not unlike that found in an interactive first-person experience with Sony Playstations and other simulated reality games. With discontinuous access panels, consumption, attitudes, and intentions can be vividly collected for existing products, new product introductions, and new package concepts.

The power of simulation will provide a greater degree of specificity to the Web. No longer will questions be general,[1] but rather they will be vivid and situationally specific. The experience can vary for people on the basis of key segmentation variables, such as their age, the age and genders of their children, and so forth. Their experiences can also be varied systematically to provide modal tests, such as 2×2 experimental designs that vary consumption-related scenarios in four systematic ways and then compare the different responses in each of the four conditions.

Richer Data for Panel Researchers

Right now, the speed of some panel research approaches the speed of light, or at least the speed of a modem. In the future, the largest difference for panel researchers will not be in the speed that data are collected as much as it will be in their richness. One historical drawback of panel data is that they were not effective in providing qualitative explanations of behavior. Most conventional questionnaires do not allow the space, time, or cost considerations to collect these data or code and interpret them.

Instead of being largely constrained to categorical or interval-scaled data, data in the future will be given a colorful qualitative dimension that will be made possible by two technologies. Voice-recognition technology and coding technology will enable researchers to collect, code, and translate a panelist's description of his or her shopping experience into any major language of interest.

Hearing Voices and Coding Thoughts

Voice-activated surveys free panelists from needing to write or type their responses. This in turn saves them time and effort and allows for more questions to be asked. This voice-recognition software allows consumers to complement or supplement their quantitative responses with qualitative verbal information. They can then explain the process they went through when deciding on a purchase or making a trade-off. Furthermore, voice-recognition software will allow panelists to describe

---

[1]Attitudes toward products, for example, are not general. They are specific to products in specific situations. Asking a person about his or her attitude about eating cranberry sauce for Thanksgiving dinner versus eating it for a weekday dinner or with chicken yields a much more positive attitude measure.

the thoughts and feelings they had when using a product, seeing an ad, tasting a product, or comparing four package designs.[2] This information can help determine causality and generate insights.

These verbal protocols will be worth nothing, however, if they are not organized in a systematic way that enables analysis. Fortunately, advances in new generations of qualitative software will continue to help transform this data into a usable systematic form. This software can be used to code data in several ways. For example, when capturing a person's thoughts and feelings toward using a particular product, each statement can be categorized as to whether it is positive or negative and whether it is a general evaluative statement or a more attribute-specific statement. The exact nature of each statement can then be subcategorized on the basis of the attributes it reflects.

Cross-Country Coordination

"Smart databases" will facilitate a researcher's ability to develop a global perspective. These automated databases will be able to search for a stratified or diversified panel, including one that consists of members from many different countries, for each survey.

The databases will be supported by an increase in the availability of instantaneous language translation programs that enable an unprecedented opportunity for cross-country comparisons. When there is a desire to make comparisons across languages, translation software will make near instantaneous conversions of a panel survey into other languages. This software will offer backward translation to double-check meaning (e.g., from English to Mandarin and back to English). Furthermore, the same voice recognition software that allows for qualitative responses will also allow words to be translated and coded into whatever language is desired.

These advances will bring global markets together more quickly into one heterogeneous but coordinated market. Our understanding of the

---

[2]When measuring verbal responses, the general wording for the questions eliciting these responses is "Please describe in your own words the thoughts and feelings you had after _____ (seeing this ad for the product, using this brand, comparing these two new package designs, and so on). It is important to understand that there are no right or wrong answers. We are interested in the thoughts and feelings you have, so please do not worry about your grammar or about speaking in full sentences." These directions can also be given in a more guided manner toward specific types of thoughts, and there are pretesting methods that can be used to ensure that such wording does not bias or guide panelists (see Wansink, Ray, and Batra 1994).

diversity of these different groups will increase, and our ability to provide recommendations and understand why they differ will help companies better satisfy the groups while enabling them to keep their identity. In this way, the global potential for certain products can be assessed early in their development. Changes can then be made to the product that make it most promising for a world market or that make it customizable by different panelists in different markets.

What Will Not Change?

In 1982, it was widely predicted that by the year 2000, we would be living in a paperless society. There would be no more daily newspapers distributed to our doors. Our shopping would be done from home while our kitchens automatically cooked our meals. These futurists were partly right. Today, there are online newspapers and online grocery delivery companies. They also were largely wrong. Many of us are still starting our mornings reading an inky, smudgy morning newspaper while pouring and eating the cereal we bought at the grocery store last weekend.

Indeed, the technology of the future will have a tremendous impact on consumer panels, but there will still be an important need for offline panels. Incentives will still play an important part in increasing panel representativeness, and the value of the data will still be enhanced even as they become more accessible and usable.

The Need for Traditional Offline Panels

Most newspapers are available online, but they have not yet replaced the hard copy form that can be moved from the kitchen table to the couch to the train station to the office. Multimedia forms of consumer panels provide some convenience, but they do not always have the convenience of portability. They are convenient in some respects but inconvenient in others. They are preferred by some people and not preferred by others. These issues are partly issues of targeting panelists according to their preferences. It may eventually get to the point that multiple panel instruments will be used according to what a panelist prefers. Although this brings concerns of method bias, it reduces sample bias.

In addition to panel member preferences, the longevity of offline panels will also be guaranteed by privacy concerns. For sensitive issues or potentially embarrassing topics, greater anonymity is required. In these circumstances, the virtual hostess mentioned at the beginning of this chapter becomes intimidating, and panelists fear their log-on addresses might be traced. A cold, unexciting, black-and-white survey booklet may seem old-fashioned 20 years from now. It will also still be the best way to collect representative data on sensitive or embarrassing topics.

The Importance of Incentives

One online researcher recently boasted that his company's online panels required fewer incentives than its offline panels. He also noted that the company was going to test cutting back online incentives even further.

Assuming the level of incentives given to offline panels are well calibrated and not overly generous, there can be only two reasons online panels currently need fewer incentives. First, these panels could require fewer incentives if they are less representative (more biased) than the general population. That is, these people might have time that is less valuable, or they may need the money more desperately. Second, these people might accept lower incentives because the initial novelty of working online is worth the extra effort. In the long run, both reasons result in unrepresentative results and in turnover after the novelty of the technology wears off.

Improving Data Accessibility and Usability

In recent years, increased efforts have been made to make data both accessible and usable to the brand manager who wants to manipulate them. As data become more complicated, it will be convenient—but foolish—to stop investing effort in continuing to make them accessible and usable. It will be too easy—but foolish—to believe it is too complicated for anyone but the researchers to understand. With that perspective, the perceived value of what panel researchers offer will be eroded rather than enhanced.

Pull-down menus, voice-activated commands, host- or hostess-guided instruction—all of these can be designed to give the brand manager easy access to however much or little information he or she wants. The Reformation occurred as the printing press made literature more accessible and literacy made it more usable. It is not clear what a consumer panel reformation would bring. It is clear that it will only be possible as panel data become more accessible and analytical literacy makes them more usable. From the perspective of some brand managers, few industry-level initiatives would be more welcome than a focus on improving the accessibility and usability of the panel data they commission.

Future Fears

Science fiction movies and books are replete with the theme of technology outpacing humans' ability to control it. The future brings the ability to collect more and better data and to make the panel experience richer and more satisfying for the consumer. It is less clear if we will know what to do with these data when we have them.

One concern is that the focus on cost and speed will lead to the death of answering "why?" When a person is not trained to "get behind" the numbers, the marginal benefit of sophisticated data will not commensurately add to his or her ability to make more insightful decisions. Perhaps the core of the problem is in how we train graduate students, particularly the MBAs who use panel results in positions as brand managers. MBAs are trained to see the "big picture" and develop vision. This often subjugates technical skills in favor of strategic thinking and team management. Yet, at some point, it is insights about consumers that constitute the mosaic behind the big picture of successful companies. Learning how to run regressions, ANOVAs, and chi-square tests can be reasonably easily taught. The value in doing so, however, is in being able to ask the next level of question that moves from numbers in a table to insights. Is the purpose of research merely to describe the data or to tell a story? Is it to "tag and bag," or is it to solve a mystery? We often do the former, not the latter.

The Commodification of Research

Research costs have been increasingly dropping as the use of the Web and standardized procedures reduce the time and labor necessary to execute a study. Yet, the same aspects that make online panel research so efficient also make it prone to commodification. When the positioning statement of an online panel company is "we're faster and cheaper," that will unfortunately be the yardstick by which they will be evaluated as other online competitors emerge. Higher speed, lower costs, and lower margins will have a predictable impact on quality. As one sign in a computer consultant's office reads, "Cheap, fast, and good: Pick two."

If the incremental value of a panel researcher is not made clear, clients might overweight cost and speed. That is, a client might find him- or herself price shopping for eight cross-tabs he or she wants on a specified population of a prescribed size. Having articulated this, it is now time to find the lowest bidder.

Such technology will commodify the panel research industry. No longer will there be a premium on being the firm that goes beyond the numbers and provides insights or explanations that move the understanding of consumers to another level. To a low bidder, there is no time for thoughtful analyses. The costly hiring of people who are talented and clever enough to generate these insights will be forgone in favor of a less expensive technician who can click a "cross-tabs" button. This will drive out much of the diversity in the marketing research area in favor of large, low cost suppliers.

Low cost panel research may often be worth even *less* than what one pays for it. In contrast, users who pay a premium price deserve more. There is no shame in asking panel researchers what value-added benefits they provide beyond simply the basic findings their "generic" competitor offers. This makes sure users get their money's worth. It also pushes that provider to hire better, look deeper, and continue to develop the analytic expertise that will keep it competitive.

The progress in any industry is never linear. This is also true with consumer research. Some techniques and some companies move our understanding directly forward, other techniques take us on a creative side road, and others make us step back and rethink our progress. But if the widespread decision to select a vender is based only on speed and cost, the progress in this industry and our advancement will become dormant.

Rationalization Research and Marketing Schizophrenia

There are two dangerous extremes of the research continuum: Underresponding to research and overresponding to it. The first leads to rationalization research; the second leads to marketing schizophrenia.

Rationalization Research

Consider the danger of underresponding to research. More than $6 billion is spent each year on professional marketing research. A sizable amount of this is devoted to justifying, fortifying, or rationalizing a business decision that has already been made and that needs to be supported with data. As the cost and speed to ask questions go down, the temptation to ask more rationalization-related questions goes up.

When research is so easy to conduct, what keeps it from being commissioned and recommissioned until results fit expectations and it comes out the way management wants? In such circumstances, there will be little trouble and little cost to recommission it and send it back until it is "right." In the end, the casualness by which we commission studies will be matched with the casualness with which we regard the results.

Marketing Schizophrenia

Now let us consider the opposite danger—that of overresponding to research findings. Brand managers often look for instantaneous change, and the convenience and affordability of online research can nearly instantly satisfy this curiosity. Yet, continuous data may lead to continuous change. Too much change can lead companies to lose sight of who they are and what their products stand for.

Consider continuous tracking in political polls. Small changes in public opinion create corresponding changes in political strategies. But brands are different. Part of what makes a brand or company valuable is that it stands for consistency in quality and in image. Many of the most powerful brands—Marlboro, Coca-Cola, Federal Express—seldom stray from their image. When brands change their images with the changing of every new brand manager, they leave a confusing or schizophrenic impression in the eyes of consumers.

Just because data are available does not mean they have to be continually accessed and acted on. "Stay the course" is unfortunately a foreign phrase to many brand managers. The fear of staying the course is often related to the fear of being left behind and becoming a forgotten manager of a forgotten product. Although it is good to make midcourse corrections to stay with changes in the winds, there is often a tendency toward overcorrection. Large companies tend to dampen out what might otherwise be a manager's tendency to overrespond to the data. Yet even if a company can save a person from his or her own best intentions, it is important to acknowledge a tendency toward this bias.

The accessibility of continuous online information brings with it the warning to resist making continuous changes that correspond with the continuous change in attitudes. The key is knowing what changes are worth responding to and which are not. That is why "brand stewards" have a different career trajectory than "brand administrators."

Privacy and Regulation

Underlying all of these methods and the techniques for their collection is the ever-present danger that a person's responses can be stolen or abused (Baculski 2001). Publicized attacks of online systems of the CIA, FBI, Microsoft, and other organizations by hackers have not reduced the public's unease regarding the security of the personal information they give to marketing agencies and Web sites.

With new developments in personal encryption, the use of personal keys to enter information online, and the practice of sending a respondent's answers as packets of information instead of as a unified whole, hackers are having a harder time making this type of data meaningful or relating this information back to the respondent. The infinite routes that data travel along the Internet today make even the best hackers practically harmless to the research respondent.

Whereas some believe security will be a less sensitive issue in the future, many do not. In the end, the future of panel research rests on the shoulders of consumers. They are one asset with which we cannot gamble.

It might be easy to assume that if only, say, 20% of the population is concerned with privacy, it will not be a notable problem. That would be dangerous. Because of their fear of privacy violations, this 20% might give biased or incomplete answers. They might not even respond or participate at all. Given the concern our industry has with representativeness, biased responses, incomplete responses, or even nonresponses from this group begin to make a notable impact on the reliability and generalizability of our findings. This is even more troubling if this 20% also has a common characteristic, such as being savvy shoppers. Indeed, the fear of privacy is a fear that is very much worth our industry's time, effort, and resources to minimize.

Originally, the Federal Trade Commission (FTC) held a stance of industry self-regulation. Identifying five core principles that it would like the industry to follow was the first step to a structure, or set of guidelines, for federal regulation (Gillin 2000). The FTC offers five principles of fair information practices that should be followed:

1. Notice. Communicating how data are collected, the uses of the information, and what third parties may receive the information.
2. Choice. Giving consumers options as to how any personal information collected from them may be used (opt-in or opt-out).
3. Access. Allowing people the ability to access data about themselves and to correct any inaccuracies.
4. Security. Taking reasonable steps to ensure the security of information collected.
5. Enforcement. The core principles of privacy protection can only be effective if there is a mechanism in place to enforce them.

Increasing regulation is imminent if companies and Congress do not see eye to eye. Although it should not be necessary to make new laws regarding this medium, education is vital if marketers and researchers want to continue the relationship and maintain the trust of the public they are so eager to analyze. The ability to "reach out and touch someone" brings opportunities and responsibilities. We can assume the best intentions, but we must guard these systems against the worst.

Recommendations for Future Consumer Panel Researchers

In Chapter 9, 12 suggestions were given as to how managers can get the most out of their panel service. In this section, we focus on how panel researchers can better manage their future.

No competitive advantage lasts forever, particularly in a service industry. As soon as a new tool is developed, it is only a matter of time before it is replicated and improved on by competitors. Nevertheless, the pioneering advantage has enduring benefits and halos, one of them being financial solvency. The basic theme of this section is that innovative thinking will be one of the biggest assets of the future. Innovative thinking is based on developing the ability to ask and answer "why?" and on the ability to envision and develop new products.

Ask and Answer "Why?"

One off-putting but illustrative description of what differentiates insightful researchers from less insightful ones is that insightful researchers are able to "beat the data until they confess." This underscores one way that many great researchers have learned how to generate insights. It is the iterative three-step process of going from data results to head scratching to data analysis until the picture is clear and the "whys" are answered. Insights from a data set are not found in the first eight sets of cross-tabs conducted. The real value might be in explaining why certain segments differ from others.

"Beat the data until they confess." What you want the data to confess is "why." For example, you may want the data to confess ...

- Why do people with shopping lists make more impulse purchases?
- Why do people buy multiple units of products that are not on sale?
- Why has restaurant patronage decreased except for expensive restaurants?
- Why would someone who says they "buy American" own a Japanese car?
- Why do people buy products they never use?
- Why do women like unhealthy "comfort foods" and men like healthy ones?

Research analysts can become accustomed to analyzing data in prespecified, preformatted ways, but this efficiency can also cause them to lose the ability to look deeper into the meaning behind the results. Many researchers begin to get a flavor for asking why and why not in their graduate training. If their day-to-day responsibilities do not develop this, the skill is lost.

Educate for Insights

It is important to educate analysts to dig deep and look for insightful ways in which to better understand the whys behind the data. There are at least two ways this can be done. One is through theory-based education; the second is through data-driven insights. The first is top-down, the second is bottom-up.

Theory-Based Education

Theory-based education is built on the belief that the best insights behind how consumers behave can be derived from basic models about how they think. That is, even a handful of basic models of how consumers make decisions, or how they shop, or why they eat what they do can be used to stimulate questions, insights, and analyses that are relevant to a client's basic Monday morning problems.

Although theory-based education can be accomplished through high-level graduate courses in psychology, sociology, and consumer behavior, it can also be achieved through in-house programs. One common version of this is the form of "journal clubs." Instead of simply keeping up with the trade press, the purposes of journal clubs are to push thinking beyond day-to-day needs and stretch people into thinking beyond their comfort level.[3] This increases comfort and skill in asking and answering "why" questions. One way to encourage this is to try and build process-related models that force researchers to draw arrow and bubble diagrams or flow charts that cause them to think about why consumers behave the ways they do.

Data-Driven Education

Instead of, or in addition to, using theory-based education to generate insights, data-driven education can also be used. This is more difficult to structure, but it can be done in the form of data-driven mysteries. Each week's discussion is led by a different researcher. The objective is to present a data-related mystery that he or she faced on a prior project and

---

[3]Many companies support Friday afternoon journal clubs. One form these take is a weekly box-lunch affair for which one journal article has been preassigned for reading and discussion. In the fall and spring, six to ten individuals scan academic journals for articles that might be of interest, and they agree on one for each week. Articles are scheduled, and discussion leaders are assigned. The responsibility of each discussion leader is to assign reading-related questions, direct the discussion, and provide a one-page summary of the insights and implications of the discussion by the following Monday. With some companies, these summaries are distributed to the relevant departments.

subsequently solved. By walking other researchers through the experience, it provides a case study opportunity to look beyond the numbers and ask why questions.

This can be in the form of a presentation, but data-driven education appears to be more effective (and more enjoyable to the participants) when it is limited to a minimal number of slides and a good deal of give-and-take discussion. Because the goal of such a process is to put analysts in the shoes of the person leading the discussion, there are several ways the discussion can be structured. One way is for the discussion leader to present only the background and importance of the research, then present the dilemma, and then open it up for discussion as to how to solve the dilemma. People cannot just casually throw out half-thought-out suggestions. They must explain their reasoning and the assumptions behind their suggestions. It is important that the whole group be involved in the discussion and converge on the solution. It is only toward the end of the session that the actual results are revealed. After discussing the results, it is productive to ask two questions: (1) Who else has faced a problem similar to this, and how did you solve it? and (2) What are you working on, or have you worked on, where this technique might be useful?

Consider the following example:

> *Background and Importance of Research.* Knowing what types of measures best predict consumers' consumption of a packaged good, such as canned soup, gelatin, or cranberry sauce, would be useful. These sorts of products are often stockpiled, and typical measures of purchase intentions do not capture the true impact of an ad. That is, an ad might stimulate people to want to eat soup, but they will eat a can from their inventory instead of immediately buying a new one. For this reason, it is important to know what type of measure of consumption intention best predicts subsequent consumption.

> *Data-Related Dilemma.* In designing the panel research, there were two types of consumption measures that were taken for a number of products. These were consumption likelihood questions ("How likely are you to consume canned soup in the next two weeks?" 1 = unlikely and 9 = likely) and consumption quantity questions ("How many cans of soup do you think you might consume in the next two weeks?"). A second wave of the panel asked consumers for the actual consumption of these products, along with the three target products we were interested in (soup, gelatin, and cranberry sauce).

> Which measure best predicted actual usage? Herein lies the dilemma. Neither consumption likelihood measures nor consumption quantity

measures correlated with actual usage. The correlation with the first was .04 and –.07 with the second.

Rationale for Possible Solutions to the Dilemma. In solving this mystery, it is important to understand that these two different measures of usage intent have different relative strengths. With infrequent users of a brand, volume estimates will be skewed toward 0 units (especially over a relatively short period of time). This is a drawback of numerical estimates that provide no gradation between 0 and 1 units. In such cases, volume estimates would provide less variance and less information than an estimate of usage likelihood. As a result, usage likelihood estimates would allow a greater gradation in response and would be more sensitive to detecting any potentially different effects these ads might have on usage.

In contrast, with frequent or heavy users of a brand, a volume estimate is likely to be more accurate than a likelihood estimate. This is because the distribution of these volume estimates is more likely to be normally distributed. As a result, a volume estimate of usage intent is likely to provide more variance and more information about the intended usage of heavy users than is a likelihood measure, which would undoubtedly be at or near 1.0 (100% probable). In these circumstances, volume estimates would be more accurate estimates of a heavy user's usage volume of a brand.

Reanalysis of Data to Test Possible Explanation. For heavy users, an intended usage volume measure was correlated at a respectable .60 with actual usage. For light users, a usage likelihood measure was correlated .47 with actual usage. This was much more diagnostic and useful than the aggregated results that were first found.

This illustrates one example of a data-driven form of education (excerpted from Wansink and Ray 1992, 1997). It begins with an important context in which there is a data dilemma, inconsistency, or mystery. Following a discussion—possibly even a series of yes and no questions—a general hypothesized theory about consumers is developed. The last part of the discussion is the outcome of the reanalysis, the solution. The more interactive data-driven sessions are, the more effectively they are burned into the minds of the researchers.

Develop These Breakthrough Products

Although no competitive advantage lasts forever, innovation is the backbone of most service-related companies. Some would consider it pretentious to claim that certain products have more potential than others for providing breakthroughs in our understanding of consumer behavior.

There will undoubtedly be bigger fish to fry at some point in the future. In the meantime, three areas that are ripe for progress are developing user profiles, determining consumption clusters and preference affiliation, and linking Web browsing with purchase predictions.

User Profile Analysis

When trying to facilitate the adoption of a product or behavior, it can be useful to know how segments of current users of the product differ psychographically, behaviorally, or attitudinally from segments of nonusers. Having this information can help identify predisposed segments to precisely target them. For example, knowing the ways in which consumers (users) of soy products differ from nonusers helps determine more precisely the types of soy-related products that will be most successful in these segments and how these products should be positioned.

Attempts are also being made to determine the extent to which media preferences—primarily in the form of magazine subscriptions—can provide personality clusters that predict consumption preference across a wide range of products. Although it may not be surprising that a person who subscribes to *Architectural Digest* is more likely to buy a luxury car than a reader of *TV Guide*, it would be useful to know if other magazines this person subscribes to will help predict the type of luxury car he or she would buy (even before the person knows).

Consumption Clusters and Preference Affiliation

The Internet has brought about an ability to track consumer search patterns and purchase preferences across a wider range of product categories and services than ever before. This volume of data provides a range of possibilities to understand consumers on the basis of the clusters of products they prefer and purchase. These preference affiliations are a target of interest for academics who want to determine the extent to which preferences in one category can predict preferences in other categories.

Recent studies of heavy users of consumer packaged goods have examined what personality variables are correlated with heavy usage of a particular brand or category (Wansink and Park 2000). By cross-correlating this with heavy usage in other categories, researchers can determine why these particular personality variables drive brand preference and category usage.

Web Browsing and Purchase Predictions

Many believe that correlating Web surfing behavior with long-term behavior will be the Holy Grail for Web-based researchers and managers. Yet without brilliant, theory-driven analysts, even the most powerful software will yield few surprising insights. The relationship between Web surfing and buying behavior (or preferences) is likely to be either so painfully obvious it is not interesting (e.g., people who frequently visit fishing-related Web sites are more likely to buy fishing gear than the average person) or so subtle that the potentially interesting or useful relationships are invisible. If most of us were asked how the Web influenced our behavior as consumers, it is not clear we could even point to direct influences. Perhaps this is because the effects are so ubiquitous that we, like the fish in the water, cannot see them. Or perhaps the effects are so subtle that any attempt to try and explain them will be an exercise in futility. The challenge here is knowing what to look for. If we do not know what to look for, we are unlikely find it. Nevertheless, new researchers will be in a better position to correlate Web behavior with offline buying behavior than panel researchers are currently.

Summary

The future of panel data is on the technological side. The future of panel success is on the people side. The future for consumer panels is rich. The data collection experience will be rich for consumers, the data will be rich for researchers, and we hope the value will be rich for managers. What must be remembered is that part of the value that panel research has for managers is driven by its availability and usability. Recall that the Reformation occurred as the printing press made literature more accessible and literacy made it more usable. Few industry-level initiatives would have a higher long-term pay-off than making panel data accessible and usable for decision makers.

Much of the future of panel data research is limited by our creativity and our vision. It is seductive to see the future as only technology based. Our greatest assets are the consumers who constitute our panels and the researchers who ask and answer "why?" We can sometimes become mesmerized by the gleam of technology, but it is important not to lose sight of the fact that people—panelists and researchers and managers—will always be the core of what drives the value of panel research.

References

Ahl, David H. (1970), "New Product Forecasting Using Consumer Panels," *Journal of Marketing Research*, 7 (May), 160–67.

Baculski, Jason (2001), "Privacy Issues and Regulations," working paper, Food & Brand Lab, University of Illinois.

Black, Thomas W. (1948), "Using the Consumer Panel to Measure Department-Store Buying," *Journal of Retailing*, 24 (December), 151–57, 170.

Boyd, Harper W., Jr. and Ralph L. Westfall (1960), *An Evaluation of Continuous Consumer Panel as a Source of Marketing Information*. Chicago: American Marketing Association.

Brown, George H. (1952), "Brand Loyalty—Fact or Fiction," *Advertising Age*, 23 (June 9), 53–55.

Buck, S.F., E.H. Fairclough, G. Jephcott, and D.W.C. Ringer (1997), "Conditioning and Bias in Consumer Panels—Some New Results," *Journal of the Market Research Society*, 19 (April), 23–38.

Chandon, Pierre and Brian Wansink (2002), "A Convenience-Salience Framework of Stockpiling Effects on Consumption," *Journal of Marketing Research*, 39 (May), forthcoming.

Cordell, Warren N. and Henry A Rahmel (1962), "Are Nielsen Ratings Affected by Non-Cooperation, Conditioning, or Response Error?" *Journal of Advertising Research*, 2 (September), 45–49.

Day, Alice B. (1948), "Consumer Panels React Well to Friendly, Personal Letters," *Printers' Ink*, 225 (November 26), 38–39, 75, 78.

Drayton, Leslie E. (1954), "Bias Arising in Wording Consumer Questionnaires," *Journal of Marketing*, 19 (October), 140–45.

Dunn, S. Watson (1952), "Overlapping of Listening among Radio Audiences," *Journal of Marketing*, 16 (January), 315–21.

Ehrenberg, Andrew S.C. (1959), "The Pattern of Consumer Purchases," *Applied Statistics*, 8 (March), 26–41.

211

—— (1960), "A Study of Some Potential Biases in the Operation of a Consumer Panel," *Applied Statistics*, 9 (March), 20–27.

Eskin, Gerald J. (1973), "Dynamic Forecasts of New Product Demand Using a Depth of Repeat Model," *Journal of Marketing Research*, 10 (May), 115–29.

Ferber, Robert (1949), "Twelve Pointers on Selecting a Consumer Panel Service," *Printer's Ink*, 226 (March 4), 42–47.

Fourt, Louis A. and Joseph W. Woodlock (1960), "Early Prediction of Market Success for New Grocery Products," *Journal of Marketing*, 25 (October), 31–38.

Gillin, Donna (2000), "The Federal Trade Commission and Internet Privacy," *Marketing Research*, 12 (Fall), 39–41.

Goodwin, Ron (1972), "Consumer Response to Promotional Activity," *ADMAP*, 8 (January), 10–12, 40.

Gupta, Sachin, Pradeep Chintagunta, Anil Kaul, and Dick R. Wittink (1996), "Do Household Scanner Data Provide Representative Inferences from Brand Choices? A Comparison with Store Data," *Journal of Marketing Research*, 33 (November), 383–98.

Jenkins, John G. (1938), "Dependability of Psychological Brand Barometers: I. The Problem of Reliability," *Journal of Applied Psychology*, 22, 1–7.

Lansing, John B., Gerald P. Ginsburg, and Kaisa Braaten (1961), *An Investigation of Response Errors.* Urbana, IL: Bureau of Economic and Business Research, University of Illinois.

Lazarsfeld, Paul F. (1940), "'Panel' Studies," *Public Opinion Quarterly*, 4 (March), 122–28.

—— and Ruth Durant (1942), "National Morale, Social Cleavage and Political Allegiance," *Journalism Quarterly*, 19 (June), 150–58.

—— and Marjorie Fiske (1938), "The 'Panel' as a New Tool for Measuring Opinion," *Public Opinion Quarterly*, 2 (October), 596–612.

Lewis, Harrie F. (1948), "A Comparison of Consumer Responses to Weekly and Monthly Purchase Panels," *Journal of Marketing Research*, 12 (April), 449–54.

Magazine Advertising Bureau (1960), *The Profitable Difference.* New York: Magazine Publishers Association.

Massy, William F. (1969), "Forecasting the Demand for New Convenience Products," *Journal of Marketing Research*, 6 (November), 405–12.

McDonald, Colin (1970), "What Is the Short-Term Effect of Advertising?" *ESOMAR Congress Papers*, 463–85.

Metz, Joseph F., Jr. (1956), *Accuracy of Response Obtained in a Milk Consumption Study*, Methods of Research in Marketing, Paper No. 5. Ithaca, NY: Cornell University Agricultural Experiment Station.

Neter, John and Joseph Waksberg (1961), "Measurement of Nonsampling Errors in a Survey of Homeowners' Expenditures for Alterations and Repairs," in *Proceedings of the American Statistical Association*, Social Statistics Section. Alexandria, VA: American Statistical Association, 201–10.

Nielsen, Arthur C. (1945), "Two Years of Commercial Operation of the Audimeter and the Nielsen Radio Index," *Journal of Marketing*, 9 (January), 239–55.

Parfitt, John and B.J.K. Collins (1968), "Use of Consumer Panels for Brand-Share Prediction," *Journal of Marketing Research*, 5 (May), 131–45.

———— and Ivor McGloughlin (1968), "The Use of Consumer Panels in the Evaluation of Promotional and Advertising Expenditures," in *ESOMAR Congress Papers*, Part II, 697–729.

Quackenbush, G.G. and J.D. Shaffer (1960), *Collecting Food Purchase Data by Consumer Panel: A Methodological Report on the MSU Consumer Panel*, 1951–58. Technical Bulletin 279. East Lansing, MI: Agricultural Experiment Station, Michigan State University.

Quenon, E.L. (1951), "A Method for Pre-Evaluating Merchandise Offerings," *Journal of Marketing*, 16 (October), 158–71.

Response Analysis (1976), "Panel Bias Reviewed; Results Inconclusive," *The Sampler*, 7 (Fall), 2.

Robinson, R.A. (1947), "Use of the Panel in Opinion and Attitude Research," *International Journal of Opinion and Attitude Research*, 1 (March), 83–86.

Roper, Elmo (1941), "Checks To Increase Polling Accuracy," *Public Opinion Quarterly*, 5 (March), 87–90.

Sandage, Charles H. (1951), *Building Audiences for Educational Radio Programs*. Urbana, IL: Institute of Communications Research, University of Illinois.

Sellers, Marie (1942), "The Testing of Products by Consumer Juries," *Journal of Marketing*, 6 (April), 76–80.

Shaffer, James D. (1955), "The Reporting Period for a Consumer Purchase Panel," *Journal of Marketing*, 19 (January), 252–57.

Silvey, Robert (1951), "Methods of Viewer Research Employed by the British Broadcasting Corporation," *Public Opinion Quarterly*, 15 (Spring), 89–104.

Stonborough, Thomas H.W. (1942), "Fixed Panels in Consumer Research," *Journal of Marketing*, 7 (October), 129–38.

Sudman, Seymour (1964a), "On the Accuracy of Recording of Consumer Panels: I," *Journal of Marketing Research*, 1 (May), 14–20.

———— (1964b), "On the Accuracy of Recording of Consumer Panels: II," *Journal of Marketing Research*, 1 (August), 69–83.

———— and Robert Ferber (1971), "Experiments in Obtaining Consumer Expenditures by Diary Methods," *Journal of the American Statistical Association*, 66 (December), 725–35.

———— and ———— (1974), "A Comparison of Alternative Procedures for Collecting Consumer Expenditure Data for Frequently Purchased Products," *Journal of Marketing Research*, 1 (May), 128–35.

———— and ———— (1979), *Consumer Panels*. Chicago: American Marketing Association.

————, Wallace Wilson, and Robert Ferber (1976), *The Cost-Effectiveness of Using the Diary as an Instrument for Collecting Health Data in Household Surveys.* Springfield, VA: National Technical Information Service.

Tuten, Tracy L., Michael Bosnjak, and Wolfgang Bandilla (2000), "Banner-Advertised Web Surveys," *Marketing Research*, 11 (4), 17–21.

U.S. Department of Agriculture (1952), *Problems of Establishing a Consumer Panel in the New York Metropolitan Area.* Marketing Research Report No. 8. Washington, DC: U.S. Government Printing Office.

Wansink, Brian (1994), "Developing and Validating Useful Consumer Prototypes," *Journal of Targeting, Measurement, and Analysis for Marketing*, 3 (1), 18–30.

———— (2002), "Fifty Years from the Front: Surveying Private Ryan," working paper series, University of Illinois at Champaign-Urbana.

————, S. Adam Brasel, and Stephen Amjad (2000), "The Mystery of the Cabinet Castaway: Why We Buy Products We Never Use," *Journal of Family and Consumer Science*, 92 (1), 104–108.

———— and Jennifer M. Gilmore (1999), "New Uses that Revitalize Old Brands," *Journal of Advertising Research*, 39 (April/May), 90–98.

———— and Se-Bum Park (2000), "Accounting for Taste: Prototypes that Predict Preference," *Journal of Database Marketing*, 7 (4), 308–20.

———— and ———— (2000), "Comparison Methods for Identifying Heavy Users," *Journal of Advertising Research*, 40 (July/August), 61–72.

———— and Michael L. Ray (1992), "Estimating an Advertisement's Impact on One's Consumption of a Brand," *Journal of Advertising Research*, 26 (May-June), 9–16.

———— and ———— (1996), "Advertising Strategies to Increase Usage Frequency," *Journal of Marketing*, 60 (January), 31–46.

———— and ———— (1997), "Developing Copy Tests that Estimate Brand Usage," in *Measuring Advertising's Effectiveness*, William Wells, ed. Cambridge, MA: Lexington, 359–70

————, ————, and Rajeev Batra (1994), "Increasing Cognitive Response Sensitivity," *Journal of Advertising*, 23 (June), 62–74.

Weible, Rick and John Wallace (1998), "Cyber Research: The Impact of the Internet on Data Collection," *Marketing Research*, 10 (3), 19–24+.

Recommended
Readings

Abe, Makoto (1995), "A Nonparametric Density Estimation Method for Brand Choice Using Scanner Data," *Marketing Science*, 14 (3), 300–25.

Agrawal, Deepak (1996), "Effect of Brand Loyalty on Advertising and Trade Promotions: A Game Theoretic Analysis with Empirical Evidence," *Marketing Science*, 15 (1), 86–108.

Ailawadi, Kusum L. and Scott A. Neslin (1998), "The Effect of Promotion on Consumption: Buying More and Consuming It Faster," *Journal of Marketing Research*, 35 (August), 390–98.

Allenby, Greg M. and Peter J. Lenk (1995), "Reassessing Brand Loyalty, Price Sensitivity, and Merchandising Effects on Consumer Brand Choice," *Journal of Business and Economic Statistics*, 13 (July), 281–89.

Anderson, T.W. (1954), "Probability Models for Analyzing Time Changes in Attitudes," in *Mathematical Thinking in the Social Sciences*, Paul F. Lazarsfeld, ed. Glencoe, IL: The Free Press, 17–66.

Andrews, Rick L. and T.C. Srinivasan (1995), "Studying Consideration Effects in Empirical Choice Models Using Scanner Panel Data," *Journal of Marketing Research*, 32 (February), 30–41.

Anscombe, F.J. (1961), "Estimating a Mixed-Exponential Response Law," *Journal of the American Statistical Association*, 56 (September), 493–502.

Askew, Rachel, Peyton M. Craighill, and Cliff Zukin (2000), "Internet Surveys: Fast, Easy, Cheap, and Representative of Whom?" paper presented at the 55th Annual Conference of American Association for Public Opinion Research, Portland, Oregon (May 18–21).

Bach, Michael (2000), "Using the Power of the Internet as a Strategic Research Tool," paper presented at the Mastering Web-based Surveys & Online Research Techniques Conference, San Diego (June 12–14).

Barclay, William D. (1943), "A Probability Model for Early Prediction of New Product Market Success," *Journal of Marketing*, 27 (January), 63–68.

Barton, Samuel G. (1943), "The Consumption Pattern of Different Economic Groups under War Changes," *Journal of Marketing*, 8 (July), 50–53.

Basi, R.K. (1999), "WWW Response Rates to Socio-demographic Items," *International Journal of Market Research*, 41 (4), 397–401.

Batagelj, Zenel, Katja Lozar Manfreda, Vasja Vehovar, and Metka Zaletel (2000), "Cost and Errors of Web Surveys in Establishment Surveys," paper presented at the International Conference on Establishment Surveys—II, Buffalo, New York (June 17–21).

Bates, Brian and John Bermingham (1968), "Short Term Diaries: Their Use in Collecting Detailed Consumption Data," in *ESOMAR Congress Papers*, Part II, 651–67.

Bauman, Sandra, Natlie Jobity, Jennifer Airey, and Hakan Atak (2000), "Invites, Intros, and Incentives: Lessons from a Web Survey," paper presented at the 55th Annual Conference of American Association for Public Opinion Research, Portland, Oregon (May 18–21).

Beard, Christel and Betsey Wiesendanger (1993), "The Marketer's Guide to Online Databases," *Sales & Marketing Management*, 145 (January), 36–41.

Blattberg, Robert C. and Subrata K. Sen (1976), "Market Segments and Stochastic Brand Choice Models," *Journal of Marketing Research*, 13 (February), 34–45.

Bosnjak, Michael and Wolfgang Bandilla (2000), "Participation in Non-Restricted Web Surveys: A Typology and Further Suggestions," paper pre-sented at the Fifth International Conference on Social Science Methodology, Cologne, Germany (October 3–6).

Bowers, Diane (1998), "FAQ's on Online Research," *Marketing Research: A Magazine of Management & Applications*, 10 (Winter), 45–48.

Bremer, John, George Terhanian, and Reece Smith (2000), "A Propensity Score Adjustment for Selection Bias in Online Surveys," paper presented at the JSM 2000, Indianapolis, Indiana (August 13–17).

Bresnahan, Brian W., Mark Dickie, and Shelby Gerking (1997), "Averting Behavior and Urban Air Pollution," *Land Economics*, 73 (August), 340–57.

Briesch, Richard A., Lakshman Krishnamurthi, Tridib Mazumdar, and S.P. Raj (1997), "A Comparative Analysis of Reference Price Models," *Journal of Consumer Research*, 24 (September), 202–14.

Brockett, Patrick L., Linda L. Golden, and Harry H. Panjer (1996), "Flexible Purchase Frequency Modeling," *Journal of Marketing Research*, 33 (February), 94–107.

Buck, Stephan (1968), "Consumer Purchasing Patterns as a Guide to Marketing Potential," *ADMAP*, 4 (May), 214–18.

Carman, James M. (1970), "Correlates of Brand Loyalty: Some Positive Results," *Journal of Marketing Research*, 7 (February), 67–76.

Cawl, Franklin R. (1943), "The Continuing Panel Technique," *Journal of Marketing*, 8 (July), 45–50.

Chandon, Pierre, Brian Wansink, and Gilles Laurent (2000), "A Congruency Framework of Sales Promotion Effectiveness," *Journal of Marketing*, 64 (October), 54–66.

Charlot, M. (1967), "The SCAL Model: Why a Readership Panel?" in *ESOMAR/WApoR Gm-gess*, 749–58.

Charlton, P. and A.S.C. Ehrenberg (1976), "An Experiment in Brand Choice," *Journal of Marketing Research*, 13 (May), 152–60.

Cherington, Paul T. (1943), "New Economic Patterns Found by Consumer Panels: Introduction," *Journal of Marketing*, 8 (July), 41.

Clark, Richard and Chase Harrison (2000), "Impact of Pre-Notification Methods on Response Rates for Web-based Surveys," paper presented at the 55th Annual Conference of American Association for Public Opinion Research, Portland, Oregon (May 18–21).

Crossley, Archibald M. (1943), "The Impact of War on American Families," *Journal of Marketing*, 8 (July), 41–45.

Day, Cameron (1965), "Consumer Testing: Mighty Power Behind the Product," *Sales and Marketing Management*, 95 (July 2), 20–22.

DiNapoli, Joanne (2000), "Sampling for Internet Surveys," paper presented at the 42nd MRA Annual Conference, Seattle (June 7–9).

Dysart, Joe (2000), "E-Mail Takes Marketing to the Next Level," *Credit Union Magazine*, 66 (February), 80–82.

Ehrenberg, Andrew S.C. (1968), "Pack-Size Rates of Purchasing," in *ESOMAR Congress Papers*, Part II, SOS-28.

———— and G.J. Goodhardt (1970), "A Model of Multi-Brand Buying," *Journal of Marketing Research*, 7 (February), 77–84.

Eichman, Caroline (2000), "Methodological Learnings: ibm.com Online Tracking Study," paper presented at the Mastering Web-based Surveys & Online Research Techniques Conference, San Diego (June 12–14).

Elig, Timothy W., Barbara Quigley, and Elizabeth C. Hoover (2000), "Response Rate Effects of Making Web or paper the Primary Mode," paper presented at the 55th Annual Conference of American Association for Public Opinion Research, Portland, Oregon (May 18–21).

Elrod, Terry and Michael P. Keane (1995), "A Factor-Analytic Probit Model for Representing the Market Structure in Panel Data," *Journal of Marketing Research*, 32 (February), 1–16.

———— and ———— (1998), "An Empirical Analysis of Umbrella Branding," *Journal of Marketing Research*, 35 (August), 339–51.

Enander, Jan and Attila Sajti (1999), "Online Survey of Online Customers: Value-Added Market Research Through Data Collection on the Internet," in *Proceedings of the ESOMAR Worldwide Internet Conference Net Effects*. London: ESOMAR, 35–51.

Erdem, Tulin (1996), "A Dynamic Analysis of Market Structure Based on Panel Data," *Marketing Science*, 15, 359–78.

Farley, John U., Donald R. Lehmann, Russell S. Winer, and Jerrold P. Katz (1982), "Parameter Stability and 'Carry-Over Effects' in a Consumer Decision-Process Model," *Journal of Consumer Research*, 8 (March), 465–71.

Fowler, R.F. and L. Moss (1961), "The Continuous Budget Survey in the United Kingdom," in *Family Living Studies: A Symposium*, Studies and Reports, New Series, No. 63. Geneva, Switzerland: International Labour Office, 36–53.

Frank, Ronald E. (1962), "Brand Choice as a Probability Process," in *Quantitative Techniques in Marketing Analysis*, Ronald E. Frank, Alfred A. Kuehn, and William F. Massy, eds. Homewood, IL: Richard D. Irwin, 372–89.

——— and Charles E. Strain (1972), "A Segmentation Research Design Using Consumer Panel Data," *Journal of Marketing Research*, 9 (November), 385–90.

Gates, Bill (2000), *The Road Ahead*. New York: Penguin Books.

Godwin, Deborah D. (1997), "Dynamics of Households' Income, Debt, and Attitudes Toward Credit, 1983–1989," *Journal of Consumer Affairs*, 31 (2), 303–25.

Golany, B., F.Y. Phillips, and J.J. Rousseau (1995), "Optimal-Design of Syndicated Panels: A Mathematical-Programming Approach," *European Journal of Operations Research*, 87, 148–165.

Gonul, Fusun and Kannan Srinivasan (1996), "Estimating the Impact of Consumer Expectations of Coupons on Purchase Behavior: A Dynamic Structural Model," *Marketing Science*, 15, 262–79.

Goodhardt, G.J. and A.S.C. Ehrenberg (1967), "Conditional Trend Analysis: A Breakdown by Initial Purchasing Level," *Journal of Marketing Research*, 4 (May), 155–61.

Hamlin, Charlie (1997), "Market Research and the Wired Consumer," *Marketing News*, 31 (June 9), 6.

Hardin, David K. and Richard M. Johnson (1971), "Patterns of Use of Consumer Purchase Panels," *Journal of Marketing Research*, 8 (August), 364–67.

Hatley, Suzanne and Susanne Stoessl (1974), "A Panel Measurement of Viewing and Reading," *ADMAP*, 10 (June), 171–79.

Heien, Dale and Cathy Durham (1991), "A Test of the Habit Formation Hypothesis Using Household Data," *The Review of Economics and Statistics*, 73 (May), 189–99.

Holbrook, Morris B. and Donald R. Lehmann (1981), "Allocating Discretionary Time: Complementarity Among Activities," *Journal of Consumer Research*, 7 (March), 395–406.

Hollingswortb, D.F. and A.H.J. Baines (1961), "A Survey of Food Consumption in Great Britain," in *Family Living Studies: A Symposium*. Studies and Reports,

New Series, No. 63. Geneva, Switzerland: International Labour Office, 120–38.

Honomichl, Jack (1983), "Getting a Line on On-Line Panel Databases," *Advertising Age*, 54 (March 14), 47.

Hunt, Janet C. and B.F. Kiker (1981), "The Effect of Fertility on the Time Use of Working Wives," *Journal of Consumer Research*, 7 (March), 380–87.

Internationales Zentralinstitut für das Jugend-und Bildungfernsehen (1971), *Methods of Audience Research Applied by Western European Broadcasting Stations*. Strasbourg: Council of Europe.

Irons, Karl (2000), "The Promise and Pitfalls of On-Line Research," *Marketing News*, 56 (4), 13.

Jackson, Ralph W., Stephen W. McDaniel, and C.P. Rao (1985), "Food Shopping and Preparation: Psychographic Differences of Working Wives and Housewives," *Research in Brief*, (January), 110–13.

Jacoby, Jacob and David B. Kyner (1973), "Brand Loyalty vs. Repeat Purchasing Behavior," *Journal of Marketing Research*, 10 (February), 1–9.

Jones, R. and N. Pitt (1999), "Health Surveys in the Workplace: Comparison of Postal, E-Mail, and World Wide Web Methods," *Occupational Medicine*, 49 (8), 556–58.

Keane, Michael P. (1997), "Modeling Heterogeneity and State Dependence in Consumer Choice Behavior," *Journal of Business and Economic Statistics*, 15 (July), 310–27.

Kim, Byung-Do, Robert C. Blattberg, and Peter E. Rossi (1995), "Modeling the Distribution of Price Sensitivity and Implications for Optimal Retail Pricing," *Journal of Business and Economic Statistics*, 13 (July), 291–303.

Kotter, Herbert and Jaochim Lunze (1961), "A Farm Household Budget Survey in Germany (Federal Republic)," in *Family Living Studies: A Symposium*. Studies and Reports, New Series, No. 63. Geneva, Switzerland: International Labour Office, 87–102.

Kuehn, Alfred (1961),"Consumer Brand Choice—A Learning Process?" in *Quantitative Techniques in Marketing Analysis*, Ronald E. Frank, Alfred A. Kuehn, and William F. Massy, eds. Homewood, IL: Richard D. Irwin, 390–403.

Lawrence, Raymond J. (1969), "Patterns of Buyer Behavior: Time for a New Approach?" *Journal of Marketing Research*, 6 (May), 137–44.

――― (1975), "Consumer Brand Choice—A Random Walk?" *Journal of Marketing Research*, 12 (August), 314–24.

Le Maire, P., Y. Evrard, and S. Douglas (1973), "Profiling Customers Based on Product Purchasing Characteristics,"in *ESOMAR/WAPOR Congress-ESOMAR Main Sessions*, 285–300.

Levine, Phil, Bill Ahlhauser, Dale Kulp, and Rick Hunter (1999), "Pro and Con: Internet Interviewing," *Marketing Research: A Magazine of Management & Applications*, 11 (Summer), 33–36.

Lozar Manfreda, Katja (1999), "Participation in Web Surveys," paper presented at the 9th International Meeting Dissertation Research in Psychometrics and Sociometrics, Oegstgeest, The Netherlands (December 16–17).

Lusardi, Annamaria (1996), "Permanent Income, Current Income, and Consumption: Evidence from Two Panel Data Sets," *Journal of Business and Economic Statistics*, 14 (January), 81–90.

Market Research Corporation of America (no date), *The National Consumer Panel: A Brief Description for Marketers*. New York: Market Research Corporation of America.

Massy, William F. (1966), "Order and Homogeneity of Family Specific Brand-Switching Processes," *Journal of Marketing Research*, 3 (February), 48–54.

Morgan, James N. (1985), "Comparing Static and Dynamic Estimates of Behavioral Responses to Changes in Family Composition or Income," *Journal of Consumer Research*, 12 (June), 83–89.

Morrison, Donald G. (1966), "Interpurchase Time and Brand Loyalty," *Journal of Marketing Research*, 3 (August), 289–91.

Pacula, Rosalie Liccardo (1995), "Women and Substance Use: Are Women Less Susceptible to Addiction?" *Women, Health, and Aging*, 87, 454–59.

Parfitt, John (1975), "Tailor-Made Panels—Combining the Advantages of Ad-hoc Survey and Consumer Panel Methods," in *ESOMAR/WAPOR Congress—Main Sessions*, 147–75.

Pearl, Robert B. (1968), *Methodology of Consumer Expenditures Surveys*. Working Paper No. 27. Washington, DC: U.S. Bureau of the Census.

Pedrick, James H. and Fred S. Zufryden (1993), "Measuring the Competitive Effects of Advertising Media Plans," *Journal of Advertising Research*, 33 (November/December), 11–20.

Postnikov, S.V. (1961), "The Continuous Budget Survey in the U.S.S.R.," in *Family Living Studies: A Symposium*, Studies and Reports, New Series, No. 63. Geneva, Switzerland: International Labour Office, 54–66.

Quackenbush, G.G. (1954), "Demand Analysis from the M.S.C. Consumer Panel," *Journal of Farm Economics*, 36 (August), 415–27.

Rao, Vithala R. and Darius Jal Sabavala (1981), "Inference of Hierarchical Choice Processes from Panel Data," *Journal of Consumer Research*, 8 (June), 85–96.

Reisz, A.B. (1961), "A Budget Survey in the Urban Areas of Greece," in *Family Living Studies: A Symposium*, Studies and Reports, New Series, No. 63. Geneva, Switzerland: International Labour Office, 67–86.

Renwick, Mary E. and Sandra O. Archibald (1998), "Demand Side Management Policies for Residential Water Use: Who Bears the Conservation Burden?" *Land Economics*, 74 (August), 343–59.

Richmond, Cecilia and Tim Maginn (2000), "Action Steps for Successful Internet-based Surveys," paper presented at the Third Annual Advanced Marketing Reseach Conference, Las Vegas (June 6–7).

Root, Alfred R. and Alfred C. Welch (1942), "The Continuing Consumer Study: A Basic Method for the Engineering of Advertising," *Journal of Marketing*, 7 (July), 3–21.

Rossi, Peter E. and Greg M. Allenby (1993), "A Bayesian Approach to Estimating Household Parameters," *Journal of Marketing Research*, 30 (May), 171–82.

Roy, Rishin, Pradeep K. Chintagunta, and Sudeep Haldar (1996), "A Framework for Investigating Habits, 'The Hand of the Past,' and Heterogeneity in Dynamic Brand Choice," *Marketing Science*, 15 (3), 280–99.

Sandage, Charles H. (1936), *Advertising Theory and Practice*. Homewood, IL: Richard D. Irwin.

—— (1956), "Do Research Panels Wear Out?" *Journal of Marketing*, 20 (April), 397–401.

Sethuraman, Raj and John Mittelstaedt (1992), "Coupons and Private Labels: A Cross-Category Analysis of Grocery Products," *Psychology and Marketing*, 9 (November/December), 487–500.

Sherwood, R. and W.A. Twyman (1973), "Operating Effective Panels for TV Audience Measurement," *ESOMAR/WAPOR Congress-Special Groups*, 1–31.

Shuchman, Abe and Peter C. Riesz (1975), "Correlates of Persuasibility: The Crest Case," *Journal of Marketing Research*, 12 (February), 7–11.

Stauber, B.R. (1966), *The Collection of Agricultural Statistics in Japan*. Washington, DC: Statistical Reporting Service, U.S. Department of Agriculture.

Sudman, Seymour (1962), "On the Accuracy of Recording of Consumer Panels," doctoral dissertation, University of Chicago.

—— (1982), "Estimating Response to Follow-Ups in Mail Surveys," *Public Opinion Quarterly*, 46, 582–84.

—— (1983), "Response Effects to Behavior and Attitude Questions," in *Statistical Methods and the Improvement of Data Quality*, Tommy Wright, ed. New York: Academic Press, 85–115.

—— (1983), "Survey Research and Technological Change," *Sociology and Social Research*, 12, 217–30.

—— (1985), "Efficient Screening Methods for the Sampling of Geographically Clustered Special Populations," *Journal of Marketing Research*, 22 (February), 20–29.

—— (1985), "Mail Surveys of Reluctant Professionals," *Evaluation Review*, 9, 349–60.

——, Barbara Bickart, Johnny Blair, and Geeta Menon (1993), "A Comparison of Self- and Proxy Reporting," in *Autobiographical Memory and the Validity of Retrospective Reports*, Norbert Schwarz and Seymour Sudman, eds. New York: Springer, 251–66.

—— and Norman M. Bradburn (1973), "Effects of Time and Memory Factors on Response in Surveys," *Journal of the American Statistical Association*, 68, 805–15.

——— and ——— (1974), *Response Effects in Surveys: A Review and Synthesis*. Chicago: Aldine.

——— and ——— (1982), *Asking Questions: A Practical Guide to Questionnaire Design*. San Francisco, CA: Jossey-Bass.

——— and Graham Kalton (1986), "New Developments in the Sampling of Special Populations," *Annual Review of Sociology*, 12, 401–29.

——— and Linda Lannom (1977), "A Comparison of Alternative Panel Procedures for Obtaining Health Data," in *Proceedings of the American Statistical Association*, Social Statistics Section. Alexandria, VA: American Statistical Association, 511–13.

——— and ——— (1978), *A Comparison of Alternative Panel Procedure for Obtaining Health Data*. Urbana, IL: Survey Research Laboratory, University of Illinois.

———, Monroe G. Sirken, and Charles D. Cowan (1988), "Sampling Rare and Elusive Populations," *Science*, 240, 991–96.

Taylor, Thayer C. (1994), "The Hidden Meaning," *Sales and Marketing Management*, 146 (October), 51–54.

Telser, Lester G. (1962), "The Demand for Branded Goods as Estimated from Consumer Pane Data," *Review of Economics and Statistics*, 44 (August), 300–24.

Tuten, Tracy L., Michael Bosnjak, and Wolfgang Bandilla (1999), "The Effect of Motive on Response Rates in Web-based Surveys: A Proposal Based on the Heuristic-Systematic Processing Model," paper presented at WebNet 99, Honolulu, Hawaii (October).

———, ———, and ——— (2000), "Banner-Advertised Web Surveys," *Marketing Research*, 11 (4), 16–21.

Van Yoder, Steven (2001), "The Limits of On-Line Research," *Brand Marketing*, (January), 42–45.

Vehovar, Vasja, Zenel Batagelj, and Katja Lozar (1998), "Who Are Nonrespondents in Web Surveys?" paper presented at the 9th International Workshop on Household Survey Nonresponse, Bled, Slovenia.

———, ———, and ——— (1999) "Web Surveys: Can the Weighting Solve the Problem?" in *Proceedings of the American Statistical Association*, Survey Research Methods Section. Alexandria, VA: American Statistical Association.

———, ———, ———, and Metka Zaletel (1999), "Nonresponse in Web Surveys," paper presented at the International Conference on Survey Nonresponse ICSN, Portland, Oregon (October 28–31).

Vilcassim, Naufel J. and Pradeep K. Chintagunta (1995), "Investigating Retailer Product Category Pricing from Household Scanner Panel Data," *Journal of Retailing*, 71 (2), 103–28.

von Hofsten, Erland (1961), "A Budget Survey in Sweden," in *Family Living Studies: A Symposium*, Studies and Reports, New Series, No. 63. Geneva, Switzerland: International Labour Office, 15–35.

Wadsworth, Robert (1952), "The Experience of a User of a Consumer Panel," *Applies Statistics*, 1 (November), 169–78.

Wagenfuhr, Rolf (1961), "International Comparison: Budget Survey Made by the E.C.S.C.," in *Family Living Studies: A Symposium*, Studies and Reports, New Series, No. 63. Geneva, Switzerland: International Labour Office, 103–19.

Wansink, Brian (1993), "Bet You Can't Eat Just One: What Stimulates Consumption Acceleration?" *Journal of Food Products Marketing*, 1 (4), 1–26.

———— (1994), "Advertising's Impact on Category Substitution," *Journal of Marketing Research*, 21 (November), 95–105.

———— (1996), "Can Package Size Accelerate Usage Volume?" *Journal of Marketing*, 60 (July), 1–14.

———— (1997), "Developing Accurate Customer Usage Profiles," in *Values, Lifestyles, and Psychographics*, Lynn Kahle, ed. Cambridge, MA: Lexington, 183–98.

———— (2000), "New Techniques to Generate Key Marketing Insights," *Marketing Research*, 12 (Summer), 28–36.

———— and Rohit Deshpandé (1994), "'Out of Sight, Out of Mind': The Impact of Household Stockpiling on Usage Rates," *Marketing Letters*, 5 (January), 91–100.

Webber, Harold H. (1944), "The Consumer Panel: A Method of Media Evaluation," *Journal of Marketing*, 9 (October), 137–40.

Wedel, Michel, Wagner A. Kamakura, Wayne S. Desarbo, and Frenkel Ter Hofstede (1995), "Implications for Asymmetry, Nonproportionality, and Heterogeneity in Brand Switching from Piecewise Exponential Mixture Hazard Models," *Journal of Marketing Research*, 32 (November), 457–62.

Womer, Stanley (1944), "Some Applications of the Continuous Consumer Panel," *Journal of Marketing*, 9 (October), 132–36.

Wydra, Donna and Ted Davies (2000), "An Examination of Online Sampling Techniques," paper presented at the ESOMAR Worldwide Internet Conference Net Effects, Dublin, Ireland (April 10–12).

Index